3D Graphics for
Game Programming

3D Graphics for Game Programming

JungHyun Han

Korea University, Seoul, South Korea

CRC Press
Taylor & Francis Group
Boca Raton London New York

CRC Press is an imprint of the
Taylor & Francis Group, an **informa** business

A CHAPMAN & HALL BOOK

The cover image of green and yellow barley is titled "When Barley is Ripening" and is by artist Lee Sook Ja.

Chapman & Hall/CRC
Taylor & Francis Group
6000 Broken Sound Parkway NW, Suite 300
Boca Raton, FL 33487-2742

© 2011 by Taylor and Francis Group, LLC
Chapman & Hall/CRC is an imprint of Taylor & Francis Group, an Informa business

No claim to original U.S. Government works

Printed in the United States of America on acid-free paper
10 9 8 7 6 5 4 3 2 1

International Standard Book Number: 978-1-4398-2737-6 (Hardback)

Visit the Taylor & Francis Web site at
http://www.taylorandfrancis.com

and the CRC Press Web site at
http://www.crcpress.com

Dedication

To my pride and joy, Jeehee, who is stepping into a new world.

Contents

Preface

Many of computer graphics classes in colleges are focused on real-time rendering and animation. However, it is not easy to find an appropriate textbook, which presents the state of the art in interactive graphics, is balanced between theory and practicality, and is of a proper length to be covered in a semester. This book is written for answering the need and presents the *must-know* in interactive graphics. This book fits the advanced undergraduate or beginning graduate classes for 'Computer Graphics' and 'Game Programming.'

Another primary reader group of this book may be composed of game developers, who have experience in graphics APIs and shader programming but have felt lack of theoretical background in 3D graphics. A lot of programming manual-like books can be found in the bookstore, but they do not provide a sufficient level of mathematical background for the game developers. Assuming that the readers have minimal understanding of vectors and matrices, this book provides an opportunity to combine their experiences with the background theory of computer graphics.

At the core of contemporary interactive graphics is the evolution of GPU. The content of this book is organized around GPU programming. The GPU is partitioned into programmable stages and hard-wired stages. This book presents a variety of algorithms for the programmable stages, and the indispensable knowledge required to configure the hard-wired stages.

The organization and presentation of this book have been carefully designed so as to enable the readers to easily understand the key aspects of interactive graphics. Over the chapters, a lot of 3D presentations are provided in order to help the readers quickly grasp the complicated topics. An important organizational feature of this book is that theoretical or technical details are presented in separate notes (in shaded boxes) and in optional sections (marked by asterisk). They can be safely skipped without any difficulty in understanding the main stream of the book.

Two well-known graphics APIs are Direct3D and OpenGL. This book is API-neutral but presents the sample programs bit by bit in many places. They help the readers understand how the interactive graphics algorithms are implemented. However, the sample programs are located at the optional part and can be safely skipped.

If the optional parts are not taught, the content of this book would be appropriate for being covered in a semester for the undergraduate class. If needed, additional choices may be made among the required parts. For example, Sections 6.3 and 7.4 may be skipped.

A Web site is provided for this book, http://media.korea.ac.kr/book, which contains full lecture notes in PowerPoint files and additional materials including video clips. Especially, the lecture notes contain *all* figures presented in this book.

Acknowledgements

This book is a byproduct of a project supported by Nexon Corporation and Korea Creative Content Agency. Many people from Nexon contributed to the content of this book. Jubok Kim has worked together with the author from the proposal stage of this book, and also proofread the alpha and beta versions. Seungwon Han provided the key 3D models used in this book and performed various art works requested by the author. Hyunwoo Ki, Joongwon Gouk, and Minsun Song also provided valuable images.

Many people from Korea University supported writing this book. Virtually all visual presentations given in this book are generated by Seungjik Lee, who has an exceptional talent in both programming and visual art. Without the dedicated efforts of Dr. Nguyen Trung Kien, three chapters on texturing could never be completed. Dr. Hanyoung Jang has made great contributions to the chapters on shader models and physics-based simulation. Kiwon Um helped the author keep reorganizing the chapters. The author has been deeply indebted to his students at the 3D Interactive Media Lab: Dong-young Kim, Hyun Ju Shin, YoungBeom Kim, EunSeok Han, GwangHyun Park, Seungho Baek, and Junhoo Park. The content of this book has been gradually built through the courses offered at Korea University and Carnegie Mellon University. The students in the classes have provided the author with a lot of feedback.

Prof. Young J. Kim at Ewha Womans University, Prof. Kyoung-Su Oh at Soongsil University, Prof. Kang Hoon Lee at Kwangwoon University, Prof. Jorg Peters at the University of Florida, and Dongwook Ha at Crytek reviewed the draft of this book and provided invaluable comments. Li-Ming Leong, the acquisitions editor of CRC Press, proposed this book, and since then has considerately supported the author not to miss the planned dates.

The greatest thanks go to the brightest faces I have met in my life, Kyung-Ok, Jeehee, and Jihoon. Thank you for always being with me. I love you so much.

Chapter 1

Modeling in Game Production

The process of game development is typically partitioned into three stages: pre-production, production, and post-production. The specific steps of each stage may vary from game genre to genre and also from studio to studio. In general, the pre-production stage includes sketching the game characters, composing the storyline, creating the storyboards (visual representations of the storyline), and writing the design document. The game design document is the blueprint from which a game is to be built, and states what the goals and rules of the game are, how the maps and levels are defined, how the characters and objects are controlled, and how the screen and menus are organized.

In the production stage, a crew of level designers[1], artists, programmers, and sound engineers is made up. They cooperate under the supervision of producers. The design document is usually updated during the production stage. For example, levels can be added or removed. The output of the production stage is a game program and a bunch of game assets to be consumed by the game program. The assets include 3D models, images, and animation data.

The final stage is post-production. The output of the production stage is passed to the game testers. The flaws and bugs are reported, and then the programmers and artists fix them. This process is iterated, and the game evolves into the final version.

This book is about the 3D graphics aspect of the production stage. The first step of the 3D game production stage is *modeling*. This chapter presents the topics in modeling.

1.1   Game Production Pipeline

Compared with the pre- and post-production stages, the production stage for 3D games has rather universal steps. They compose the *game production*

---

[1] The major components of level design include laying out the game map, placing the game characters and objects (such as enemies and obstacles), and specifying their behaviors in response to the user actions or the events of the game world.

Fig. 1.1:   Three major steps of the game production pipeline.

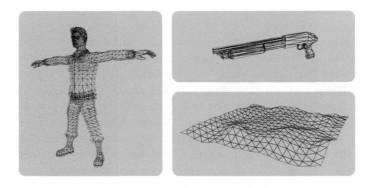

Fig. 1.2:   Almost all 3D models in games are represented in polygon meshes.

pipeline shown in Fig. 1.1. It is called pipeline in the sense that the output of one step is taken as the input of the next step. The pipeline in Fig. 1.1 is defined from the graphics viewpoint, and therefore graphic artists and programmers are the key players. The artists create graphics assets and are in charge of modeling and 'half' of animation. The programmers are in charge of the other half of animation and rendering. Roughly speaking, the animation step is partitioned into off-line tasks and run-time tasks, which are handled by artists and programmers, respectively.

In the modeling step, the artists create the components of the game environment. Consider a shooting game in an outdoor environment. We need soldiers, guns, terrain maps, etc. See Fig. 1.2. They are usually modeled in *polygons*, and such a representation is named *polygon mesh*. It is the most popular modeling method in games.

The scope of modeling is not limited to constructing 3D models, but includes creating *textures* that are added to 3D models to increase their visual realism. The simplest form of a texture is a bitmap image that is pasted to an object surface. Fig. 1.3-(a) shows an image texture created for the soldier model. The texture is applied to the surface of the soldier at run time, to produce the result shown in Fig. 1.3-(b).

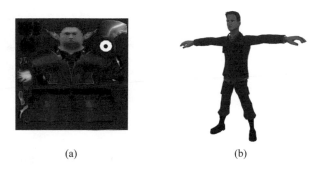

(a) (b)

Fig. 1.3: An image texture applied to the surface of a polygon mesh. (a) This example is a collection of small images, each of which is for a part of the soldier's body. At first glance, the texture may look weird. Section 4.1 presents how to create such an image texture. (b) The texture is pasted to the soldier's polygon mesh at run time.

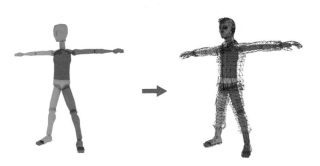

Fig. 1.4: A skeleton is composed of bones and is embedded into the polygon mesh. This figure illustrates the bones as if they were surfaces, but the bones do not have explicit geometric representations. They are conceptual entities that are usually represented as matrices. Chapter 11 presents this issue in detail.

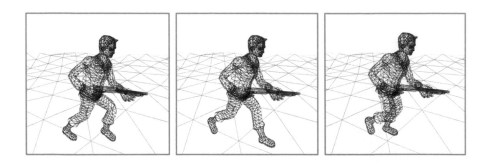

Fig. 1.5:   The polygon mesh can be animated by controlling its skeleton.

Fig. 1.6:   Results of rendering the animated scenes.

The soldier should be able to walk, run, and crawl, i.e., it needs to be animated. For this purpose, we usually specify the skeletal structure of the soldier and then define how the skeletal motion deforms the soldier's polygon mesh such that, for example, the polygons of the thigh are made to move when the thigh-bone moves. This process is often referred to as *rigging*. Fig. 1.4 shows a skeleton embedded into the polygon model. A rigged model is animated by artists. (The animations are then replayed at run time.) Fig. 1.5 shows a few snapshots of an animated soldier in wireframes.

The artists perform modeling and animation in an off-line mode. Dedicated programs such as Autodesk 3ds Max and Autodesk Maya are popularly used. This book uses 3ds Max for demonstrating the artists' work.

Computer games generate an illusion of movement on the screen by quickly displaying a sequence of changing images, called *frames*. When replaying an object's animation created by artists, distinct shape and pose (position and orientation) of the object are computed per frame. In addition, run-time dynamics caused by external forces and collisions among the game objects is handled, and the states of the involved objects are updated per frame. (This process is referred to as physics-based simulation and is presented in Chapter 12.) Furthermore, lighting conditions and viewing specifications can be changed per frame. When all such parameters are determined, the rendering module is invoked. Rendering is the process of generating a 2D image from a 3D scene. The image makes up a frame. Fig. 1.6 shows the results of rendering the animated scenes.

Unlike modeling and off-line animation conducted by artists, run-time animation and rendering are executed by a game program. It is typically built upon graphics APIs (Application Programming Interfaces) such as Direct3D [1] and OpenGL (Open Graphics Library) [2]. Direct3D is part of Microsoft's DirectX API and is available only for Microsoft platforms. OpenGL is managed by a non-profit consortium, the Khronos Group, and is a cross-platform standard API.

Graphics APIs provide application programmers with essential graphics functions. Today, such functions are implemented in hardware, named GPU (Graphics Processing Unit), which is a processor specialized for graphics. A graphics API can be taken as a software interface of the GPU. The API translates the application's graphics command to instructions that can be executed by the GPU.

This book is not intended to be a manual for Direct3D or OpenGL, but presents the sample programs bit by bit. They help the readers understand how the real-time graphics algorithms are implemented. For programming with the APIs, their SDK manuals should be referenced. For example, Direct3D SDK [3] provides tutorials and samples for beginners.

1.2 Polygon Mesh

In 3D computer graphics, various modeling techniques are used. Consider a sphere of radius r that is centered at (C_x, C_y, C_z). Its simplest representation is to use the sphere equation. See Fig. 1.7-(a). It is an example of an *implicit surface* based on an implicit function $f(x, y, z) = 0$. Suppose that, when a point (x, y, z) is inserted into the implicit function, the result is zero. Then, the point is on the implicit surface.

We can represent the sphere explicitly in terms of its topological entities such as vertices. A good example of such an explicit representation is the

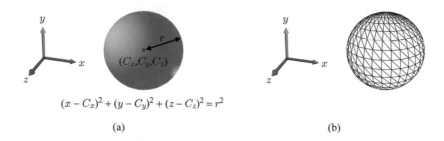

$$(x - C_x)^2 + (y - C_y)^2 + (z - C_z)^2 = r^2$$

(a)   (b)

Fig. 1.7: Two different representations of a sphere. (a) Implicit surface. (b) Polygon mesh.

convex polygons   concave polygons

Fig. 1.8: Concave polygons are harder to process than convex ones and therefore are rarely used.

polygon mesh shown in Fig. 1.7-(b). Real-time applications prefer the polygon mesh representation because the GPU has been optimized for processing the representation. Note that the mesh vertices are the points sampling the smooth surface, and therefore the polygon mesh is not an accurate but an approximate representation.

OpenGL supports a general polygon having an arbitrary number of vertices, but the polygon must be convex. Fig. 1.8 compares convex and concave polygons. The restriction on convexity is placed because the algorithm for processing concave polygons is slow. Another restriction in OpenGL is that the polygon must be planar, i.e., the vertices of a polygon must lie in the same

Fig. 1.9: Triangle mesh vs. quadrilateral mesh.

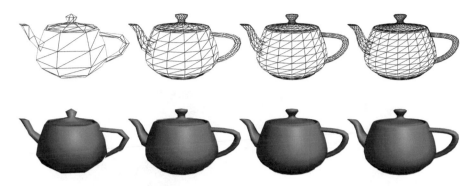

Fig. 1.10: Rendering a low-resolution mesh is fast but the model's polygonal nature is easily revealed. Rendering a high-resolution mesh is slow, but the rendering result is better in general.

plane. The simplest polygon is a triangle, and it guarantees the convexity and planarity. The polygons supported by Direct3D are limited to triangles, i.e., a polygon mesh in Direct3D implies a triangle mesh. Fig. 1.9 compares a triangle mesh and a quadrilateral mesh (simply a quad mesh) for the same object. The triangle mesh is more popular. However, the quad mesh is often preferred, especially for modeling step, as can be observed in Section 1.2.1.

When we approximate a curved surface by a polygon mesh, various *resolutions* can be considered, as shown in Fig. 1.10. There is a trade-off between accuracy and efficiency. As the resolution is increased, the mesh becomes closer to the original curved surface, but the time needed for processing the mesh is increased. Handling various resolutions of a polygon mesh has been an important research topic [4]. The process of converting a low-resolution mesh into a high-resolution mesh is called *refinement*, and the reverse process is called *simplification*.

1.2.1 Polygon Mesh Creation*

In most cases, the polygon mesh of a game object is interactively created using graphics packages. The polygon mesh is stored in a file and is then input to the game program which animates and renders it at run time. A programmer may not have to understand how a polygon mesh is created. It is the job of an artist. If you want, you can skip this subsection[2]. However, understanding the basics of the modeling step is often helpful for developing a game as well as communicating with an artist. This section roughly sketches how a polygon mesh of a character is created.

---

[2]In this book, the asterisk-marked parts can be skipped, and no difficulty will be encountered for further reading.

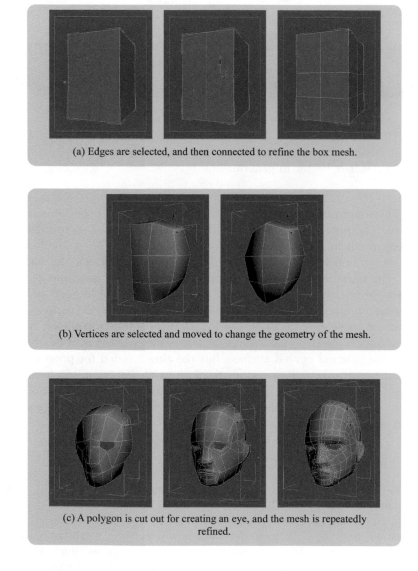

(a) Edges are selected, and then connected to refine the box mesh.

(b) Vertices are selected and moved to change the geometry of the mesh.

(c) A polygon is cut out for creating an eye, and the mesh is repeatedly refined.

Fig. 1.11:   A polygon mesh is created by manual operations.

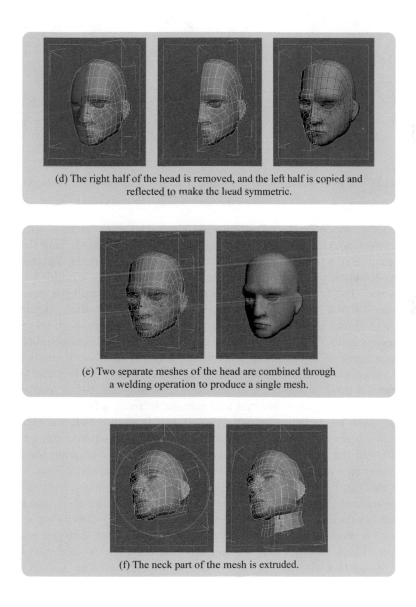

(d) The right half of the head is removed, and the left half is copied and reflected to make the head symmetric.

(e) Two separate meshes of the head are combined through a welding operation to produce a single mesh.

(f) The neck part of the mesh is extruded.

Fig. 1.11:   A polygon mesh is created by manual operations (*continued*).

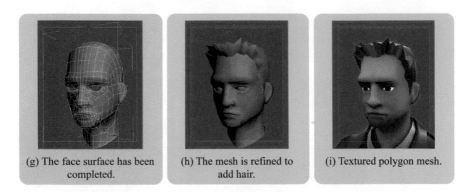

(g) The face surface has been completed.

(h) The mesh is refined to add hair.

(i) Textured polygon mesh.

Fig. 1.11:   A polygon mesh is created by manual operations (*continued*).

In general, modeling packages provide the artist with various operations such as selection, translation, rotation, and scaling for manipulating the topological entities of a polygon mesh, i.e., vertices, edges, and faces. Further, such topological entities can be cut, extruded, and connected. Consider modeling a character's head. There are many ways of creating its polygon mesh, and we choose starting from a box and modifying its topology and geometry.

Fig. 1.11 shows the step-by-step process of editing a box mesh to generate a character's head. In Fig. 1.11-(a), edges are selected and connected to refine the coarse mesh of the box, i.e., to produce a larger number of smaller polygons. Consequently, the topology is changed. In Fig. 1.11-(b), the vertices of the refined mesh are selected and moved to change the mesh geometry. In Fig. 1.11-(c), a polygon is selected and cut out to make a hole for an eye, and then the mesh keeps being refined. Fig. 1.11-(d) shows that, for creating a symmetric object, one side of the mesh is copied, reflected, and pasted to the other side. In the modeling process, refining one side and copying the refined to the other side are often repeated to create a well-balanced object.

Note that, in Fig. 1.11-(d), the right- and left-hand sides of the head are separate meshes. However, they share the boundaries, and there are one-to-one correspondences between their vertices. Fig. 1.11-(e) shows that a pair of vertices at a single position can be combined into a vertex through a welding operation. Then, two adjacent meshes are combined into a single mesh. Fig. 1.11-(f) shows that the neck of the mesh is extruded, and Fig. 1.11-(g) shows the result. The mesh is further refined to add hair, as shown in Fig. 1.11-(h). A complete character can be created by continuing such operations. Fig. 1.11-(i) shows the bust of the textured mesh.

Note that the model in Fig. 1.11 is a quad mesh, not a triangle mesh. The quad mesh makes various operations easy. However, the modeling packages provide a triangle mesh of the same object, and therefore we can use it for rendering.

1.2.2 Polygon Mesh Representation

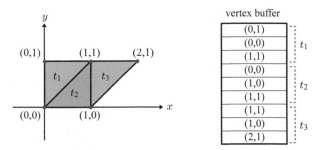

Fig. 1.12: Non-indexed triangle list. For a mesh of n triangles, $3n$ vertices are stored in the vertex buffer.

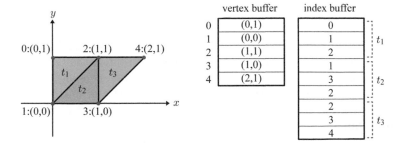

Fig. 1.13: Indexed triangle list. Vertices are stored with no duplication in the vertex buffer, and the index buffer stores the triangle information.

An obvious method to represent a triangle mesh is to enumerate its vertices, where three vertices are read in linear order to make up a triangle. See the 2D triangles in Fig. 1.12. The vertices are stored in a memory space, named *vertex buffer*[3], and define three triangles. This representation is called a *triangle list*.

---

[3] Vertex buffer is the terminology of Direct3D. OpenGL calls it *vertex array*.

The triangle list representation is quite intuitive. However, it is inefficient because the vertex buffer contains redundant data. In Fig. 1.12, for example, the vertex at (1,1) is shared by three triangles and appears three times in the vertex buffer.

In a triangle mesh, a vertex is almost always shared by multiple triangles. Then, the vertex buffer can be made compact by using a separate *index buffer*. The vertices are stored in the vertex buffer with no duplication, and three indices per triangle are stored in the index buffer. Fig. 1.13 shows the vertex and index buffers for the same mesh of Fig. 1.12. This representation is called *indexed triangle list*.

In general, the vertex data stored in the vertex buffer include not only positions but also normals, texture coordinates, and many more. (All of these data will be presented throughout this book.) Therefore, the vertex buffer storage saved by removing the duplicate data outweighs the additional storage needed for the index buffer. The representation illustrated in Fig. 1.12 is often called *non-indexed*, and it is rarely used because there are very few cases where the indices are not needed.

In Direct3D, the formats for index buffer data are either 16- or 32-bit unsigned integers. If 16-bit index is used, we can represent 2^{16} (65,536) vertices. With 32-bit index, 2^{32} (4,294,967,296) vertices can be represented. When fewer than 65,536 vertices are put into the vertex buffer, 16-bit format is preferred because it results in a smaller index buffer.

The indexed triangle list brings not only storage efficiency but also performance increase. For rendering, a triangle mesh is sent to the GPU. As will be presented in Chapter 2, each vertex of a mesh is independently transformed by the so-called *vertex processing stage* of the GPU and is stored in a *post-transform cache*. If a triangle references a vertex located in the cache, the vertex is simply fetched from the cache instead of being transformed again by the vertex processing stage. When searching the cache for the vertex referenced by a triangle, the vertex index is used. (The triangle formed by assembling three vertices of the cache is further processed for rendering.)

Only when the cache is missed, the vertex is processed. Therefore, the average number of vertices processed per triangle is called the *average cache miss ratio* (ACMR). It is often used to measure the rendering performance. In a typical closed mesh, the number of triangles is approximately twice the number of vertices, i.e., given n vertices, we have about $2n$ triangles. See note in the next page for discussion on this ratio[4]. If the post-transform cache is large enough to contain all vertices of the mesh, no vertex will be processed multiple times. Then, the ACMR will be approximately $\frac{n}{2n}$, i.e., 0.5.

---

[4]Note presented in a shaded box contains the background theory, technically detailed discussions, or advanced issues. If you are not interested, it can be skipped with no difficulty in following the main stream of the book.

[Note: Vertex-triangle ratio in a triangle mesh]

For a closed mesh with no hole, the Euler's polyhedron formula asserts

$$v - e + f = 2 \qquad (1.1)$$

where v, e, and f are respectively the numbers of vertices, edges, and faces of the mesh. In a closed triangle mesh, every edge is shared by two faces, and every face has three edges. Therefore, if we count two faces per edge, the counted number will be three times the number of faces of the mesh, i.e.,

$$2e = 3f \qquad (1.2)$$

(As an example, consider a tetrahedron, where e is 6 and f is 4.) When we replace e in Equation (1.1) by $\frac{3}{2}f$ derived from Equation (1.2), we obtain the following:

$$f = 2v - 4$$

As the mesh size increases, the number of faces (f) converges to twice the number of vertices (v).

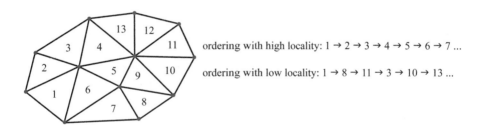

ordering with high locality: $1 \rightarrow 2 \rightarrow 3 \rightarrow 4 \rightarrow 5 \rightarrow 6 \rightarrow 7 ...$

ordering with low locality: $1 \rightarrow 8 \rightarrow 11 \rightarrow 3 \rightarrow 10 \rightarrow 13 ...$

Fig. 1.14: Triangle orders influence the rendering performance.

The cache has a limited size. If the triangles are randomly ordered, the cache may not be very helpful. See Fig. 1.14. In the first ordering, the vertices of triangle 1 are processed and stored in the cache. Then, among the three vertices of triangle 2, two are fetched from the cache, and only one is processed. The same applies to triangle 3. It is less likely to process a vertex multiple times. Consider the second ordering. Triangle 8 follows triangle 1, and all of its vertices need to be processed. The same applies to triangle 11. When triangle 3 is processed, its vertex shared with triangle 1 might have been replaced if the cache is quite small. Then, the vertex has to be

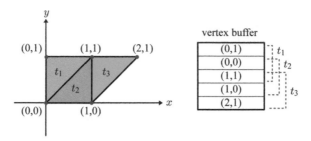

Fig. 1.15:   Triangle strip. Except for the first triangle, each triangle shares two vertices with the previous triangle.

processed again. In the worst case, where three vertices referenced by each triangle are not found in the cache, the ACMR will be 3. These examples show that ACMR depends on the order of the triangles fed into the GPU.

The ACMR can be reduced if the triangles of a polygon mesh are ordered to increase the *locality* of vertex reference. There have been efforts for reducing ACMR by reordering the triangles [5, 6]. A few utilities are available, and an example is `ID3DXMesh::Optimize`[5]. With such an effort to provide a triangle mesh with high locality, ACMR can be maintained between 0.5 and 1 in most applications.

Another interesting representation of a polygon mesh is a *triangle strip*. It describes a mesh as a series of adjacent triangles. See Fig. 1.15. The first triangle (t_1) is rendered by processing the first three vertices in the vertex buffer. When rendering the second triangle (t_2), the last two vertices of the first triangle, (0,0) and (1,1) in the example, are simply fetched from the cache. Then, only a single vertex, (1,0) in the example, is taken from the vertex buffer and processed. Similarly, the third triangle (t_3) is rendered by fetching two vertices, (1,1) and (1,0), from the cache, and processing a new vertex, (2,1).

Let us consider the rendering performance of the triangle strip. In the ideal case, three vertices are processed for the first triangle, and then a single vertex is processed for each of the remaining triangles. Then, rendering n triangles requires $(n+2)$ vertices to be processed, i.e., ACMR is $\frac{n+2}{n}$. As n increases, the ACMR approaches 1, which is usually worse than that of the indexed triangle list. However, the triangle strip outperforms the triangle list for some specific applications. For example, displaying a quadrilateral of four vertices can be performed best by using the triangle strip with no index buffer.

---

[5]D3DX is a library of utilities designed to provide additional graphics functionality on top of Direct3D. `ID3DXMesh` is an interface of D3DX, and `Optimize` is a method of `ID3DXMesh`.

1.2.3 Surface Normal

In the real world, light emitted from a light source is reflected by object surfaces and then reaches our eye. Such an interaction between light sources and object surfaces is *simulated* in computer graphics. It is called *lighting* and is essential for creating a photorealistic image of 3D models. In lighting, surface normal plays a key role, as is the case in the real-world physics. (Lighting will be presented in Chapter 5.)

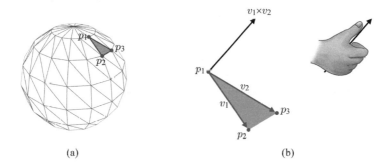

(a)   (b)

Fig. 1.16: Triangle normal. (a) The triangle is composed of three vertices, p_1, p_2, and p_3. (b) The cross product $v_1 \times v_2$ is computed using the right-hand rule and defines the triangle normal.

Consider the triangle $\langle p_1, p_2, p_3 \rangle$ in Fig. 1.16-(a). Its normal is obtained by taking the edges as vectors and calculating their *cross product*[6]. Let us denote the vector connecting the first vertex (p_1) and the second (p_2) by v_1, as shown in Fig. 1.16-(b). Similarly, the vector connecting the first vertex (p_1) and the third (p_3) is denoted by v_2. Then, the triangle normal is computed as follows:

$$\frac{v_1 \times v_2}{||v_1 \times v_2||} \tag{1.3}$$

where $\times$ denotes the cross product operation. The cross product is divided by its length to make a unit vector. In computer graphics, every normal vector is made to be a unit vector by default.

Equation (1.3) follows the *right-hand rule*: The thumb of the right hand indicates the direction of the cross product when the remaining fingers curl from the first argument vector (v_1) to the second (v_2).

---

[6]Consider two 3D vectors, a and b. When their coordinates are (a_x, a_y, a_z) and (b_x, b_y, b_z), respectively, the cross product $a \times b$ is defined to be $(a_y b_z - a_z b_y, a_z b_x - a_x b_z, a_x b_y - a_y b_x)$. The cross product is perpendicular to both a and b, i.e., perpendicular to the plane spanned by a and b.

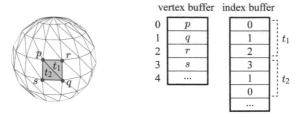

Fig. 1.17: In the representation of indexed triangle list, the index buffer records the vertices in the CCW order.

What if the vertices of the triangle are ordered as p_1, p_3, and p_2? The first vertex (p_1) and the second (p_3) are connected to generate v_2, and the first (p_1) and the third (p_2) generate v_1. The right-hand rule applied to v_2 and v_1 defines the triangle normal as follows:

$$\frac{v_2 \times v_1}{||v_2 \times v_1||} \tag{1.4}$$

Note that Equations (1.3) and (1.4) represent opposite directions. The normal direction depends on the vertex order, i.e., whether $\langle p_1, p_2, p_3 \rangle$ or $\langle p_1, p_3, p_2 \rangle$.

Observe that, in Fig. 1.16-(a), $\langle p_1, p_2, p_3 \rangle$ represents the counter-clockwise (CCW) order of vertices whereas $\langle p_1, p_3, p_2 \rangle$ represents the clockwise (CW) order. According to the right-hand rule, the CCW order makes the normal point out of the object whereas the CW order makes the normal inward. The convention in computer graphics is to make the normal point outward. For this purpose, the triangle vertices are always ordered CCW. Fig. 1.17 shows an example of the indexed triangle list with the CCW vertex ordering.

We have so far discussed the triangle normals, but more important in computer graphics are the *vertex normals*. The vertex normals might be less intuitive than the triangle normals. Then, recall that the mesh vertices are the points sampling the smooth surface, as illustrated in Fig. 1.18. A normal can be assigned to a vertex such that the vertex normal approximates the normal of the smooth surface at the sampled point.

Given a polygon mesh only, computing the vertex normals is an underconstrained problem, and rules of thumb and heuristics are often adopted [7]. A simple method is to average the normals of all triangles sharing the vertex, as shown in Fig. 1.19. In many cases, the vertex normals are automatically computed by the modeling packages, stored as vertex attributes in the vertex buffer, and then passed to the rendering step.

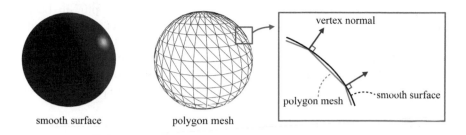

smooth surface   polygon mesh

Fig. 1.18: A vertex normal corresponds to the surface normal at the point sampled by the vertex.

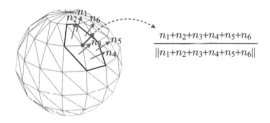

$$\frac{n_1+n_2+n_3+n_4+n_5+n_6}{\|n_1+n_2+n_3+n_4+n_5+n_6\|}$$

Fig. 1.19: A vertex normal is often computed as a mean of the normals of the triangles sharing the vertex.

1.3 Model Export and Import

As discussed earlier in this chapter, game objects and animation data created using off-line graphics packages are stored in files and passed to the run-time game program. The process of outputting the data in a format suitable for other applications is called *export*. On the other hand, taking such exported data is called *import*.

Export can be done using *plug-ins* or *scripts*. A plug-in is referred to as an add-on program that is designed for a specific application. It interacts with the host program (for example, 3ds Max in the current context) to provide a set of functions not supported by the host. A plug-in is coded in high-level languages such as C and using the APIs provided by the host program. It is compiled into a machine code and then run by CPU.

In contrast, a script is usually interpreted and run by the host program. Many graphics packages provide their own script languages to manipulate and output the data created by the packages. The script language of 3ds Max is MAXScript. In general, a script is less versatile than a plug-in because a script language is domain-specific. A script is interpreted for execution and consequently is slower than a plug-in that performs the same function. Despite these drawbacks, a script is preferred in many applications because it is easy to code and often provides an optimized access to the data of the host program. Shown below are the pseudo script code that exports an indexed triangle list and a fraction of the output text file.

```
Specify Out as the output file
foreach polygon mesh
  Write the number of vertices to Out
  foreach vertex
    Write its position and normal to Out
  endforeach
  Write the number of polygons to Out
  foreach polygon
    Write its vertex indices to Out
  endforeach
endforeach
```

```
vertices 530
49.2721 0.809525 85.6266 -0.966742 0.0 0.255752
48.5752 0.809525 88.2606 -0.966824 0.0 0.255444
49.3836 0.809525 89.1386 -0.092052 0.0 0.995754
...

faces 1024
0 5 6
6 1 0
1 6 7
...
```

In the above example, the exported polygon mesh is composed of 530 vertices and 1024 triangles. A vertex is described by six floating-point values: three for position and three for normal. The vertex index is implicitly specified such that the first vertex is 0, the second is 1, and so on. A triangle is described by three indices. For example, the first triangle is composed of the 0th, 5th and 6th vertices.

Game-developing studios usually have their own proprietary data representations and exporters that are optimized for the games under development.

The exported polygon mesh is loaded into the run-time game program, also by a proprietary importer. The polygon mesh represented in an indexed triangle list is usually loaded into two CPU arrays: one for vertices and the other for indices. A series of graphics API functions is invoked to pass the arrays to GPU. Then, the GPU renders the polygon mesh.

[Note: Vertex/index buffers and drawcall in Direct3D]

In Direct3D 9, `IDirect3DDevice9` interface is the software controller of the graphics device hardware. Through its methods, application programs instruct the GPU to create resources such as buffers and textures, draw 3D geometry, work with system-level variables, etc. For creating a vertex buffer and an index buffer within the GPU, `IDirect3DDevice9::CreateVertexBuffer` and `IDirect3DDevice9::CreateIndexBuffer` are invoked, respectively. The vertex/index data stored in the CPU arrays may then be copied to the vertex/index buffers using `memcpy`, for example. Finally, the polygon mesh represented in the vertex/index buffers is drawn by invoking `IDirect3DDevice9::DrawIndexedPrimitive`. It is called the *drawcall* for the indexed triangle list. The drawcall for the non-indexed triangle list is `IDirect3DDevice9::DrawPrimitive`. (Not only triangles but also line segments and points can be rendered as independent entities. They are collectively called *primitives*.)

1.4 Coordinate Systems

The Cartesian coordinate system can be either right-handed or left-handed. See Fig. 1.20-(a). In the right-hand system (RHS), the thumb of the right hand points toward the positive end of the z-axis when the other four fingers curl from the x-axis to the y-axis. In the left-hand system (LHS), the same rule is applied to the left hand.

In Section 1.2.3, we implicitly assumed RHS and used the right hand for defining the triangle normal. In LHS, however, the triangle normal is defined using the left hand, i.e., the triangle vertices are traversed by the left hand's four fingers, making the thumb indicate the direction of the triangle normal.

Recall that, in Section 1.2.3, the triangle vertices were made to be ordered counter-clockwise (CCW). It was also based on the assumption of RHS. If we maintained the CCW vertex order in LHS, the triangle normal would point inward. It violates the convention of computer graphics. Therefore, the triangle vertices are ordered clockwise (CW) in LHS.

When a polygon mesh created in an RHS-based package is ported to an LHS-based one, a sort of *remodeling* is needed. First of all, the vertex order

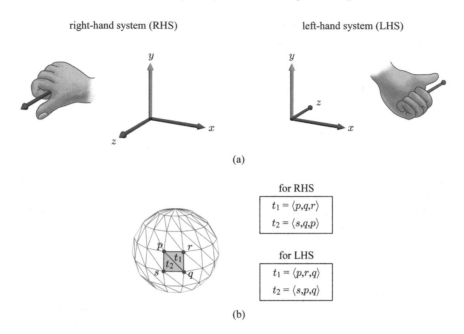

right-hand system (RHS)

left-hand system (LHS)

(a)

for RHS

$t_1 = \langle p,q,r \rangle$	
$t_2 = \langle s,q,p \rangle$	

for LHS

$t_1 = \langle p,r,q \rangle$	
$t_2 = \langle s,p,q \rangle$	

(b)

Fig. 1.20: The handedness of a coordinate system determines the vertex order of each triangle. (a) RHS vs. LHS. (b) CCW ordering for RHS vs. CW ordering for LHS.

of each triangle is changed such that the triangle normal points out of the polyhedron. If the vertex order is $\langle p_1, p_2, p_3 \rangle$, the changed is $\langle p_1, p_3, p_2 \rangle$, as shown in Fig. 1.20-(b).

Let us discuss another remodeling task. Fig. 1.21-(a) shows an object composed of a triangle and a square. It is defined at the $-z$ side of the RHS. When a model is viewed, a synthetic camera's position and view direction have to be defined, as will be presented in Chapter 2. Assume that the camera is positioned at the origin and its view direction is $(0, 0, -1)$. Then, the camera captures the image shown in the right-hand side of Fig. 1.21-(a).

Suppose that the object is ported *as is* into the LHS-based package. Shown in the left of Fig. 1.21-(b) is the object placed in the LHS. Let us use the same view parameters specified in the RHS-based package. Then, the resulting image will be the one at the right of Fig. 1.21-(b), which is the *reflection* of the image shown in Fig. 1.21-(a).

A solution to resolve this inconsistency is simple. At the remodeling stage, the z-coordinates of the object and view parameters are negated. It has the effect of reflecting the object and camera with respect to the xy-plane. Fig. 1.21-(c) shows the z-negated object and view parameters. Then, the correct image is obtained.

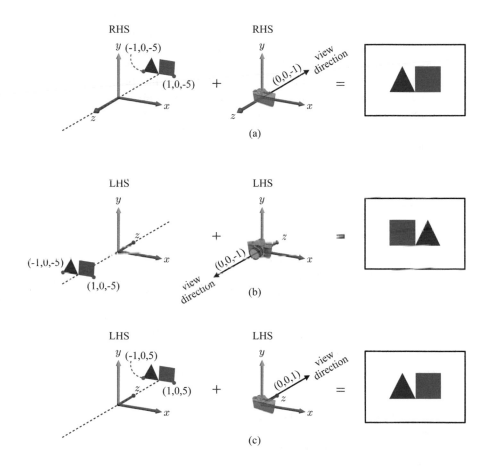

Fig. 1.21: Reflection needed for converting from RHS to LHS. (a) An object and the view parameters are defined in an RHS. (b) The object is imported *as is* to an LHS. Note that the vertex coordinates are not changed. The view parameters are also used without change. The captured image in the LHS is different from the one captured in the RHS shown in (a). (c) The z-coordinates of both the object and view parameters are negated. Then, the image captured in the LHS is identical to the one shown in (a).

In summary, porting an application between RHS and LHS requires two tasks: vertex order change and z-negation. Whereas the z-negation is required, the vertex order change is optional. There exists a roundabout way. These issues will be presented more rigorously in Chapter 3.

OpenGL and Direct3D adopt different handedness. The default coordinate system of OpenGL is right-handed whereas that of Direct3D is left-handed. The difference constructed a barrier hard to cross over for inexperienced programmers. However, the barrier has crumbled away, and we can run an RHS-based application on top of Direct3D, for example. It has been due to GPU's *programmability*, which will be presented in the next chapters.

This book uses RHS by default because it is much more familiar to the ordinary readers. Therefore, the triangle vertices are listed in the CCW order unless specified otherwise.

Exercises

1. Consider the simplest 3D closed mesh, *tetrahedron*. Suppose that it is composed of four vertices, (0,0,0), (1,0,0), (0,1,0), and (0,0,1). The triangle normals should point out of the tetrahedron.

    (a) Assuming that the tetrahedron is exported to a *right-hand* system, draw the vertex and index buffers for its indexed triangle list representation.

    (b) Assuming that the tetrahedron is exported to a *left-hand* system, do the same.

2. Let v, e, and f denote the numbers of vertices, edges and faces of a closed triangle mesh, respectively. In [Note: Vertex-triangle ratio in a triangle mesh], we have derived $f = 2v - 4$. Derive a similar relation between v and e.

3. ATVR stands for average transform to vertex ratio, and measures the number of vertex-transforms per vertex. (It is different from ACMR.)

    (a) What would be the best-case ATVR?

    (b) What would be the worst-case ATVR?

Chapter 2

Vertex Processing

In computer architecture, a *pipeline* refers to a sequence of data processing elements, where the output of one element is used as the input of the next one. The *rendering pipeline* of GPU accepts a representation of a 3D scene as input, which is mainly composed of polygons. The pipeline transforms a stream of polygons to the 2D form. The colors of the pixels comprising the 2D polygons are computed, and finally the image of the scene is output.

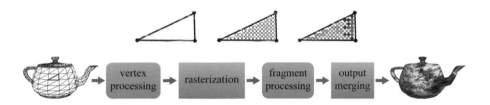

Fig. 2.1: The vertex processing and fragment processing stages (in rounded boxes) are programmable, and the rasterization and output merging stages (in rectangles) are hard-wired.

The main component of the rendering pipeline consists of the stages for vertex processing, rasterization, fragment processing, and output merging. Fig. 2.1 uses a polygon of a 3D model to illustrate the process of filling its interior that occurs during the four stages. The vertex processing stage operates on every input vertex stored in the vertex buffer and performs various operations such as transform. The rasterization stage assembles polygons from the vertices and converts each polygon to a set of *fragments*. A fragment refers to a set of data needed to update a pixel[1] in the color buffer. (The color buffer is a memory space storing the pixels to be displayed on the screen.) The fragment processing stage operates on each fragment and determines its

---

[1]In Direct3D, the word *pixel* is used for both fragment and pixel, but it often brings confusion.

color through various operations such as texturing. In the output merging stage, the fragment compotes or combines with the pixel in the color buffer to update the pixel's color.

The rendering pipeline architecture has continuously evolved. (Chapter 7 presents the state of the art.) Despite the evolution, the above four stages compose the main component of the pipeline. The stages are either *programmable* or *fixed*. The vertex and fragment processing stages are programmable. The programs for the stages are called *vertex program* and *fragment program*. Using the programs, you can apply any transform you want to the vertex, and you can determine the fragment color through any way you want.

In contrast, the rasterization and output merging stages are fixed or hardwired. They are not programmable but are just *configurable* through user-defined parameters. Throughout this book, you will learn how to write the vertex and fragment programs and how to configure the rasterization and output merging stages.

This chapter covers the vertex processing stage, and Chapters 3 and 4 cover the remaining stages. Typical operations on a vertex include transform, lighting, and animation. This chapter focuses on vertex transform and briefly shows how a vertex can be lit. Chapter 5 gives a detailed discussion on vertex lighting, and Chapter 11 presents how vertices can be animated.

2.1 World Transform

Fig. 2.2: Transforms and spaces in the vertex processing stage. Sections 2.1, 2.2, and 2.4 present the three transforms in order.

Chapter 1 presented how a 3D model is created. The coordinate system used for creating the model is named *object space*, which is also called model space or local space. (Throughout this book, we use the terms *space* and *coordinate system* interchangeably.) In the vertex processing stage, the object-space model goes though several spaces and finally arrives at the clip space, as illustrated in Fig. 2.2.

2.1.1 Affine Transforms and Homogeneous Coordinates

The world and view transforms in Fig. 2.2 are built upon the very basic transforms, such as *scaling, rotation,* and *translation.* Scaling and rotation are instances of a specific class of functions named *linear transform.* A combination of linear transform and translation is called *affine transform.*

Three-dimensional scaling is represented by a 3×3 matrix:

$$\begin{pmatrix} s_x & 0 & 0 \\ 0 & s_y & 0 \\ 0 & 0 & s_z \end{pmatrix} \tag{2.1}$$

where s_x, s_y and s_z are the scaling factors along the principal axes. If all of the scaling factors are identical, the scaling is called uniform. Otherwise, it is a non-uniform scaling. A vector is scaled through *matrix multiplication:*

$$\begin{pmatrix} s_x & 0 & 0 \\ 0 & s_y & 0 \\ 0 & 0 & s_z \end{pmatrix} \begin{pmatrix} x \\ y \\ z \end{pmatrix} = \begin{pmatrix} s_x x \\ s_y y \\ s_z z \end{pmatrix}$$

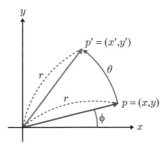

Fig. 2.3: A vector p is rotated by θ to define a new vector p'.

Now consider rotating a vector. Fig. 2.3 illustrates 2D rotation, where p is rotated about the origin by θ to define p'. If p's length is r, the coordinates of p are defined as follows:

$$x = r cos\phi$$
$$y = r sin\phi$$

The length of p' is also r, and its x-coordinate is computed as follows:

$$\begin{aligned} x' &= r cos(\phi + \theta) \\ &= r cos\phi cos\theta - r sin\phi sin\theta \\ &= x cos\theta - y sin\theta \end{aligned} \tag{2.2}$$

Its y-coordinate is similarly computed:

$$
\begin{aligned}
y' &= r sin(\phi + \theta) \\
&= r cos\phi sin\theta + r sin\phi cos\theta \\
&= x sin\theta + y cos\theta
\end{aligned}
\tag{2.3}
$$

Equations (2.2) and (2.3) are combined into a matrix multiplication form:

$$
\begin{pmatrix} x' \\ y' \end{pmatrix} = \begin{pmatrix} cos\theta & -sin\theta \\ sin\theta & cos\theta \end{pmatrix} \begin{pmatrix} x \\ y \end{pmatrix}
\tag{2.4}
$$

The 2×2 matrix in Equation (2.4) represents the 2D rotation matrix.

A 3D rotation requires the *axis of rotation*. First, consider rotation about the z-axis, which we denote by R_z. Suppose that it rotates (x, y, z) into (x', y', z'). Obviously, the z-coordinates are not changed by R_z:

$$
z' = z
\tag{2.5}
$$

On the other hand, Equations (2.2) and (2.3) hold for the xy-coordinates. Then, Equations (2.2), (2.3), and (2.5) are combined into a matrix multiplication form:

$$
\begin{pmatrix} x' \\ y' \\ z' \end{pmatrix} = \begin{pmatrix} cos\theta & -sin\theta & 0 \\ sin\theta & cos\theta & 0 \\ 0 & 0 & 1 \end{pmatrix} \begin{pmatrix} x \\ y \\ z \end{pmatrix}
\tag{2.6}
$$

The 3×3 matrix in Equation (2.6) represents R_z.

In Equations (2.2), (2.3), and (2.5), let us apply *cyclic permutation* to the xyz-coordinates, i.e., x, y, and z are replaced by y, z, and x, respectively. Then, we obtain the rotation about the x-axis:

$$
R_x = \begin{pmatrix} 1 & 0 & 0 \\ 0 & cos\theta & -sin\theta \\ 0 & sin\theta & cos\theta \end{pmatrix}
\tag{2.7}
$$

Applying the cyclic permutation one more time leads to the rotation about the y-axis:

$$
R_y = \begin{pmatrix} cos\theta & 0 & sin\theta \\ 0 & 1 & 0 \\ -sin\theta & 0 & cos\theta \end{pmatrix}
\tag{2.8}
$$

Another frequently used transform in computer graphics is translation, which displaces (x, y, z) to $(x + d_x, y + d_y, z + d_z)$. Translation does not fall into the class of linear transforms and is represented as *vector addition*:

$$
\begin{pmatrix} x \\ y \\ z \end{pmatrix} + \begin{pmatrix} d_x \\ d_y \\ d_z \end{pmatrix} = \begin{pmatrix} x + d_x \\ y + d_y \\ z + d_z \end{pmatrix}
\tag{2.9}
$$

Fortunately, we can describe translation as matrix multiplication if we use the *homogeneous coordinates*. Given the 3D Cartesian coordinates (x, y, z) of a point, we can simply take $(x, y, z, 1)$ as its homogeneous coordinates. Then, translation is represented by a 4×4 matrix and is applied to the homogeneous coordinates of the point through matrix multiplication:

$$\begin{pmatrix} 1 & 0 & 0 & d_x \\ 0 & 1 & 0 & d_y \\ 0 & 0 & 1 & d_z \\ 0 & 0 & 0 & 1 \end{pmatrix} \begin{pmatrix} x \\ y \\ z \\ 1 \end{pmatrix} = \begin{pmatrix} x + d_x \\ y + d_y \\ z + d_z \\ 1 \end{pmatrix} \quad (2.10)$$

Note that Equations (2.9) and (2.10) show the same result, one in Cartesian coordinates and the other in homogeneous coordinates.

For handling the homogeneous coordinates, the 3×3 matrices for scaling and rotation need to be altered. For example, the scaling matrix in Equation (2.1) is extended into a 4×4 matrix and applied to a point in homogeneous coordinates as follows:

$$\begin{pmatrix} s_x & 0 & 0 & 0 \\ 0 & s_y & 0 & 0 \\ 0 & 0 & s_z & 0 \\ 0 & 0 & 0 & 1 \end{pmatrix} \begin{pmatrix} x \\ y \\ z \\ 1 \end{pmatrix} = \begin{pmatrix} s_x x \\ s_y y \\ s_z z \\ 1 \end{pmatrix}$$

The fourth row of the 4×4 matrix is (0 0 0 1) and serves to copy the fourth coordinate of the point into the transformed. In Section 2.4, however, you will find a new class of transforms, whose fourth row is not (0 0 0 1).

In general, the fourth component of the homogeneous coordinates is not necessarily 1 and is denoted by w. The homogeneous coordinates (x, y, z, w) correspond to the Cartesian coordinates $(\frac{x}{w}, \frac{y}{w}, \frac{z}{w})$. For example, (1,2,3,1), (2,4,6,2) and (3,6,9,3) are different homogeneous coordinates for the same Cartesian coordinates (1,2,3). In other words, $(x, y, z, 1)$ are just an instance of the infinitely many homogeneous coordinates for the Cartesian coordinates (x, y, z).

The w-component of the homogeneous coordinates is used to distinguish between vectors and points. If w is 0, (x, y, z, w) represent a vector, not a point.

2.1.2 World Matrix

Once an object is modeled, it can be thought of as being stuck to its object space. Each vertex of the object is fixed and immovable in the object space. The object space for a model is typically unrelated to that of another model. The first task in the rendering pipeline is to assemble all the component models defined in their own object spaces into a single space named *world space*, which is the coordinate system used for the entire game environment. This is performed by *world transform*.

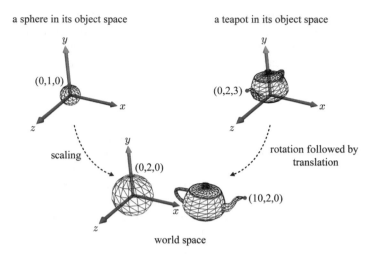

Fig. 2.4: The sphere and teapot are defined in their own object spaces and are assembled into a single space, the world space.

Given a sphere and a teapot created in their own object spaces, let us construct the scene shown in Fig. 2.4. The world transform needed for the sphere is simply a scaling. Suppose that the scaling factors are all 2s. Then, we have the following scaling matrix:

$$\begin{pmatrix} 2 & 0 & 0 & 0 \\ 0 & 2 & 0 & 0 \\ 0 & 0 & 2 & 0 \\ 0 & 0 & 0 & 1 \end{pmatrix}$$

Consider the north pole of the sphere located at $(0,1,0)$ of the object space. The world matrix transforms it into $(0,2,0)$ in the world space:

$$\begin{pmatrix} 2 & 0 & 0 & 0 \\ 0 & 2 & 0 & 0 \\ 0 & 0 & 2 & 0 \\ 0 & 0 & 0 & 1 \end{pmatrix} \begin{pmatrix} 0 \\ 1 \\ 0 \\ 1 \end{pmatrix} = \begin{pmatrix} 0 \\ 2 \\ 0 \\ 1 \end{pmatrix}$$

The world transform needed for the teapot is a rotation about the y-axis (R_y) followed by a translation, as illustrated in Fig. 2.5. R_y is defined in Equation (2.8). The *sign* of the rotation angle θ is determined as follows: Look at the origin of the coordinate system such that the axis of rotation points toward you. If the rotation is counter-clockwise, θ is positive. If the rotation is clockwise, θ is negative. (See [Note: Clockwise and counter-clockwise rotations] for more on this.) In Fig. 2.5, the rotation angle is $90°$, and we have

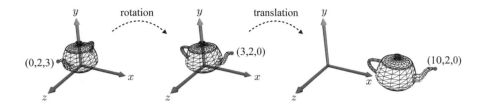

Fig. 2.5: The teapot is rotated about the y-axis by 90° and is then translated along the x-axis by seven units. The teapot's mouth is rotated from (0,2,3) to (3,2,0) and then translated to (10,2,0). The combined matrix of the rotation and the translation instantly transforms (0,2,3) to (10,2,0).

the following rotation matrix:

$$R_y(90°) = \begin{pmatrix} 0 & 0 & 1 & 0 \\ 0 & 1 & 0 & 0 \\ -1 & 0 & 0 & 0 \\ 0 & 0 & 0 & 1 \end{pmatrix} \tag{2.11}$$

The teapot's mouth positioned at (0,2,3) is rotated to (3,2,0) by $R_y(90°)$:

$$\begin{pmatrix} 0 & 0 & 1 & 0 \\ 0 & 1 & 0 & 0 \\ -1 & 0 & 0 & 0 \\ 0 & 0 & 0 & 1 \end{pmatrix} \begin{pmatrix} 0 \\ 2 \\ 3 \\ 1 \end{pmatrix} = \begin{pmatrix} 3 \\ 2 \\ 0 \\ 1 \end{pmatrix}$$

Now we consider translation. In Fig. 2.5, the teapot is translated by seven units along the x-axis by the following matrix:

$$T = \begin{pmatrix} 1 & 0 & 0 & 7 \\ 0 & 1 & 0 & 0 \\ 0 & 0 & 1 & 0 \\ 0 & 0 & 0 & 1 \end{pmatrix} \tag{2.12}$$

The teapot's mouth located at (3,2,0) is translated to (10,2,0) by T:

$$\begin{pmatrix} 1 & 0 & 0 & 7 \\ 0 & 1 & 0 & 0 \\ 0 & 0 & 1 & 0 \\ 0 & 0 & 0 & 1 \end{pmatrix} \begin{pmatrix} 3 \\ 2 \\ 0 \\ 1 \end{pmatrix} = \begin{pmatrix} 10 \\ 2 \\ 0 \\ 1 \end{pmatrix}$$

[Note: Clockwise and counter-clockwise rotations]

Fig. 2.6: The teapot shown in the middle is rotated CCW to define the one on the left. If rotated CW, we have the result on the right.

Fig. 2.6 illustrates the counter-clockwise (CCW) and clockwise (CW) rotations about the y-axis. If the rotation angle is positive, the rotation is CCW with respect to the axis pointing toward us. If it is negative, the rotation is CW by the absolute value of the given rotation angle.

Note that rotation by $-\theta$ is equivalent to rotation by $(2\pi-\theta)$. For example, rotation by $-90°$ is equivalent to rotation by $270°$. The matrix for rotation by $-90°$ about the y-axis is as follows:

$$
\begin{aligned}
R_y(-90°) &= \begin{pmatrix} cos(-90°) & 0 & sin(-90°) & 0 \\ 0 & 1 & 0 & 0 \\ -sin(-90°) & 0 & cos(-90°) & 0 \\ 0 & 0 & 0 & 1 \end{pmatrix} \\
&= \begin{pmatrix} cos\,270° & 0 & sin\,270° & 0 \\ 0 & 1 & 0 & 0 \\ -sin\,270° & 0 & cos\,270° & 0 \\ 0 & 0 & 0 & 1 \end{pmatrix} \\
&= \begin{pmatrix} 0 & 0 & -1 & 0 \\ 0 & 1 & 0 & 0 \\ 1 & 0 & 0 & 0 \\ 0 & 0 & 0 & 1 \end{pmatrix}
\end{aligned}
$$

The above discussion assumes the right-hand system. In the left-hand system, a positive angle leads to a CW rotation, and a negative one leads to a CCW rotation. Recall that, unless otherwise specified, all of the coordinate systems presented in this book are right-handed.

$R_y(90°)$ in Equation (2.11) and T in Equation (2.12) can be combined into a single matrix, the world matrix:

$$TR_y(90°) = \begin{pmatrix} 1 & 0 & 0 & 7 \\ 0 & 1 & 0 & 0 \\ 0 & 0 & 1 & 0 \\ 0 & 0 & 0 & 1 \end{pmatrix} \begin{pmatrix} 0 & 0 & 1 & 0 \\ 0 & 1 & 0 & 0 \\ -1 & 0 & 0 & 0 \\ 0 & 0 & 0 & 1 \end{pmatrix}$$

$$= \begin{pmatrix} 0 & 0 & 1 & 7 \\ 0 & 1 & 0 & 0 \\ -1 & 0 & 0 & 0 \\ 0 & 0 & 0 & 1 \end{pmatrix} \qquad (2.13)$$

The teapot's mouth that is originally located at (0,2,3) in the object space is transformed to (10,2,0) in the world space by the world matrix:

$$\begin{pmatrix} 0 & 0 & 1 & 7 \\ 0 & 1 & 0 & 0 \\ -1 & 0 & 0 & 0 \\ 0 & 0 & 0 & 1 \end{pmatrix} \begin{pmatrix} 0 \\ 2 \\ 3 \\ 1 \end{pmatrix} = \begin{pmatrix} 10 \\ 2 \\ 0 \\ 1 \end{pmatrix}$$

Thanks to the homogeneous coordinates, the linear transform and the translation can be combined into a single 4×4 affine matrix. No matter how many transforms are concatenated, the resulting 4×4 affine matrix is decomposed into two parts: the upper-left 3×3 sub-matrix representing a combined linear transform, and the fourth column representing a combined translation.

2.1.3 Euler Transform

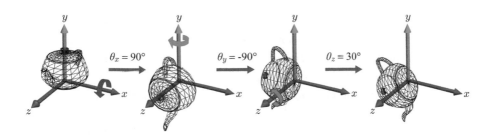

Fig. 2.7: The teapot is successively rotated using the Euler angles and acquires an orientation.

When we successively rotate an object about the x-, y-, and z-axes, the object acquires a specific orientation. See Fig. 2.7. The rotation angles, θ_x,

θ_y, and θ_z, are called the *Euler angles*, and are popularly used for representing an arbitrary orientation.

When three rotations are combined into one, it is called *Euler transform*. Concatenating the matrices of the rotations presented in Fig. 2.7 produces a single matrix:

$$R_z(30°)R_y(-90°)R_x(90°) = \begin{pmatrix} \frac{\sqrt{3}}{2} & -\frac{1}{2} & 0 & 0 \\ \frac{1}{2} & \frac{\sqrt{3}}{2} & 0 & 0 \\ 0 & 0 & 1 & 0 \\ 0 & 0 & 0 & 1 \end{pmatrix} \begin{pmatrix} 0 & 0 & -1 & 0 \\ 0 & 1 & 0 & 0 \\ 1 & 0 & 0 & 0 \\ 0 & 0 & 0 & 1 \end{pmatrix} \begin{pmatrix} 1 & 0 & 0 & 0 \\ 0 & 0 & -1 & 0 \\ 0 & 1 & 0 & 0 \\ 0 & 0 & 0 & 1 \end{pmatrix}$$

$$= \begin{pmatrix} 0 & -\frac{\sqrt{3}}{2} & \frac{1}{2} & 0 \\ 0 & -\frac{1}{2} & -\frac{\sqrt{3}}{2} & 0 \\ 1 & 0 & 0 & 0 \\ 0 & 0 & 0 & 1 \end{pmatrix}$$

If we multiply the combined matrix with the teapot, we obtain the oriented teapot shown at the right end of Fig. 2.7.

2.1.4 Transform of Surface Normals

Let M denote a matrix transforming a polygon mesh, i.e., all of its vertices are transformed by M. Can M be used for transforming its surface normals? The answer is yes if M is a rotation, a translation, a uniform scaling, or a combination of those. The answer is no if M includes a non-uniform scaling. See the 2D example in Fig. 2.8, where the line segment represents the cross section of a triangle perpendicular to the xy-plane of the coordinate system. Suppose that M is a 2D non-uniform scaling where $s_x = 0.5$ and $s_y = 1$. Fig. 2.8-(a) shows that the triangle's normal scaled by M is not any longer orthogonal to the triangle scaled by M. (As shown in Fig. 2.8, the transformed normal should be normalized when the transform includes a scaling.)

[Note: Normal transform] shows that the *transpose of the inverse* of M, $(M^{-1})^T$, is used for transforming the normals[2]. Fig. 2.8-(b) depicts the result of applying $(M^{-1})^T$ to the triangle normal. The normal transformed by $(M^{-1})^T$ remains orthogonal to the triangle transformed by M.

Fig. 2.8 uses triangle normals for easy discussions. More important are the vertex normals, which are usually computed at the modeling step. The vertex normals are also transformed by $(M^{-1})^T$. (Readers are referred to [8] for more rigorous discussions on transforming normals.)

---

[2]The *identity matrix* is a square matrix with ones on the main diagonal (from the upper-left element to the lower-right element) and zeros elsewhere. It is denoted by I. When two square matrices A and B are multiplied to make an identity matrix, i.e., $AB = I$, B is called the *inverse* of A and is denoted by A^{-1}. The *transpose* of a matrix A is created by reflecting A with respect to its main diagonal and is denoted by A^T. The rows of A^T are identical to the columns of A.

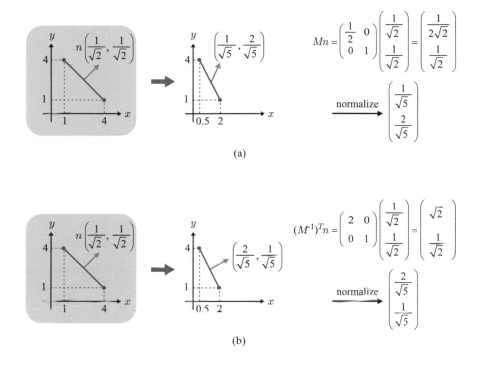

(a)

(b)

Fig. 2.8: Vertex transform vs. normal transform (modified from [8]). (a) The vertices and normal are transformed by a single matrix M. The transformed normal is not orthogonal to the transformed triangle. (b) Whereas the vertices are transformed by M, the normal is transformed by $(M^{-1})^T$. After the transforms, the normal remains orthogonal to the triangle.

[Note: Normal transform]

Consider the triangle $\langle p,q,r \rangle$ in Fig. 2.9. Its normal n is orthogonal to the vector connecting p and q. The dot product of orthogonal vectors is zero, and we have the following:

$$n^T(q - p) = 0 \qquad (2.14)$$

where p, q, and n are represented as column vectors, and n^T denotes the transpose of n. M transforms p and q to p' and q', respectively, i.e., $Mp = p'$ and $Mq = q'$. Using the *inverse* transform M^{-1}, we can rewrite Equation (2.14) as follows:

$$n^T(M^{-1}q' - M^{-1}p') = 0 \qquad (2.15)$$

Rearranging Equation (2.15) leads to the following:

$$n^T M^{-1}(q' - p') = 0 \qquad (2.16)$$

Let us take the *transpose* of Equation (2.16):

$$(q' - p')^T (M^{-1})^T n = 0 \qquad (2.17)$$

Equation (2.17) asserts that $(M^{-1})^T n$ is a vector orthogonal to $(q' - p')$ which is the edge vector of the transformed triangle.

The same discussion can be made for the vector connecting p and r, and we obtain the following:

$$(r' - p')^T (M^{-1})^T n = 0 \qquad (2.18)$$

As shown in Equations (2.17) and (2.18), the vector $(M^{-1})^T n$ is orthogonal to both $(q' - p')$ and $(r' - p')$, and therefore can be taken as the normal vector n' of the transformed triangle. It concludes that $(M^{-1})^T$ is the correct transform to be applied to n.

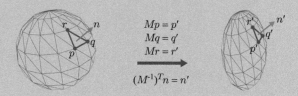

Fig. 2.9:   Before transforms, n is orthogonal to the triangle $\langle p,q,r \rangle$. Whereas $\langle p,q,r \rangle$ is transformed by M, n is transformed by $(M^{-1})^T$. Then, the transformed normal n' remains orthogonal to the transformed triangle $\langle p',q',r' \rangle$.

2.2   View Transform

Suppose that the world transform has been completed and all objects are now defined in the world space. We then have to specify the pose of the *camera* (which is often called the *viewer* or *eye*) in the world space, in order to capture the scene. Given the camera pose, the *camera space* is defined. Then, the world-space objects are transformed into the camera space.

2.2.1 Camera Space

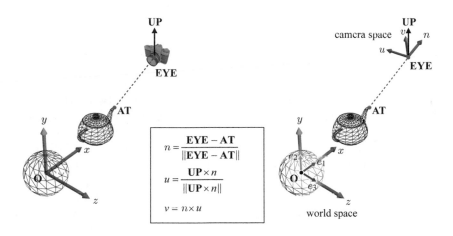

$$n = \frac{\mathbf{EYE} - \mathbf{AT}}{\|\mathbf{EYE} - \mathbf{AT}\|}$$

$$u = \frac{\mathbf{UP} \times n}{\|\mathbf{UP} \times n\|}$$

$$v = n \times u$$

Fig. 2.10: Given **EYE**, **AT**, and **UP**, the camera space is defined. Its origin is **EYE**, and the basis is $\{u,v,n\}$. In terms of the camera space, the camera is located at the origin and points in the $-n$ direction, i.e., the *view direction* is $-n$.

The camera pose is specified in terms of three parameters, **EYE**, **AT**, and **UP**, as shown in Fig. 2.10. They are called the *view parameters*.

- **EYE** is the camera position in the world space.

- **AT** is a reference point in the scene at which the camera is pointing. (It is typically somewhere in the middle of the scene. In the example, **AT** is set to the position of the teapot's mouth.)

- **UP** is a vector that roughly describes where the top of the camera is pointing. (In most cases, **UP** is set to the y-axis of the world space.)

The view parameters are used to build the camera space, which is also called view space or eye space. Its origin is **EYE**. The box in Fig. 2.10 shows the sequential process of building the *basis* $\{u,v,n\}$ of the camera space. First, the vector connecting **AT** and **EYE** is normalized to compose a unit vector n. The cross product of **UP** and n is normalized to define another unit vector u. Finally, the cross product of n and u determines a unit vector v. Observe that $\{u,v,n\}$ is an *orthonormal basis*, which is defined as an orthogonal set of unit vectors. (See [Note: Orthonormal basis] at the end of this section.)

2.2.2   Space Change and View Matrix

We have two distinct spaces, world space and camera space. The world space has the standard basis $\{e_1,e_2,e_3\}$, where $e_1 = (1,0,0)$, $e_2 = (0,1,0)$, and $e_3 = (0,0,1)$. The standard basis is obviously an orthonormal basis. We denote the world space by $\{\mathbf{O},e_1,e_2,e_3\}$. The camera space is denoted by $\{\mathbf{EYE},u,v,n\}$.

A point is given different coordinates in distinct spaces. See the first box in Fig. 2.11. Suppose that the teapot's mouth is located at $(10,2,0)$ in the world space. In terms of the camera space, however, it is on the $-n$ axis, and therefore its u- and v-coordinates are 0. The distance between the teapot's mouth and $\mathbf{EYE}$ located at $(20,3,0)$ is $\sqrt{101}$. Therefore, in the camera space $\{\mathbf{EYE},u,v,n\}$, the coordinates of the teapot's mouth are $(0,0,-\sqrt{101})$.

It becomes much easier to develop the rendering algorithms if all the world-space objects are redefined into the camera space in the manner of the teapot's mouth. It is called *space change* from the world space $\{\mathbf{O},e_1,e_2,e_3\}$ to the camera space $\{\mathbf{EYE},u,v,n\}$, and is performed by the *view transform*. This subsection presents how the view transform is derived. You have to clearly understand the concept of space change because it is frequently used in this book. (It also plays an important role in many key algorithms of robotics and computer vision.)

The view transform for space change can be intuitively described by the process of *superimposing* the camera space $\{\mathbf{EYE},u,v,n\}$ onto the world space $\{\mathbf{O},e_1,e_2,e_3\}$ while maintaining the relative poses of the scene objects with respect to the camera space. It will be helpful if you imagine invisible rods connecting the scene objects and the camera space. As illustrated in Fig. 2.11, the camera space is translated and then rotated to be superimposed onto the world space. Accordingly, the scene objects are translated and then rotated. Then, the world-space coordinates of the transformed objects can be taken as the camera-space coordinates because the camera space becomes identical to the world space.

The camera space is translated such that $\mathbf{EYE}$ is moved to $\mathbf{O}$. The translation vector is $\mathbf{O}-\mathbf{EYE}$, i.e., $(-\mathbf{EYE}_x,-\mathbf{EYE}_y,-\mathbf{EYE}_z)$. This results in the following translation matrix:

$$T = \begin{pmatrix} 1 & 0 & 0 & -\mathbf{EYE}_x \\ 0 & 1 & 0 & -\mathbf{EYE}_y \\ 0 & 0 & 1 & -\mathbf{EYE}_z \\ 0 & 0 & 0 & 1 \end{pmatrix} \tag{2.19}$$

$\mathbf{EYE}$ is located at $(20,3,0)$ in the world space, and T is a known matrix. It translates the teapot's mouth originally located at $(10,2,0)$ into $(-10,-1,0)$:

$$\begin{pmatrix} 1 & 0 & 0 & -20 \\ 0 & 1 & 0 & -3 \\ 0 & 0 & 1 & 0 \\ 0 & 0 & 0 & 1 \end{pmatrix} \begin{pmatrix} 10 \\ 2 \\ 0 \\ 1 \end{pmatrix} = \begin{pmatrix} -10 \\ -1 \\ 0 \\ 1 \end{pmatrix}$$

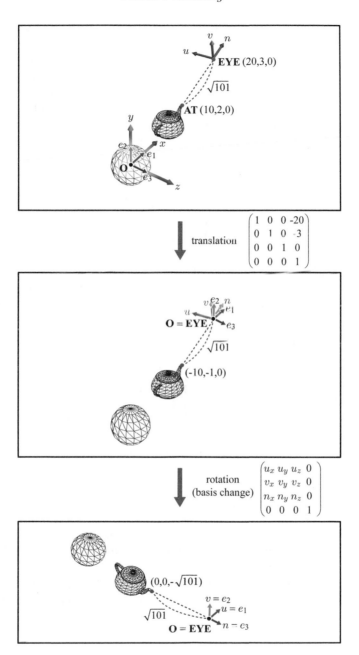

Fig. 2.11: The camera space $\{\mathbf{EYE}, u, v, n\}$ is superimposed onto the world space $\{\mathbf{O}, e_1, e_2, e_3\}$. It is done by a translation followed by a rotation. The two transforms are combined to produce the view transform, which converts the world-space objects into the camera space.

See the second box of Fig. 2.11. The world space and the camera space now share the origin, due to translation. We then need a rotation that transforms u, v, and n into e_1, e_2, and e_3, respectively. The rotation performs *basis change* from $\{e_1,e_2,e_3\}$ to $\{u,v,n\}$. By the basis-change matrix, the vertex coordinates defined in terms of the basis $\{e_1,e_2,e_3\}$, e.g., $(-10,-1,0)$, are redefined in terms of the basis $\{u,v,n\}$. Note that the problem of space change is decomposed into translation and basis change.

Consider the following matrix R, where the *rows* of the upper-left 3×3 matrix are filled by u, v, and n:

$$R = \begin{pmatrix} u_x & u_y & u_z & 0 \\ v_x & v_y & v_z & 0 \\ n_x & n_y & n_z & 0 \\ 0 & 0 & 0 & 1 \end{pmatrix} \tag{2.20}$$

We have already computed $\{u,v,n\}$ using the view parameters, **EYE**, **AT**, and **UP**, and therefore R in Equation (2.20) is a known matrix. Because $\{u,v,n\}$ is an orthonormal basis, it is obvious that $u \cdot u = 1$, $u \cdot v = 0$ and $u \cdot n = 0$, where $\cdot$ denotes the dot product operation[3]. Consequently, we have the following result:

$$Ru = \begin{pmatrix} u_x & u_y & u_z & 0 \\ v_x & v_y & v_z & 0 \\ n_x & n_y & n_z & 0 \\ 0 & 0 & 0 & 1 \end{pmatrix} \begin{pmatrix} u_x \\ u_y \\ u_z \\ 0 \end{pmatrix} = \begin{pmatrix} 1 \\ 0 \\ 0 \\ 0 \end{pmatrix} = e_1$$

Similarly, $Rv = e_2$ and $Rn = e_3$. R is the matrix that rotates $\{u,v,n\}$ so as to be superimposed onto $\{e_1,e_2,e_3\}$. It is the basis-change matrix.

Keep imagining the invisible rods connecting the scene objects and the camera space $\{$**EYE**$,u,v,n\}$. The matrix R rotates the scene objects, as shown in the last box of Fig. 2.11. The teapot's mouth is accordingly rotated. Its final coordinates in the world space should be $(0,0,-\sqrt{101})$. The coordinates are taken as the camera-space coordinates because the world and camera spaces are now identical.

So far, we have found that the view transform is defined as translation T in Equation (2.19) followed by rotation R in Equation (2.20). They are

---

[3]Consider two vectors, a and b. When their coordinates are $(a_1, a_2, \ldots, a_n)$ and $(b_1, b_2, \ldots, b_n)$, respectively, the dot product $a \cdot b$ is defined to be $\sum_{i=1}^{n} a_i b_i = a_1 b_1 + a_2 b_2 + \ldots + a_n b_n$. If a is a unit vector, $a \cdot a = (a_1)^2 + (a_2)^2 + \ldots + (a_n)^2 = 1$. In Euclidean geometry, $a \cdot b = ||a||\,||b||cos\theta$, where $||a||$ and $||b||$ denote the lengths of a and b, respectively, and θ is the angle between a and b. If a and b are perpendicular to each other, $a \cdot b = 0$. The camera-space basis $\{u,v,n\}$ is *orthonormal*, and therefore it is straightforward to derive that $u \cdot u = 1$, $u \cdot v = 0$ and $u \cdot n = 0$.

combined into a single 4×4 matrix, the view matrix:

$$M_{view} = RT$$
$$= \begin{pmatrix} u_x & u_y & u_z & 0 \\ v_x & v_y & v_z & 0 \\ n_x & n_y & n_z & 0 \\ 0 & 0 & 0 & 1 \end{pmatrix} \begin{pmatrix} 1 & 0 & 0 & -\mathbf{EYE}_x \\ 0 & 1 & 0 & -\mathbf{EYE}_y \\ 0 & 0 & 1 & -\mathbf{EYE}_z \\ 0 & 0 & 0 & 1 \end{pmatrix}$$
$$= \begin{pmatrix} u_x & u_y & u_z & -\mathbf{EYE} \cdot u \\ v_x & v_y & v_z & -\mathbf{EYE} \cdot v \\ n_x & n_y & n_z & -\mathbf{EYE} \cdot n \\ 0 & 0 & 0 & 1 \end{pmatrix}$$
(2.21)

M_{view} is applied to the world-space objects to transform them into the camera space. In the example of Fig. 2.11, M_{view} transforms the coordinates of the teapot's mouth from $(10,2,0)$ to $(0,0,-\sqrt{101})$. At the next page, [Note: View matrices in OpenGL and Direct3D] presents how to obtain M_{view} using the graphics APIs.

[Note: Orthonormal basis]

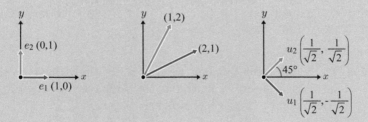

Fig. 2.12: The first is the standard basis for R^2. The second is a valid basis for R^2, but is neither standard nor orthonormal. The third is not the standard but an orthonormal basis.

The vectors $v_1, v_2, \ldots, v_n$ form a *basis* for the vector space V if and only if (1) $v_1, v_2, \ldots, v_n$ are linearly independent, and (2) $v_1, v_2, \ldots, v_n$ span V. Fig. 2.12 shows three examples of the basis for the 2D Euclidean vector space R^2. The *standard basis* is denoted by $\{e_1, e_2\}$, where $e_1 = (1,0)$ and $e_2 = (0,1)$. There are many other bases that can be chosen for R^2. An example is $\{(2,1),(1,2)\}$. However, it is generally easier to work with an *orthonormal basis*, an orthogonal set of unit vectors, rather than an arbitrary basis. The standard basis $\{e_1, e_2\}$ is an instance of the orthonormal basis. Another instance is $\{u_1, u_2\}$ shown in Fig. 2.12.

[Note: View matrices in OpenGL and Direct3D]

The view matrix in Equation (2.21) can be created using the OpenGL utility function gluLookAt:

```
void gluLookAt(
  GLdouble Eye_x, GLdouble Eye_y, GLdouble Eye_z,
  GLdouble At_x, GLdouble At_y, GLdouble At_z,
  GLdouble Up_x, GLdouble Up_y, GLdouble Up_z
);
```

The xyz-coordinates of the view parameters (Eye, At, and Up) are provided as input to gluLookAt. Then, the view matrix created by gluLookAt is stored in an OpenGL internal structure named *matrix stack* and can be popped for later use.

In Direct3D, the view matrix can be obtained using the D3DX utility function D3DXMatrixLookAtRH:

```
D3DXMATRIX * D3DXMatrixLookAtRH(
  D3DXMATRIX *pOut,
  CONST D3DXVECTOR3 *Eye,
  CONST D3DXVECTOR3 *At,
  CONST D3DXVECTOR3 *Up
);
```

Given Eye, At, and Up, the function returns pOut, the pointer to the view matrix. However, the returned matrix is the *transpose* of the 4×4 matrix presented in Equation (2.21), as shown below:

$$\begin{pmatrix} u_x & v_x & n_x & 0 \\ u_y & v_y & n_y & 0 \\ u_z & v_z & n_z & 0 \\ -\mathbf{EYE}\cdot u & -\mathbf{EYE}\cdot v & -\mathbf{EYE}\cdot n & 1 \end{pmatrix}$$

To understand why D3DXMatrixLookAtRH returns the transpose, consider the difference between a *column vector* and a *row vector*. Choice between them changes the matrix representation. When a column vector v is multiplied by a matrix M, v is located at the right-hand side of M, i.e., the matrix-vector multiplication is represented as Mv. In contrast, a row vector v^T is located at the left-hand side of M^T, i.e., $v^T M^T$. Whereas this book uses the column vectors and the vector-on-the-right notation for matrix-vector multiplication, Direct3D uses the row vectors and the vector-on-the-left convention. Therefore, Direct3D returns $(M_{view})^T$ instead of M_{view}.

2.3   Per-vertex Lighting

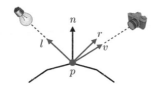

Fig. 2.13:   The vertex position and normal are denoted by p and n, respectively. Once the light source and camera positions are defined, l, r, and v are obtained. Then, lighting can be computed per vertex.

Light emitted from a light source is reflected by the object surface and then reaches the camera. Fig. 2.13 roughly describes what kinds of parameters are needed for lighting computation. The light source is defined in the world space. For a vertex p of a polygon mesh, the light vector l is computed by connecting p and the light source position. Together with the vertex normal n, l determines how much light is incident on p. If l is closer to n, for example, p would receive more light. Given n and l, the reflection vector r can be computed. The view vector v connects p and the camera position (**EYE**). If v is closer to r, for example, the camera would receive more reflected light. All the parameters shown in Fig. 2.13 are combined to determine p's color perceived by the camera.

In the procedure briefly sketched above, lighting is computed per vertex. It is called *per-vertex lighting* and is done by the vertex program. However, per-vertex lighting is old-fashioned. More popular is *per-fragment lighting*. It is performed by the fragment program and produces a better result. Chapter 5 presents both the per-vertex lighting and the per-fragment lighting.

2.4   Projection Transform

The view transform has converted all vertices of the world-space objects into the camera space $\{\mathbf{EYE}, u, v, n\}$. We need not consider the world space any longer. Then, let us denote the basis of the camera space by $\{x, y, z\}$, instead of $\{u, v, n\}$, because $\{x, y, z\}$ is more familiar to us.

2.4.1 View Frustum

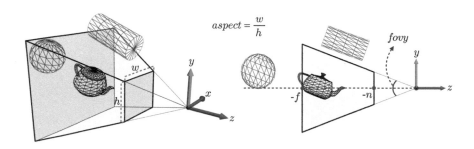

$$aspect = \frac{w}{h}$$

Fig. 2.14: The pyramid-like volume is named view frustum. The polygons outside the view frustum (illustrated in red) are considered invisible.

In general, a camera cannot capture all objects in the scene because its *field of view* is limited. The visible region in a scene is called the *view volume* and is specified in terms of four parameters: *fovy*, *aspect*, n, and f. See Fig. 2.14. First of all, *fovy* specifies the vertical field of view, and *aspect* denotes the aspect ratio of the view volume, i.e., the width divided by the height of the view volume. The shape of the view volume can then be considered an infinite pyramid. Its apex is located at the origin and its axis is the $-z$ axis. In Fig. 2.14, the cylinder is invisible because it is out of the field of view.

The other parameters of the view volume, n and f, denote the distances from the origin to the *near plane* and *far plane*, respectively. The infinite pyramid defined by *fovy* and *aspect* is truncated by the planes, $z = -n$ and $z = -f$. The truncated pyramidal view volume is called the *view frustum*. Observe that, in Fig. 2.14, not only the cylinder but also the sphere is invisible because it is outside the view frustum. The near and far planes run counter to the real-world camera or human vision system, but have been introduced for the sake of computational efficiency.

Recall that, for constructing the view transform, we defined only the *external* parameters of the camera, i.e., **EYE**, **AT**, and **UP**. In contrast, the view frustum controls the camera's *internals*, and it is analogous to choosing a lens for the camera.

Consider the cylinder and sphere in Fig. 2.14. Such out-of-frustum objects do not contribute to the final image. If they can be discarded before entering the GPU pipeline, the overall performance will increase. *View-frustum culling* serves the purpose [9]. In a typical implementation of view-frustum culling, a large enough box or sphere bounding a polygon mesh is computed at the preprocessing step, and then at run time a CPU program tests if the bounding

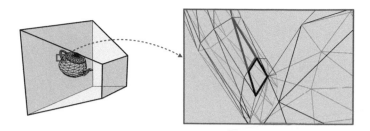

Fig. 2.15: If a polygon intersects the view frustum's boundary, the part of the polygon outside the view frustum is discarded.

volume is outside the view frustum. If it is, the polygon mesh is discarded and does not enter the rendering pipeline. (Section 3.7.2 presents how to compute the bounding volumes.) View-frustum culling can save a fair amount of GPU computing cost with a little CPU overhead, especially when a polygon mesh comprises a large number of vertices.

In Fig. 2.14, only the teapot would survive the view-frustum culling. However, its handle intersects the far plane of the view frustum. If a polygon intersects the boundary of the view frustum, it is *clipped* with respect to the boundary, and only the portion inside the view frustum is processed for display. See Fig. 2.15. The clipped polygons with black edges are further processed whereas those with red edges are discarded.

Fig. 2.15 clearly shows the concept of clipping, but in reality clipping is not performed in the camera space. The *projection transform* is the last operation in the vertex processing stage, and it converts the camera-space objects into the *clip space*. Then, clipping is done at the clip space, as the space name implies[4]. The projection transform is presented in the next subsection.

2.4.2 Projection Matrix

The projection transform *deforms* the pyramidal view frustum into the axis-aligned $2\times2\times1$-sized cuboidal view volume, as shown in Fig. 2.16-(a). The x- and y-ranges of the cuboid are $[-1,1]$, and the z-range is $[-1,0]$. Note that the projection transform does not produce a 2D image, but deforms the 3D objects of the scene.

---

[4]If view-frustum culling is not enabled, the cylinder and sphere in Fig. 2.14 enter the rendering pipeline. Their vertices are processed by the vertex program and are defined in the clip space. However, all of their polygons lie outside the view frustum and are discarded by the clipping algorithm. This shows a lack of efficiency because the computation done by the vertex program is in vain.

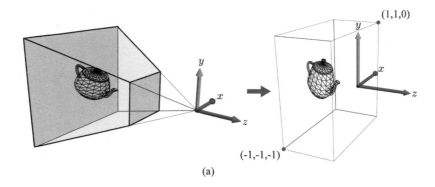

(a)

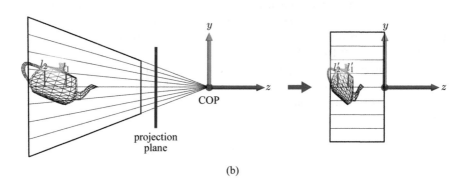

(b)

Fig. 2.16:   Projection transform. (a) The view frustum is deformed into a cuboid. The deformation named projection transform is in fact applied to the objects in the scene. Observe how the teapot is deformed. (b) Cross-section views show how the perspective projection effect (called *foreshortening*) is achieved through projection transform.

The cross section of the view frustum is shown at the left-hand side of Fig. 2.16-(b). The view frustum can be taken as a convergent pencil of *projection lines*. The lines converge on the origin, where the camera is located. The origin is often called the *center of projection* (COP). Imagine a *projection plane* that is parallel to the *xy*-plane and is located between the view frustum and the COP. The projection lines would form the image of the scene in the projection plane.

All 3D points on a projection line would be mapped onto a single point in the projection plane. Consider the line segments l_1 and l_2 in Fig. 2.16-(b). They would appear to be of equal length in the projection plane even though l_2 is longer than l_1 in the 3D space. It is the effect of *perspective projection*, where objects farther away look smaller.

Now see the right-hand side of Fig. 2.16-(b). The projection transform ensures that the projection lines become parallel, i.e., we have a universal projection line. Take a closer look at the teapot deformed by the projection transform. The polygons near the COP are relatively expanded whereas those at the rear side of the view frustum are relatively shrunken. Consequently, the projection-transformed line segments l_1' and l_2' are made to be of equal length. When viewed along the universal projection line, l_1' and l_2' appear to be of equal length. (Viewing along the universal projection line is called the *orthographic projection*.) Surprisingly, the projection transform has brought the effect of perspective projection in a 3D space.

Shown below is the projection matrix that converts the view frustum into the cuboid:

$$\begin{pmatrix} \frac{cot(\frac{fovy}{2})}{aspect} & 0 & 0 & 0 \\ 0 & cot(\frac{fovy}{2}) & 0 & 0 \\ 0 & 0 & \frac{f}{f-n} & \frac{nf}{f-n} \\ 0 & 0 & -1 & 0 \end{pmatrix} \tag{2.22}$$

It is defined using the view frustum parameters, *fovy, aspect, n,* and *f.* (The next subsection presents how to derive the projection transform.) An important feature of the projection matrix is that, unlike affine transforms, the last row is not (0 0 0 1), and consequently the *w*-coordinate of the projection-transformed vertex is $-z$, not 1 in general. Its implication will be discussed in Section 3.2.

Note that the projection-transformed teapot in Fig. 2.16 is defined in the right-handed clip space. The projection transform is the last operation in the vertex processing stage, and the teapot's vertices will then enter the hard-wired stage for rasterization. In the rasterization stage, the clip space is assumed to be left-handed. Therefore we need to switch from the right-hand system (RHS) to the left-hand system (LHS). It requires two remodeling tasks presented in Section 1.4: (1) vertex order change, and (2) *z*-negation.

When we move from the camera space (RHS) to the clip space (LHS) in the rendering pipeline, the first task need not be done. It is because the vertex

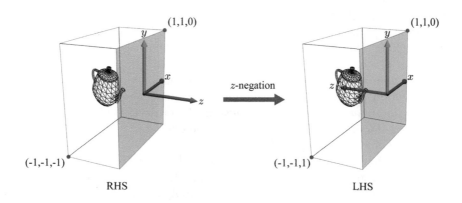

Fig. 2.17: The z-coordinates are negated for switching from the right-handed clip space to the left-handed clip space. Z-negation is equivalent to the z-axis inversion.

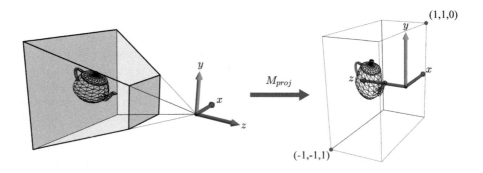

Fig. 2.18: The last transform in the vertex processing stage, M_{proj}, converts the right-handed camera-space objects into the left-handed clip space. This illustrates the combination of Fig. 2.16-(a) and Fig. 2.17.

order problem can be resolved by *configuring* the hard-wired rasterization stage. (Sections 3.3 and 3.4 discuss this issue in detail.) Then, the only thing to do now is to negate the z-coordinates. Fig. 2.17 shows the result of z-negation, which is equivalent to inverting the z-axis. Compare the cuboid's z-ranges. Due to z-negation, the z-range has been changed from $[-1,0]$ to $[0,1]$, whereas the x- and y-ranges remain the same, i.e., $[-1,1]$.

When a vertex v is transformed into v' by a matrix M, the z-coordinate of v' is determined by the third row of M. Therefore, negating the z-coordinate of v' (This is the task assigned to us!) is achieved by negating the third row of M. This observation enables us to simply negate the third row of the projection matrix in Equation (2.22) in order to make it compatible with the left-handed clip space:

$$M_{proj} = \begin{pmatrix} \frac{cot(\frac{fovy}{2})}{aspect} & 0 & 0 & 0 \\ 0 & cot(\frac{fovy}{2}) & 0 & 0 \\ 0 & 0 & -\frac{f}{f-n} & -\frac{nf}{f-n} \\ 0 & 0 & -1 & 0 \end{pmatrix} \quad (2.23)$$

Fig. 2.18 shows that M_{proj} transforms the object defined in the right-handed camera space to that of the left-handed clip space.

[Note: Projection matrices in Direct3D and OpenGL]

A D3DX utility function `D3DXMatrixPerspectiveFovRH` computes the projection matrix for RHS:

```
D3DXMATRIX * D3DXMatrixPerspectiveFovRH(
    D3DXMATRIX *pOut,
    FLOAT fovy,
    FLOAT aspect,
    FLOAT n,
    FLOAT f
);
```

where `fovy` is in radian. Given `fovy`, `aspect`, `n`, and `f`, the function returns `pOut`, the pointer to the following 4×4 projection matrix:

$$\begin{pmatrix} \frac{cot(\frac{fovy}{2})}{aspect} & 0 & 0 & 0 \\ 0 & cot(\frac{fovy}{2}) & 0 & 0 \\ 0 & 0 & -\frac{f}{f-n} & -1 \\ 0 & 0 & -\frac{nf}{f-n} & 0 \end{pmatrix} \quad (2.24)$$

This matrix is the transpose of the projection matrix presented in Equation (2.23) because Direct3D uses the row vectors whereas this book uses the column vectors.

In OpenGL, the role of D3DXMatrixPerspectiveFovRH is taken by gluPerspective:

```
void gluPerspective(
  GLdouble fovy,
  GLdouble aspect,
  GLdouble n,
  GLdouble f
);
```

The OpenGL projection matrix transforms the view frustum into a cube, the xyz-ranges of which are all $[-1,1]$. Note the z-range difference: $[-1,1]$ in OpenGL and $[0,1]$ in Direct3D and this book. Such a z-range difference makes the OpenGL projection matrix slightly different from our projection matrix in Equation (2.23). Shown below is the OpenGL matrix. Take a look at the third row.

$$\begin{pmatrix} \frac{cot(\frac{fovy}{2})}{aspect} & 0 & 0 & 0 \\ 0 & cot(\frac{fovy}{2}) & 0 & 0 \\ 0 & 0 & -\frac{f+n}{f-n} & -\frac{2nf}{f-n} \\ 0 & 0 & -1 & 0 \end{pmatrix} \qquad (2.25)$$

To derive Equation (2.25), Section 2.4.3 should be understood. Derivation of Equation (2.25) is left as an exercise.

2.4.3 Derivation of Projection Matrix*

This subsection derives the projection matrix presented in Equation (2.22). It converts the view frustum into the $2\times2\times1$-sized cuboid. Consider a point v located in the view frustum, whose coordinates are (x, y, z). If v is projection-transformed into v' at (x', y', z'), x' and y' are in the range of $[-1,1]$, and z' is in $[-1,0]$. Based on this observation, x', y' and z' are calculated.

Let us first compute y'. Fig. 2.19-(a) shows the view frustum's cross section. In the figure, v and v' are represented as (y, z) and (y', z'), respectively. A conceptual projection plane is defined: $z = -cot\frac{fovy}{2}$. Then, y' is confined in the range of $[-1,1]$ and is computed using similar triangles:

$$y' = -cot\frac{fovy}{2} \cdot \frac{y}{z} \qquad (2.26)$$

Let us now compute x'. It should also be in the range of $[-1,1]$. If $fovx$ were given as the horizontal field of view, we could find that

$$x' = -cot\frac{fovx}{2} \cdot \frac{x}{z} \qquad (2.27)$$

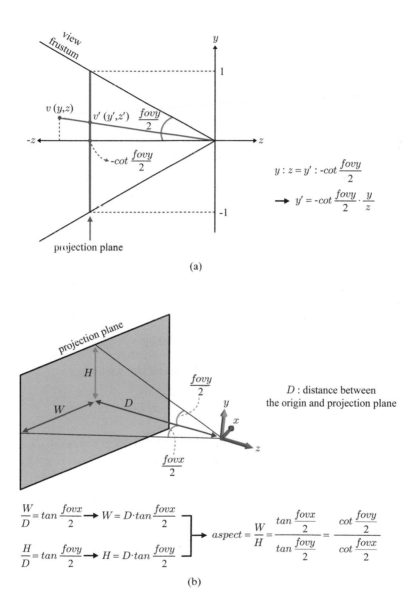

(a)

$$y : z = y' : -cot\frac{fovy}{2}$$

$$\rightarrow y' = -cot\frac{fovy}{2}\cdot\frac{y}{z}$$

D : distance between the origin and projection plane

$$\frac{W}{D}=tan\frac{fovx}{2}\rightarrow W=D\cdot tan\frac{fovx}{2}$$

$$\frac{H}{D}=tan\frac{fovy}{2}\rightarrow H=D\cdot tan\frac{fovy}{2}$$

$$aspect=\frac{W}{H}=\frac{tan\dfrac{fovx}{2}}{tan\dfrac{fovy}{2}}=\frac{cot\dfrac{fovy}{2}}{cot\dfrac{fovx}{2}}$$

(b)

Fig. 2.19: Computing projection matrix. (a) Normalized coordinate y' is computed. (b) The aspect ratio can be defined in terms of *fovx* and *fovy*.

through the same method used for computing y'. However, $fovx$ is not given. Let us then rewrite x' in terms of $fovy$ and $aspect$. Recall that $aspect$ denotes the width divided by the height of the view frustum. Fig. 2.19-(b) shows that

$$aspect = \frac{\cot \frac{fovy}{2}}{\cot \frac{fovx}{2}}$$

It is rewritten into

$$\cot \frac{fovx}{2} = \frac{\cot \frac{fovy}{2}}{aspect} \tag{2.28}$$

By inserting Equation (2.28) into Equation (2.27), we can obtain x':

$$x' = -\cot \frac{fovx}{2} \cdot \frac{x}{z} = -\frac{\cot \frac{fovy}{2}}{aspect} \cdot \frac{x}{z} \tag{2.29}$$

For simplicity, let us abbreviate $\cot \frac{fovy}{2}$ and $aspect$ to D and A, respectively. Then, using Equations (2.26) and (2.29), the projection-transformed point v' is represented as follows:

$$v' = (x', y', z', 1) = (-\frac{D}{A} \cdot \frac{x}{z}, -D\frac{y}{z}, z', 1) \tag{2.30}$$

where z' remains unknown. In the homogeneous coordinate system, $(p, q, r, 1)$ are identical to (cp, cq, cr, c) for any non-zero value c. Then, multiplying all coordinates of Equation (2.30) by $-z$ leads to the following:

$$(-\frac{D}{A} \cdot \frac{x}{z}, -D\frac{y}{z}, z', 1) \rightarrow (\frac{D}{A}x, Dy, -zz', -z) \tag{2.31}$$

Let us abbreviate $-zz'$ to z''. In Equation (2.31), $\frac{D}{A}x$, Dy, and $-z$ are linear combinations of x, y, and z. Then, we have the following matrix multiplication form:

$$\begin{pmatrix} \frac{D}{A}x \\ Dy \\ z'' \\ -z \end{pmatrix} = \begin{pmatrix} \frac{D}{A} & 0 & 0 & 0 \\ 0 & D & 0 & 0 \\ m_1 & m_2 & m_3 & m_4 \\ 0 & 0 & -1 & 0 \end{pmatrix} \begin{pmatrix} x \\ y \\ z \\ 1 \end{pmatrix} \tag{2.32}$$

The 4×4 matrix is the projection matrix. We will complete the matrix by filling its third row.

Note that z' (the z-coordinate of the projection-transformed point v') is independent of x and y (the xy-coordinates of v). It can be intuitively understood if you consider a quad that is parallel to the xy-plane of the camera space. When the quad is projection-transformed, it remains parallel to the xy-plane of the clip space, i.e., every point on the transformed quad has the same z' independently of its original position (x, y) within the quad. As $z'' = -zz'$, z'' is also independent of x and y. Therefore, the third row of the projection

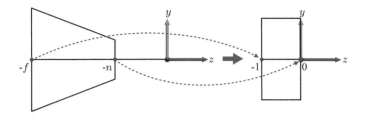

Fig. 2.20: The projection transform converts the z-range $[-f,-n]$ to $[-1,0]$.

matrix in Equation (2.32) is simplified to $(0\ 0\ m_3\ m_4)$, and we can obtain the coordinates of v' as follows:

$$
\begin{pmatrix} \frac{D}{A} & 0 & 0 & 0 \\ 0 & D & 0 & 0 \\ 0 & 0 & m_3 & m_4 \\ 0 & 0 & -1 & 0 \end{pmatrix}
\begin{pmatrix} x \\ y \\ z \\ 1 \end{pmatrix}
=
\begin{pmatrix} \frac{D}{A}x \\ Dy \\ m_3 z + m_4 \\ -z \end{pmatrix}
\rightarrow
\begin{pmatrix} \frac{D}{A} \cdot \frac{x}{z} \\ -D\frac{y}{z} \\ -m_3 - \frac{m_4}{z} \\ 1 \end{pmatrix}
= v' \quad (2.33)
$$

Observe the z-coordinate of v':

$$ z' = -m_3 - \frac{m_4}{z} \quad (2.34) $$

As shown in Fig. 2.20, the z-coordinates $-f$ and $-n$ are mapped to -1 and 0, respectively, by the projection transform. In other words, we have two known pairs of (z,z'): $(-f,-1)$ and $(-n,0)$. Putting them into Equation (2.34), we obtain the following:

$$
\begin{aligned}
-1 &= -m_3 + \frac{m_4}{f} \\
0 &= -m_3 + \frac{m_4}{n}
\end{aligned} \quad (2.35)
$$

Solving Equation (2.35) for m_3 and m_4 gives

$$
\begin{aligned}
m_3 &= \frac{f}{f-n} \\
m_4 &= \frac{nf}{f-n}
\end{aligned} \quad (2.36)
$$

The third row of the 4×4 matrix presented in Equation (2.32) is determined. Restoring D and A back to $\cot\frac{fovy}{2}$ and $aspect$, respectively, we obtain the projection matrix presented in Equation (2.22):

$$
\begin{pmatrix} \frac{\cot\frac{fovy}{2}}{aspect} & 0 & 0 & 0 \\ 0 & \cot\frac{fovy}{2} & 0 & 0 \\ 0 & 0 & \frac{f}{f-n} & \frac{nf}{f-n} \\ 0 & 0 & -1 & 0 \end{pmatrix}
$$

Exercises

1. Compute a 2D affine transform matrix that rotates a 2D point by θ about a point (a, b), not about the origin.

2. In linear algebra, it is proven that the inverse of a rotation is simply its transpose. Given two non-standard orthonormal bases $\{a,b,c\}$ and $\{d,e,f\}$, compute a 3×3 matrix that converts the vector defined in terms of $\{a,b,c\}$ into the vector of $\{d,e,f\}$.

3. Let us define a matrix for scaling along 3 orthonormal vectors, a, b, and c, which are not identical to the standard basis vectors e_1, e_2, and e_3. The scaling factors are s_a, s_b, and s_c along a, b, and c, respectively. It is also observed that $a \times b = c$ where $\times$ denotes the cross product. The scaling matrix is a combination of three 3×3 matrices. Compute the three matrices.

4. The view transform consists of a translation and a rotation. We are given the following view parameters: $\mathbf{EYE} = (0, 0, -\sqrt{3})$, $\mathbf{AT} = (0,0,0)$, and $\mathbf{UP} = (0,1,0)$.

   (a) Compute the translation.

   (b) Compute the rotation.

5. Section 2.4.3 derives the projection matrix assuming that the z-range of the cuboidal view volume is $[-1,0]$. In OpenGL, the z-range is $[-1,1]$. Derive the projection matrix for OpenGL presented in Equation (2.25).

Chapter 3

Rasterization

The vertices processed by the vertex program enter a hard-wired stage. First of all, they are assembled to build *primitives* such as triangles, using the connectivity information that accompanies the input stream of vertices. (Not only a triangle but also a line segment or a point can be a primitive. A primitive is processed as an independent entity in the rendering pipeline.) Each primitive is further processed to determine its 2D form appearing on the screen, and is *rasterized* into a set of fragments. The per-vertex data such as the vertex normals are interpolated across each primitive, and each fragment is assigned the interpolated data. The hard-wired stage is generally named *primitive assembly and rasterization.* Direct3D simply calls this stage *rasterization* or *rasterizer*, and this book follows it just for the sake of simplicity.

The substages composing the rasterizer include clipping, perspective division, back-face culling, viewport transform, and scan conversion. The rasterizer is not programmable. For some substages, it is enough just to understand what they do. An example is clipping. On the other hand, some other substages require us to understand how they work. An example is back-face culling. Without understanding its working principle, it would not be easy to *configure* the substage. Another example is scan conversion, which is taken as the key feature of the real-time graphics and needs to be fully understood for writing the fragment program. This chapter focuses on the triangle primitives and presents the substages in different depths.

3.1 Clipping

Clipping refers to the process of cutting the polygons against the cuboidal view volume. The clipping algorithm is implemented in hardware, and we cannot modify the algorithm. Just for intuitive understanding, this section presents the idea of polygon clipping "against the view frustum in the camera space." The spatial relationship between a triangle and the view frustum is classified into three cases. See Fig. 3.1. (1) Triangle t_1 is completely outside the view frustum and is discarded. (2) Triangle t_2 is completely inside and is passed to the next step *as is*. (3) Triangle t_3 intersects the view frustum and is then clipped. Only the part of the triangle located inside the view frustum

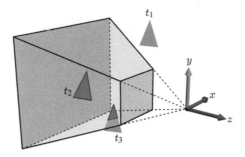

Fig. 3.1: Examples of clipping a triangle against the view frustum.

proceeds to the next step in the rendering pipeline. As a result of clipping, vertices are added to and deleted from the triangle.

3.2 Perspective Division

Fig. 3.2 shows a view frustum and the cuboidal view volume produced by the projection matrix M_{proj} presented in Equation (2.23). Unlike affine transforms, the last row of M_{proj} is not (0 0 0 1) but (0 0 −1 0). When M_{proj} is applied to $(x, y, z, 1)$, the w-coordinate of the transformed vertex is $-z$, which is not necessarily 1. See the results of applying M_{proj} to P_2 and Q_2.

In order to convert from the homogeneous (clip) space to the Cartesian space, each vertex should be divided by its w-coordinate. It equals $-z$ and is a positive value representing the *distance* from the xy-plane of the camera space. Therefore, division by w makes distant objects smaller. In Fig. 3.2, consider line segments l_1 and l_2, which are projection-transformed into l'_1 and l'_2, respectively. Even though l_1 and l_2 are of the same length in the camera space, l'_2 becomes smaller than l'_1 due to the division. This brings the effect of perspective projection or foreshortening. Division by w is called *perspective division*.

By the perspective division, a vertex in the clip space can be represented in so-called *normalized device coordinates* (NDC). The coordinates are named normalized because the x- and y-coordinates are in the range of $[-1,1]$ and the z-coordinate is in $[0,1]$[1]. The vertices P'_1, Q'_1, P'_2 and Q'_2 in Fig. 3.2 are all represented in NDC.

---

[1]Direct3D has the same range. In contrast, OpenGL's z-range is $[-1,1]$. See the shaded note in Section 2.4.2.

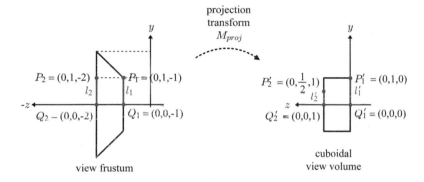

Fig. 3.2: Projection transform produces the vertices in the homogeneous clip space. Dividing each vertex by its w-coordinate converts the homogeneous coordinates into the Cartesian coordinates. This brings the effect of perspective projection and therefore is called perspective division.

3.3 Back-face Culling

In general, culling refers to the process of eliminating parts of a scene that are not visible to the camera. Whereas the view-frustum culling (presented in Section 2.4.1) discards the parts of the scene outside the view frustum, *back-face culling* discards the polygons facing away from the viewpoint of the camera, which are called *back-faces*. The polygons facing the camera are called *front-faces*.

The concept of back-face culling is best presented in the camera space. A triangle is taken as a back-face if the camera (**EYE**) is in the opposite side of the triangle's normal. In Fig. 3.3-(a), t_1 is a back-face whereas t_2 is a front-face. Such a distinction can be made by taking the dot product of the triangle normal n and the vector c connecting the camera position and the triangle. Recall that $n \cdot c = ||n||||c||cos\theta$ where θ is the angle between n and c. If n and c form an acute angle, $n \cdot c$ is positive, and the triangle is a back-face. If n and c form an obtuse angle, $n \cdot c$ is negative, and the triangle is a front-face. For t_3 in Fig. 3.3-(a), $n \cdot c = 0$, which implies that n and c are perpendicular and t_3 is an edge-on face.

However, back-face culling is not done at the camera space. Above all, it is expensive to compute the connecting vectors for all triangles. Fortunately, the projection transform makes all the connecting vectors parallel to the z-axis, as shown in the 2D illustration of Fig. 3.3-(b). The universal connecting vector represents the "parallelized projection lines" shown in Fig. 2.16. Then, by viewing the triangles along the universal connecting vector, we can distinguish the back-faces from the front-faces.

Fig. 3.3-(c) shows the projection-transformed sphere. Viewing a triangle along the universal connecting vector is equivalent to *orthographically projecting* the triangle onto the xy-plane. Fig. 3.3-(d) illustrates the back-facing triangle t_1 orthographically projected onto the xy-plane. Note that its vertices appear clockwise (CW) even though they are ordered counter-clockwise (CCW) in the 3D space[2]. It is not surprising because the CCW order in the 3D space is observed when we see t_1 from the outside of the sphere, but Fig. 3.3-(d) looks as if t_1 would be captured from the inside of the sphere. On the other hand, the 2D vertices of t_2 appear CCW, as illustrated in Fig. 3.3-(e). These two examples show that a 2D triangle with CW-ordered vertices is a back-face, and a 2D triangle with CCW-ordered vertices is a front-face.

Given a 2D triangle $\langle v_1, v_2, v_3 \rangle$, where v_i has the coordinates (x_i, y_i), it is straightforward to determine if the triangle is CW or CCW. Connect v_1 and v_2 to define a vector $(x_2 - x_1, y_2 - y_1)$, and connect v_1 and v_3 to define another

---

[2]Recall that, when we moved from the camera space to the clip space in Section 2.4.2, we did not change the vertex order. Therefore, for every triangle in Fig. 3.3-(c), the vertices are ordered CCW, i.e., $\langle v_1, v_2, v_3 \rangle$, not $\langle v_1, v_3, v_2 \rangle$.

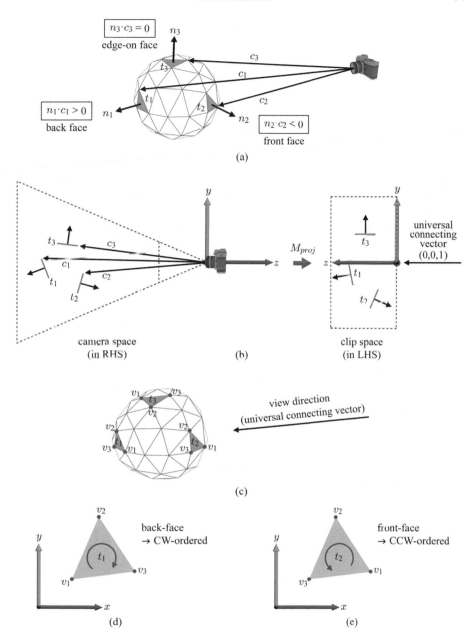

Fig. 3.3: Back-face culling. (a) In the camera space, the dot product of the triangle normal and a vector connecting the triangle and the camera could be used for back-face culling. (b) All of the connecting vectors are made parallel by the projection transform. (c) In the clip space, vertices of every 3D triangle are ordered CCW. (d) The vertices of a 2D back-face are ordered CW. (e) The vertices of a 2D front-face are ordered CCW.

vector $(x_3 - x_1, y_3 - y_1)$. Then, compute the following determinant:

$$\begin{vmatrix} (x_2 - x_1) & (y_2 - y_1) \\ (x_3 - x_1) & (y_3 - y_1) \end{vmatrix} = (x_2 - x_1)(y_3 - y_1) - (y_2 - y_1)(x_3 - x_1) \qquad (3.1)$$

If the determinant is positive, the triangle is CW. If negative, it is CCW. If zero, it is an edge-on face. The back-face culling substage uses Equation (3.1) to distinguish between back-faces and front-faces.

What if the vertices of every triangle are ordered CW in the 3D clip space? Then, the reverse of the conditions presented in Fig. 3.3-(d) and -(e) is applied, i.e., the 2D front-face has CW-ordered vertices, and the 2D back-face has CCW-ordered vertices.

Some applications do not cull the back-faces. Rendering a translucent sphere is an example. Its back-faces should show through the front-faces. OpenGL and Direct3D provide flexible face-culling mechanisms and allow the users to control face culling through the CW/CCW vertex ordering. Interested readers are referred to the following notes.

[Note: Face culling in OpenGL]
    In OpenGL, face culling is disabled by default, and both front- and back-faces are rendered. When it is enabled, `glCullFace()` specifies whether front- or back-facing polygons are culled. It accepts the following symbolic constants:
- `GL_FRONT`
- `GL_BACK`
- `GL_FRONT_AND_BACK`

The default value is `GL_BACK`, and back-faces are culled.
    Then, `glFrontFace()` specifies the vertex order of front-facing polygons. It accepts the following:
- `GL_CW`
- `GL_CCW`

The default value is `GL_CCW`. It is compatible with Fig. 3.3-(e).

[Note: Face culling in Direct3D]
    Direct3D 10 provides a functionality, which is similar to OpenGL, through a rasterizer-state object description, `D3D10_RASTERIZER_DESC`. It has a member named `CullMode`, which can be set to one of the following:
- `D3D10_CULL_NONE` (for drawing all triangles)
- `D3D10_CULL_FRONT` (for front-face culling)
- `D3D10_CULL_BACK` (for back-face culling)

The default value is `D3D10_CULL_BACK`.

Another member of D3D10_RASTERIZER_DESC is FrontCounterClockwise. If it is true, a triangle is considered front-facing when its vertices are CCW-ordered and is considered back-facing when the vertices are CW-ordered.

In our context, FrontCounterClockwise should be set to true. However, the default value in Direct3D is false. It is because, unlike our context, Direct3D adopts the left-hand system, the default ordering of vertices (in a 3D polygon mesh) is CW, and therefore the vertices of a 2D front-face appear CW.

Let us now see Direct3D 9. Various parts of the rendering pipeline can be controlled using *states*, through which we can define vertex/texture formats, the behavior of the hard-wired parts of the pipeline, etc. Direct3D supports *render state*. It is set by invoking IDirect3DDevice9::SetRenderState. One of its parameters is D3DRS_CULLMODE. It can be set to one of the following constants:

- D3DCULL_NONE (for drawing all triangles)
- D3DCULL_CW (for culling faces with CW-ordered vertices)
- D3DCULL_CCW (for culling faces with CCW-ordered vertices)

The default is D3DCULL_CCW, due to the same reason discussed above. In our context, however, it should be set to D3DCULL_CW.

Back-faces of an opaque object are culled because they cannot contribute to the final image. However, a front-face may not be able to contribute to the final image if it is occluded from the camera position by other front-faces. Such an invisible face is handled by the well-known per-fragment visibility algorithm, *z-buffering*, at the output merging stage. It will be presented in Chapter 4.

The culling operations performed by the rasterizer are not limited to back-face culling. Another important culling technique is *z-culling*. It requires understanding of the z-buffering algorithm and therefore will be presented also in Chapter 4.

3.4 Coordinate Systems - Revisited*

This section extends the discussion on the topic of conversion between right-hand system (RHS) and left-hand system (LHS) presented in Section 1.4, and further presents how the topic is related with back-face culling. This section contains informative content, but can be safely skipped if you want to quickly follow the flow of the rendering pipeline.

3.4.1   3ds Max to OpenGL - Axis Flipping

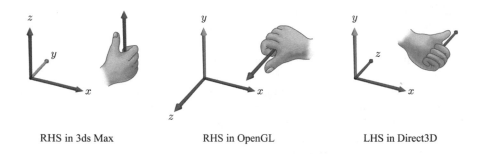

RHS in 3ds Max   RHS in OpenGL   LHS in Direct3D

Fig. 3.4:   Both 3ds Max and OpenGL use RHS, but their axis orientations are different. Direct3D uses LHS.

Consider the graphics package 3ds Max and two graphics APIs, OpenGL and Direct3D. Both 3ds Max and OpenGL use RHS whereas Direct3D uses LHS. See Fig. 3.4. Notice the difference between 3ds Max and OpenGL. The vertical axis is the z-axis in 3ds Max, but is the y-axis in OpenGL. This seemingly trivial difference often causes trouble. Fig. 3.5-(a) illustrates an example. The 3ds Max scene consists of a tetrahedron and a teapot. Suppose that the scene is exported *as is* to OpenGL. If the **UP** vector of the camera is set to the y-axis in OpenGL, as is done in most applications, we will have the image shown in the box. The objects appear flipped.

A solution to this problem is provided in 3ds Max. It is called *yz-axis flip*. As shown in Fig. 3.5-(b), it could be thought of as rotating the y- and z-axes by 90° about the x-axis while making the objects immovable. It is performed at the time of exporting. When the exported scene is rendered in OpenGL with **UP** set to the y-axis, we have a consistent view.

Implementing yz-axis flip is simple. As shown in Fig. 3.6-(a), (x, y, z) is converted into $(x, z, -y)$. This is done for every vertex of the scene. Fig. 3.6-(b) captures the export menu of 3ds Max, which supports yz-axis flip.

3.4.2   OpenGL to Direct3D - Reflection

Now, consider exporting a 3ds Max scene (defined in RHS) to Direct3D (based on LHS). Suppose that yz-axis flip has already been done. Then, the scene can be considered as the one defined in OpenGL, and the exporting issue is reduced to converting an OpenGL model into Direct3D.

Returning to Fig. 3.5-(b), notice that the objects are located at the $-z$ side in the RHS of OpenGL, and the camera is located at the $+z$ side. When

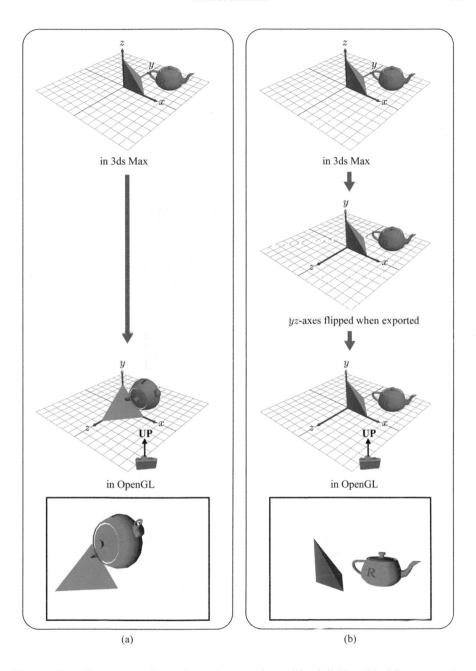

Fig. 3.5: Conversion from 3ds Max to OpenGL. (a) If a 3ds Max scene is exported to OpenGL with no modification, an inconsistent view is generated. (b) When a 3ds Max scene is exported, so-called *yz*-axis flip is done, and then a consistent view can be obtained.

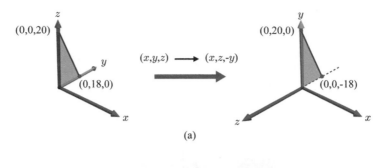

(a)

(b)

Fig. 3.6: Implementing yz-axis flip. (a) (x, y, z) are converted into $(x, z, -y)$. (b) 3ds Max supports yz-axis flip.

the objects and camera are simply put into the LHS of Direct3D, we have the configuration shown in Fig. 3.7-(a), where the objects and camera are still in the $-z$ and $+z$ sides, respectively. Compare the rendering result of Fig. 3.7-(a) with the image of Fig. 3.5-(b). They are *reflected*. Placing an RHS-based model into an LHS (or vice versa) has the effect of making the model reflected.

The problem can be easily resolved if we enforce one more reflection. Reflecting the reflected returns to the original! See Fig. 3.7-(b). Not only the scene but also the camera is reflected with respect to the xy-plane. Then, the relative pose between the scene and the camera becomes identical to that of OpenGL case shown in Fig. 3.5-(b).

Reflection with respect to the xy-plane is equivalent to negating the z-coordinates. For a polygon mesh, its vertex positions and normals are all

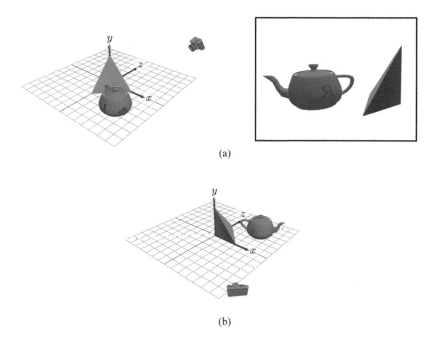

(a)

(b)

Fig. 3.7: Conversion from OpenGL to Direct3D. (a) Placing an RHS-based model into an LHS has the effect of reflection. (b) Enforced reflection restores the original relative pose between the scene and the camera.

z-negated. For the camera, the view parameters (**EYE**, **AT**, and **UP**) are z-negated.

Fig. 3.8 traces the conceptual flow from 3ds Max to Direct3D. Fig. 3.8-(a) shows a tetrahedron created in 3ds Max and its vertex/index buffers. (The tetrahedron's base triangle located at the xy-plane is not listed in the index buffer, just for simplicity. The side triangle lying at the yz-plane is blue and is currently invisible.) Fig. 3.8-(b) shows the result of flipping the yz-axes. The vertex buffer is updated, i.e., (x, y, z) are converted into $(x, z, -y)$. Fig. 3.8-(c) shows the objects placed in the LHS of Direct3D. Neither the vertex buffer nor the index buffer is changed, but the objects are reflected with respect to the xy-plane. Fig. 3.8-(d) shows the result of enforcing reflection, where the vertex buffer is updated such that all z-coordinates are negated.

Note that, when a 3ds Max model is exported to Direct3D, yz-axis flip is combined with z-negation. See Fig. 3.9, where (x, y, z) are first converted into $(x, z, -y)$ through yz-axis flip, and then z-negation converts $(x, z, -y)$ to (x, z, y). Combining the two operations is equal to swapping the y- and z-coordinates. The vertex buffer in Fig. 3.8-(d) is considered to be the result of applying yz-swap to the vertex buffer of Fig. 3.8-(a).

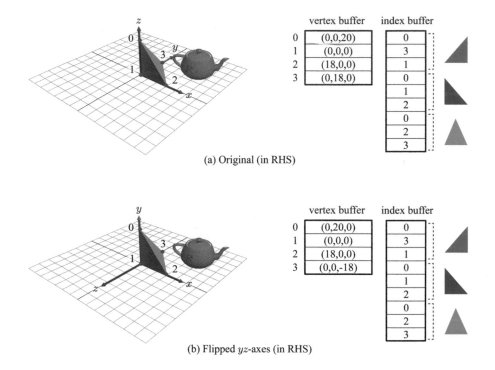

(a) Original (in RHS)

(b) Flipped yz-axes (in RHS)

Fig. 3.8:   Flow from 3ds Max to Direct3D. Between (a) and (b), yz-axes are flipped, i.e., (x, y, z) are converted into $(x, z, -y)$.

3.4.3   OpenGL to Direct3D - Vertex Reordering

Every problem may seem to be resolved. Let us then render the scene of Fig. 3.8-(d) with the "default setting of Direct3D." You would expect the image of Fig. 3.5-(b). However, we have the result shown in Fig. 3.10. Take a closer look at the image, and discover that the front-faces are culled away and the back-faces are rendered instead.

Return to Fig. 3.8-(d), and observe that the vertices are ordered counterclockwise (CCW) in the index buffer. For example, the red triangle's vertex order $\langle 0,1,2 \rangle$ is CCW. This gave rise to the problem of Fig. 3.10. In Direct3D, the default vertex order of a 3D triangle is clockwise (CW), and the vertices of a 2D back-face are assumed to appear CCW. Therefore, the default culling mode is set to D3DCULL_CCW[3]. In Fig. 3.8-(d), the red and green triangles have CCW-ordered vertices in 2D and are discarded by back-face culling. In

---

[3]This is the case of Direct3D 9. For the case of Direct3D 10, see [Note: Face culling in Direct3D] in Section 3.3.

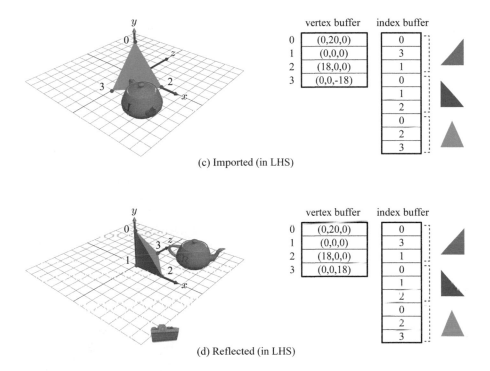

(c) Imported (in LHS)

(d) Reflected (in LHS)

Fig. 3.8: Flow from 3ds Max to Direct3D (*continued*). Between (c) and (d), z-negation is performed, i.e., (x, y, z) are converted into $(x, y, -z)$.

contrast, the other two triangles have CW-ordered vertices in 2D and survive back-face culling, leading to the rendering result of Fig. 3.10.

As presented in Section 1.4, porting an application between RHS and LHS requires two tasks: (1) the vertex order of every triangle is changed from $\langle v_1, v_2, v_3 \rangle$ to $\langle v_1, v_3, v_2 \rangle$, and (2) the z-coordinate of every vertex is negated. When we moved from Fig. 3.8-(c) to -(d), we did only the second task. We could try to complete the first task. For example, the red triangle's vertex order could be changed from $\langle 0,1,2 \rangle$ to $\langle 0,2,1 \rangle$ in the index buffer. However, a much simpler solution is to switch the culling mode from D3DCULL_CCW to D3DCULL_CW. Then, the 2D triangles with CW-ordered vertices are taken as back-faces and culled away. Consequently, we will have the correct result such as the image shown in Fig. 3.5-(b).

$$(x,y,z) \xrightarrow{\text{yz-axis flip}} (x,z,-y) \xrightarrow{\text{z-negation}} (x,z,y)$$

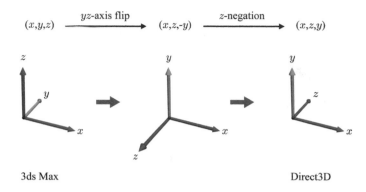

3ds Max   Direct3D

Fig. 3.9:   Conversion from 3ds Max to Direct3D requires yz-axis flip followed by z-negation. The combination is simply yz-swap.

Fig. 3.10:   An unexpected image is generated by incorrect culling mode. Instead of back-faces, front-faces are culled.

3.5   Viewport Transform

A window at the computer screen is associated with its own *screen space*. A *viewport* is defined in the screen space. It is not necessarily the entire window, but can be a sub-area of the window. The viewport can be thought of as a rectangle into which the scene is projected.

In the rendering pipeline, the screen space is 3D, and so is the viewport, as illustrated in Fig. 3.11. The screen-space origin is located at the upper-left corner of the window. The x-axis goes to right, the y-axis goes down, and the z-axis goes into the screen. The screen space is right-handed. The depth range $[MinZ,MaxZ]$ of the viewport specifies the range of z-values of the

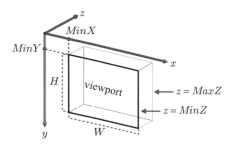

Fig. 3.11: The screen-space viewport is defined by its corner point $(MinX, MinY)$, width W, height H, and the depth-range $[MinZ, MaxZ]$.

projected scene. The z-values are needed for z-buffering. The aspect ratio of the viewport is $\frac{W}{H}$. In general, the view-frustum parameter *aspect* (presented in Section 2.4.1) is made identical to it.

[Note: Viewport definitions in graphics APIs]

In OpenGL, `glViewport(MinX,MinY,w,h)` is used to define the rectangular area of the viewport, and `glDepthRange(MinZ,MaxZ)` is used to define its z-range. Shown below are the structures used to define a viewport in Direct3D 9 and 10. They are basically the same.

```
typedef struct _D3DVIEWPORT9{
    DWORD MinX;
    DWORD MinY;
    DWORD W;
    DWORD H;
    float MinZ;
    float MaxZ;
} D3DVIEWPORT9;

typedef struct D3D10_VIEWPORT{
    INT TopLeftX;
    INT TopLeftY;
    UINT Width;
    UINT Height;
    FLOAT MinDepth;
    FLOAT MaxDepth;
} D3D10_VIEWPORT;
```

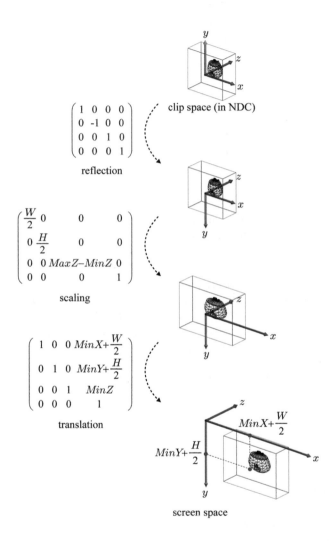

$$\begin{pmatrix} 1 & 0 & 0 & 0 \\ 0 & -1 & 0 & 0 \\ 0 & 0 & 1 & 0 \\ 0 & 0 & 0 & 1 \end{pmatrix}$$

reflection

$$\begin{pmatrix} \frac{W}{2} & 0 & 0 & 0 \\ 0 & \frac{H}{2} & 0 & 0 \\ 0 & 0 & MaxZ{-}MinZ & 0 \\ 0 & 0 & 0 & 1 \end{pmatrix}$$

scaling

$$\begin{pmatrix} 1 & 0 & 0 & MinX{+}\frac{W}{2} \\ 0 & 1 & 0 & MinY{+}\frac{H}{2} \\ 0 & 0 & 1 & MinZ \\ 0 & 0 & 0 & 1 \end{pmatrix}$$

translation

clip space (in NDC)

screen space

Fig. 3.12: Viewport transform is a combination of reflection, scaling, and translation.

The *viewport transform* converts the $2\times2\times1$-sized cuboidal view volume into the 3D viewport. Fig. 3.12 shows the conceptual sequence of three transforms composing the viewport transform. The clip space is left-handed whereas the screen space is right-handed. As their y-axes are opposite, transition from the clip space to the screen space requires the y-axis inversion. It is equivalent to the y-negation[4] and is performed by the following matrix:

$$\begin{pmatrix} 1 & 0 & 0 & 0 \\ 0 & -1 & 0 & 0 \\ 0 & 0 & 1 & 0 \\ 0 & 0 & 0 & 1 \end{pmatrix}$$

The matrix represents *reflection* with respect to the zx-plane.

[Note: Reflections]
Inverting the x-, y-, and z-axes is equivalent to negating the x-, y- and z-coordinates, respectively. When an axis is inverted, or equivalently the corresponding coordinate is negated, it has the effect of conversion between the left-hand and right-hand systems. The x-, y- and z negations are represented in the following matrices:

$$\begin{pmatrix} -1 & 0 & 0 & 0 \\ 0 & 1 & 0 & 0 \\ 0 & 0 & 1 & 0 \\ 0 & 0 & 0 & 1 \end{pmatrix}, \begin{pmatrix} 1 & 0 & 0 & 0 \\ 0 & -1 & 0 & 0 \\ 0 & 0 & 1 & 0 \\ 0 & 0 & 0 & 1 \end{pmatrix}, \begin{pmatrix} 1 & 0 & 0 & 0 \\ 0 & 1 & 0 & 0 \\ 0 & 0 & -1 & 0 \\ 0 & 0 & 0 & 1 \end{pmatrix}$$

These are the reflection matrices with respect to the yz-, zx-, and xy-planes.

In Fig. 3.12, reflection is followed by scaling and translation. Their matrices are combined into a single matrix for viewport transform:

$$\begin{pmatrix} \frac{W}{2} & 0 & 0 & MinX + \frac{W}{2} \\ 0 & -\frac{H}{2} & 0 & MinY + \frac{H}{2} \\ 0 & 0 & MaxZ - MinZ & MinZ \\ 0 & 0 & 0 & 1 \end{pmatrix} \qquad (3.2)$$

In most applications, the viewport takes the entire window, and therefore both $MinX$ and $MinY$ are zero. Further, $MinZ$ and $MaxZ$ are typically set to 0.0 and 1.0, respectively. Then, Equation (3.2) is simplified as follows:

$$\begin{pmatrix} \frac{W}{2} & 0 & 0 & \frac{W}{2} \\ 0 & -\frac{H}{2} & 0 & \frac{H}{2} \\ 0 & 0 & 1 & 0 \\ 0 & 0 & 0 & 1 \end{pmatrix} \qquad (3.3)$$

---

[4] Recall that OpenGL-to-Direct3D conversion (presented in Section 3.4.2) requires the z-axis inversion, and the z-coordinate of every vertex is negated for that purpose.

3.6   Scan Conversion

The viewport transform has converted every primitive into the screen space. The last substage in the rasterizer breaks up each screen-space primitive into a set of fragments. More specifically, it defines the screen-space pixel locations covered by the primitive and interpolates the per-vertex attributes to determine the per-fragment attributes at each pixel location. This process is often described as "rasterization in a narrow sense" and is called *scan conversion*. The graphics hardware vendors have employed various optimized algorithms for scan conversion. This section presents an implementation.

The per-vertex attributes vary from application to application and may include normal, texture coordinates[5], and color[6]. Consider a triangle within the viewport shown in Fig. 3.13-(a). For interpolating the per-vertex attributes, the xy-coordinates of the vertices are used. The z-coordinate of each vertex represents its *depth* in the screen space and is taken as another per-vertex attribute to be interpolated.

The pixels covered by a triangle are those whose centers fall inside the triangle. For example, the triangle shown in Fig. 3.13-(b) encompasses 18 pixels. For each of those, the per-fragment attributes are computed. In principle, all per-vertex attributes are interpolated in the same manner, and this section presents how the red color (R) attributes are interpolated.

First of all, the per-vertex attributes are linearly interpolated "along the edges." For this purpose, a set of *slopes* is computed per edge. An example is $\frac{\Delta R}{\Delta y}$, which denotes the ratio of R change to the vertical distance (y). Consider the edge shown in Fig. 3.13-(c). Its slopes, $\frac{\Delta R}{\Delta y}$ and $\frac{\Delta x}{\Delta y}$, are computed in the left box. The first scan line intersecting the edge is scan line 2. The right box of Fig. 3.13-(c) shows how the R value and x-coordinate are computed at the intersection. After the initialization step, the R values and x-coordinates of the next scan lines are obtained by repeatedly adding the slopes, $\frac{\Delta R}{\Delta y}$ and $\frac{\Delta x}{\Delta y}$, respectively. Fig. 3.13-(d) shows the case of R interpolation along the edge.

The process is repeated for the other two edges of the triangle. Then, for each scan line, we obtain the left- and right-bound red colors $(R_l$ and $R_r)$ and x-coordinates $(x_l$ and $x_r)$. Now is the time to interpolate the boundary attributes "along the scan lines." It is quite similar to interpolation along the edges. Fig. 3.13-(e) illustrates the process for scan line 3. First of all, $\frac{\Delta R}{\Delta x}$ is computed using ΔR $(= R_r - R_l)$ and Δx $(= x_r - x_l)$. For the pixel location of $(4,3)$, R value is initialized. Then, from left to right, R values are computed by repeatedly adding $\frac{\Delta R}{\Delta x}$.

---

[5]The texture coordinates (u, v) are used to access the 2D texture. This is presented in Section 4.1.

[6]The per-vertex color can be computed by the vertex program, or can be assigned at the modeling step.

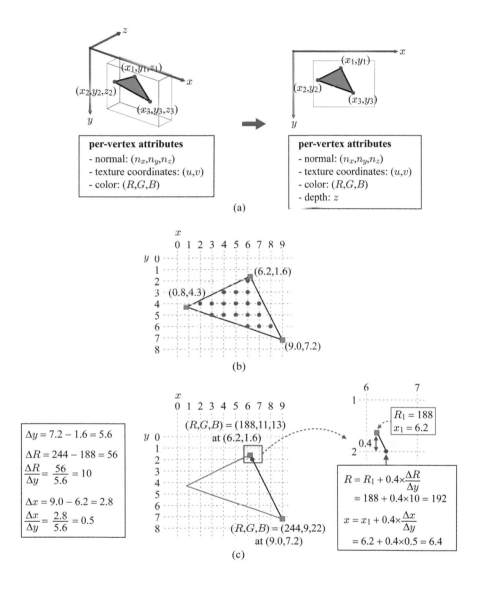

Fig. 3.13: Scan conversion through bilinear interpolation. (a) Typical examples of per-vertex attributes. (b) The per-vertex attributes are interpolated across the triangle so as to assign the interpolated attributes to each fragment within the triangle. (c) Attribute slopes are computed, and the attributes are initialized at the intersection between the edge and the first scan line.

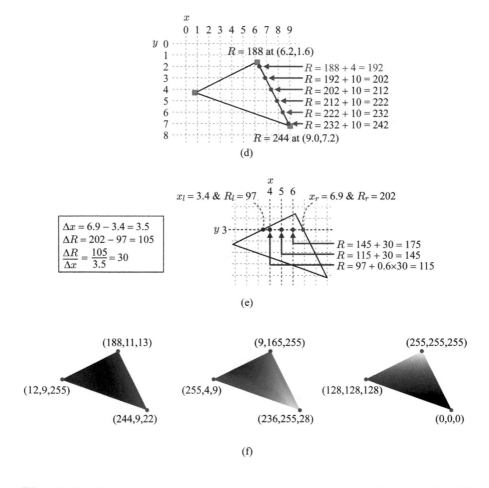

Fig. 3.13: Scan conversion through bilinear interpolation (*continued*). (d) Interpolation of the attributes along the edge. (e) Interpolation of the attributes along the scan line. (f) Examples of color-interpolated triangles.

Linear interpolation has been performed in two phases: along the edges first and then along the scan lines. It is an instance of *bilinear interpolation*. The G and B colors are interpolated using the same method, and then the per-fragment colors are obtained. Fig. 3.13-(f) shows examples of color-interpolated triangles.

The scan conversion algorithm also interpolates the vertex normals, texture coordinates, and depths. The rasterization stage is completed when all per-fragment attributes are computed. The next stage in the pipeline is the fragment processing stage (presented in Chapter 4). It processes a fragment at a time using the per-fragment attributes.

[Note: Top-left rule]

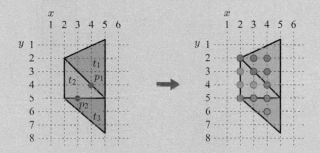

Fig. 3.14: When a pixel is located at an edge shared by two triangles, the pixel belongs to the triangle that has the edge as the top or left edge.

When a pixel is on the edge shared by two triangles, we have to decide which triangle it belongs to. Otherwise, it would be processed twice by the scan conversion algorithm. This is automatically handled by graphics APIs.

Intuitively speaking, a triangle may have right, left, top or bottom edges. For example, t_1 in Fig. 3.14 has two left edges and one right edge. In contrast, t_2 has a bottom edge, and t_3 has a top edge. Direct3D and OpenGL adopt the *top-left rule*, which declares that a pixel belongs to a triangle if it lies on the top or left edge of the triangle. In Fig. 3.14, p_1 belongs to t_1, not t_2, because it lies at the left edge of t_1. The top-left rule also judges that p_2 belongs to t_3, not t_2, because it lies at the top edge of t_3.

The top-left rule can be implemented as follows. Suppose that the y-bounds of a triangle are y_l and y_u, where $y_l < y_u$. Then, the top-most scan line to process is simply $\lceil y_l \rceil$. The bottom-most scan line is $(y_u - 1)$ if y_u is an integer. Otherwise, it is $\lfloor y_u \rfloor$. When the intersections between the triangle and a scan-line are x_l and x_r, where $x_l < x_r$, the left and right integer-bounds are similarly computed. The left bound is simply $\lceil x_l \rceil$. The right bound is $(x_r - 1)$ if x_r is an integer. Otherwise, it is $\lfloor x_r \rfloor$.

[Note: Perspective correction]

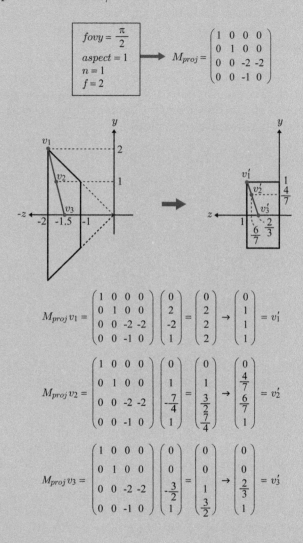

$$M_{proj} v_1 = \begin{pmatrix} 1 & 0 & 0 & 0 \\ 0 & 1 & 0 & 0 \\ 0 & 0 & -2 & -2 \\ 0 & 0 & -1 & 0 \end{pmatrix} \begin{pmatrix} 0 \\ 2 \\ -2 \\ 1 \end{pmatrix} = \begin{pmatrix} 0 \\ 2 \\ 2 \\ 2 \end{pmatrix} \to \begin{pmatrix} 0 \\ 1 \\ 1 \\ 1 \end{pmatrix} = v_1'$$

$$M_{proj} v_2 = \begin{pmatrix} 1 & 0 & 0 & 0 \\ 0 & 1 & 0 & 0 \\ 0 & 0 & -2 & -2 \\ 0 & 0 & -1 & 0 \end{pmatrix} \begin{pmatrix} 0 \\ 1 \\ -\frac{7}{4} \\ 1 \end{pmatrix} = \begin{pmatrix} 0 \\ 1 \\ \frac{3}{2} \\ \frac{7}{4} \end{pmatrix} \to \begin{pmatrix} 0 \\ \frac{4}{7} \\ \frac{6}{7} \\ 1 \end{pmatrix} = v_2'$$

$$M_{proj} v_3 = \begin{pmatrix} 1 & 0 & 0 & 0 \\ 0 & 1 & 0 & 0 \\ 0 & 0 & -2 & -2 \\ 0 & 0 & -1 & 0 \end{pmatrix} \begin{pmatrix} 0 \\ 0 \\ -\frac{3}{2} \\ 1 \end{pmatrix} = \begin{pmatrix} 0 \\ 0 \\ 1 \\ \frac{3}{2} \end{pmatrix} \to \begin{pmatrix} 0 \\ 0 \\ \frac{2}{3} \\ 1 \end{pmatrix} = v_3'$$

Fig. 3.15: The projection transform distorts the distance ratio of the camera space, and therefore bilinear interpolation using the distorted distance ratio produces incorrect results.

The projection transform maps lines to lines, i.e., collinear points remain collinear after the transform. However, it does not preserve the distance ratio of collinear points. (In contrast, affine transforms do.) Consider Fig. 3.15, where the view frustum and the projection matrix M_{proj} are the same as those of Fig. 3.2. The collinear points, v_1, v_2, and v_3, are projection-transformed to v_1', v_2', and v_3', respectively. Observe that the projected points are also collinear. However, the distance ratio is changed, i.e., $||v_1 - v_2|| : ||v_2 - v_3|| = 1 : 1$ in the camera space, but $||v_1' - v_2'|| : ||v_2' - v_3'|| = 3 : 4$ in NDC of the clip space. The clip-space ratio will be maintained in the screen space because the viewport transform is affine.

Suppose that v_1 and v_3 are the end vertices of an edge. Then, v_2 is the midpoint on the edge. Suppose also that v_1 is white and v_3 is black. Let us denote white by 1, and black by 0. The vertices are projected to v_1' and v_3', and their colors are interpolated in the screen space. Then, v_2' will be assigned a gray color $\frac{4}{7}$. It is not correct. The camera-space midpoint v_2 is projected to v_2', and therefore v_2' should be colored in $\frac{1}{2}$. We have the incorrect result because the bilinear interpolation process presented in this section uses the 'distorted' screen-space distance ratio instead of the 'undistorted' camera-space distance ratio, i.e., the ratio before the projection transform.

Using such a 'distorted' screen-space distance ratio often produces an annoying artefact especially for texturing. Therefore, the bilinear interpolation in the screen space should be modified. The modification is called *perspective correction*. It is automatically performed by the Graphics APIs.

3.7 Application: Object Picking

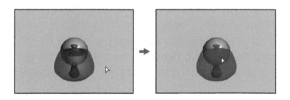

Fig. 3.16: The object at the mouse cursor's position is identified.

An operation frequently used in 3D graphics applications is to pick or select an object from the scene rendered in the screen. An example is shown in Fig. 3.16, where the teapot is picked by clicking it. The screen-space image is just an array of pixels. Mouse clicking simply returns the 2D pixel coordinates (x_s, y_s). This section presents how to identify the clicked object using (x_s, y_s).

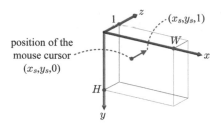

Fig. 3.17: The mouse cursor's position (x_s,y_s) leads to a *ray* that starts from $(x_s,y_s,0)$ and ends at $(x_s,y_s,1)$.

The object picking algorithm is seemingly complicated, but is implemented by combining the transforms we have learned so far. The picking algorithm would provide the readers with a chance to review the transforms.

3.7.1 Computing World-space Ray

Assume a simple viewport shown in Fig. 3.17, where *MinZ* and *MaxZ* are 0.0 and 1.0, respectively, and both *MinX* and *MinY* are zero. Given the mouse cursor position (x_s,y_s), we can consider a *ray* that starts from $(x_s,y_s,0)$ and ends at $(x_s,y_s,1)$. A ray is often described by a *start point* and a *direction vector*. The direction vector of the screen-space ray is $(0,0,1)$. The screen-space ray is transformed back to the world space. Then, the ray-object intersection test is done to find the world-space object *first* hit by the ray[7].

Let us first transform the screen-space ray back to the camera space. See Fig. 3.18. The camera-space ray is defined by its own start point and direction vector. Note that the near plane of the view frustum has been transformed to the xy-plane of the screen space, where the screen-space ray starts. Then, the camera-space ray's start point can be represented by $(x_c, y_c, -n)$, i.e., its z-coordinate is fixed to $-n$. We need to compute x_c and y_c only.

The projection matrix presented in Equation (2.23) is applied to $(x_c, y_c, -n)$.

$$\begin{pmatrix} m_{11} & 0 & 0 & 0 \\ 0 & m_{22} & 0 & 0 \\ 0 & 0 & -\frac{f}{f-n} & -\frac{nf}{f-n} \\ 0 & 0 & -1 & 0 \end{pmatrix} \begin{pmatrix} x_c \\ y_c \\ -n \\ 1 \end{pmatrix} = \begin{pmatrix} m_{11}x_c \\ m_{22}y_c \\ 0 \\ n \end{pmatrix} \rightarrow \begin{pmatrix} \frac{m_{11}x_c}{n} \\ \frac{m_{22}y_c}{n} \\ 0 \\ 1 \end{pmatrix} \quad (3.4)$$

where m_{11} and m_{22} represent $\frac{cot(\frac{fovy}{2})}{aspect}$ and $cot(\frac{fovy}{2})$, respectively, and $\rightarrow$ implies perspective division.

---

[7]The ray-object intersection is usually tested in the object spaces. It is more efficient. However, this section presents the test in the world space simply because it is more intuitive.

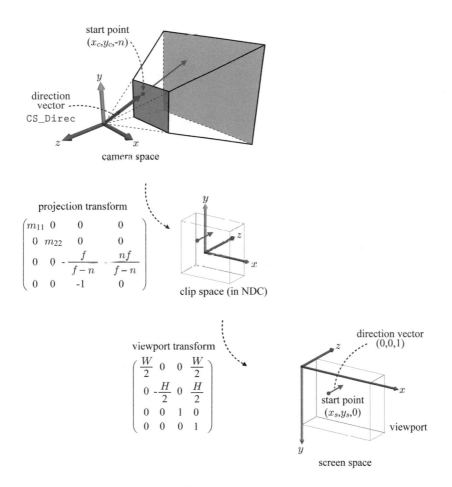

start point
$(x_c, y_c, -n)$

y

direction
vector
CS_Direc

z x

camera space

projection transform

$$\begin{pmatrix} m_{11} & 0 & 0 & 0 \\ 0 & m_{22} & 0 & 0 \\ 0 & 0 & -\dfrac{f}{f-n} & -\dfrac{nf}{f-n} \\ 0 & 0 & -1 & 0 \end{pmatrix}$$

y
z
x

clip space (in NDC)

viewport transform

$$\begin{pmatrix} \dfrac{W}{2} & 0 & 0 & \dfrac{W}{2} \\ 0 & -\dfrac{H}{2} & 0 & \dfrac{H}{2} \\ 0 & 0 & 1 & 0 \\ 0 & 0 & 0 & 1 \end{pmatrix}$$

direction vector
$(0,0,1)$

z
x

start point
$(x_s, y_s, 0)$

viewport

y

screen space

Fig. 3.18: The screen-space ray's start point is back-transformed to $(x_c, y_c, -n)$ in the camera space, and x_c and y_c can be computed using the projection and viewport transforms. The direction vector of the camera-space ray is obtained by connecting the origin and the start point.

Let us then apply the simplified matrix of the viewport transform presented in Equation (3.3) to the point obtained in Equation (3.4):

$$
\begin{pmatrix} \frac{W}{2} & 0 & 0 & \frac{W}{2} \\ 0 & -\frac{H}{2} & 0 & \frac{H}{2} \\ 0 & 0 & 1 & 0 \\ 0 & 0 & 0 & 1 \end{pmatrix} \begin{pmatrix} \frac{m_{11}x_c}{n} \\ \frac{m_{22}y_c}{n} \\ 0 \\ 1 \end{pmatrix} = \begin{pmatrix} \frac{W}{2}\left(\frac{m_{11}x_c}{n} + 1\right) \\ \frac{H}{2}\left(-\frac{m_{22}y_c}{n} + 1\right) \\ 0 \\ 1 \end{pmatrix}
\tag{3.5}
$$

Using the fact that the transformed coordinates in Equation (3.5) are identical to $(x_s, y_s, 0, 1)$, x_c and y_c can be computed. The start point of the camera-space ray is determined as follows:

$$
\begin{pmatrix} x_c \\ y_c \\ -n \\ 1 \end{pmatrix} = \begin{pmatrix} \frac{n}{m_{11}}\left(\frac{2x_s}{W} - 1\right) \\ -\frac{n}{m_{22}}\left(\frac{2y_s}{H} - 1\right) \\ -n \\ 1 \end{pmatrix}
\tag{3.6}
$$

Now compute the direction vector of the camera-space ray. Recall that the view frustum is considered to be a pencil of projection lines converging on the origin of the camera space. Therefore, if we extend the camera-space ray backward, it reaches the origin, as shown in Fig. 3.18. Consider the vector connecting the origin and the start point:

$$
\begin{pmatrix} \frac{n}{m_{11}}\left(\frac{2x_s}{W} - 1\right) \\ -\frac{n}{m_{22}}\left(\frac{2y_s}{H} - 1\right) \\ -n \\ 1 \end{pmatrix} - \begin{pmatrix} 0 \\ 0 \\ 0 \\ 1 \end{pmatrix} = \begin{pmatrix} \frac{n}{m_{11}}\left(\frac{2x_s}{W} - 1\right) \\ -\frac{n}{m_{22}}\left(\frac{2y_s}{H} - 1\right) \\ -n \\ 0 \end{pmatrix}
\tag{3.7}
$$

Equation (3.7) represents a vector whereas Equation (3.6) represents a point. (They differ only in the w-coordinate.) Observe that all of the x-, y-, and z-coordinates of the vector in Equation (3.7) contain n. Division by n leads to a simplified vector:

$$
\begin{pmatrix} \frac{\frac{2x_s}{W} - 1}{m_{11}} \\ -\frac{\frac{2y_s}{H} + 1}{m_{22}} \\ -1 \\ 0 \end{pmatrix}
\tag{3.8}
$$

Let us take this as the direction vector of the camera-space ray, and name it CS_Direc. (The length of the direction vector is of no importance, as will be clarified soon.)

We have computed the camera-space ray. Now consider transforming it back to the world space. Obviously, it is done by the inverse of the view transform. Note that, as presented in Equation (2.21), the view transform M_{view} is a translation T followed by a rotation R. Then, its inverse $(M_{view})^{-1}$ is $T^{-1}R^{-1}$. (When A and B denote matrices, $(AB)^{-1} = B^{-1}A^{-1}$.) The inverse of a rotation is simply its transpose, i.e., $R^{-1} = R^T$, as presented

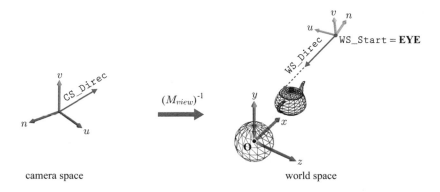

Fig. 3.19: The camera-space ray is transformed into the world space using the inverse view transform.

in [Note: Inverse rotation] of the next page. On the other hand, given a translation by an offset vector $-\mathbf{EYE}$, its inverse incurs an offset by $\mathbf{EYE}$. Then, the inverse of the view transform is defined as follows:

$$
\begin{aligned}
(M_{view})^{-1} &= (RT)^{-1} \\
&= T^{-1}R^{-1} \\
&= \begin{pmatrix} 1 & 0 & 0 & \mathbf{EYE}_x \\ 0 & 1 & 0 & \mathbf{EYE}_y \\ 0 & 0 & 1 & \mathbf{EYE}_z \\ 0 & 0 & 0 & 1 \end{pmatrix} \begin{pmatrix} u_x & v_x & n_x & 0 \\ u_y & v_y & n_y & 0 \\ u_z & v_z & n_z & 0 \\ 0 & 0 & 0 & 1 \end{pmatrix} \\
&= \begin{pmatrix} u_x & v_x & n_x & \mathbf{EYE}_x \\ u_y & v_y & n_y & \mathbf{EYE}_y \\ u_z & v_z & n_z & \mathbf{EYE}_z \\ 0 & 0 & 0 & 1 \end{pmatrix}
\end{aligned} \tag{3.9}
$$

$(M_{view})^{-1}$ is applied to the camera-space ray's direction vector `CS_Direc` defined in Equation (3.8):

$$
\begin{pmatrix} u_x & v_x & n_x & \mathbf{EYE}_x \\ u_y & v_y & n_y & \mathbf{EYE}_y \\ u_z & v_z & n_z & \mathbf{EYE}_z \\ 0 & 0 & 0 & 1 \end{pmatrix} \begin{pmatrix} \frac{\frac{2x_s}{W}-1}{m_{11}} \\ \frac{-\frac{2y_s}{H}+1}{m_{22}} \\ -1 \\ 0 \end{pmatrix} = \begin{pmatrix} u_x \frac{\frac{2x_s}{W}-1}{m_{11}} + v_x \frac{-\frac{2y_s}{H}+1}{m_{22}} - n_x \\ u_y \frac{\frac{2x_s}{W}-1}{m_{11}} + v_y \frac{-\frac{2y_s}{H}+1}{m_{22}} - n_y \\ u_z \frac{\frac{2x_s}{W}-1}{m_{11}} + v_z \frac{-\frac{2y_s}{H}+1}{m_{22}} - n_z \\ 0 \end{pmatrix} \tag{3.10}
$$

It is the direction vector of the world-space ray. Let us call it `WS_Direc`. Fig. 3.19 illustrates `CS_Direc` and `WS_Direc`.

For now, assume that the start point of the camera-space ray is the origin of the camera space, not the point computed in Equation (3.6). Such an "incorrect assumption" makes the picking algorithm simpler. Fortunately, the incorrect assumption can be easily corrected at the later stage of the algorithm, as will be presented in Section 3.7.2. $(M_{view})^{-1}$ applied to the camera-space origin returns the start point of the world-space ray:

$$
\begin{pmatrix} u_x & v_x & n_x & \mathbf{EYE}_x \\ u_y & v_y & n_y & \mathbf{EYE}_y \\ u_z & v_z & n_z & \mathbf{EYE}_z \\ 0 & 0 & 0 & 1 \end{pmatrix} \begin{pmatrix} 0 \\ 0 \\ 0 \\ 1 \end{pmatrix} = \begin{pmatrix} \mathbf{EYE}_x \\ \mathbf{EYE}_y \\ \mathbf{EYE}_z \\ 1 \end{pmatrix} \tag{3.11}
$$

The result is compatible with our understanding: The origin of the camera space corresponds to **EYE** in the world space. Notice that **EYE** is stored at the fourth column of $(M_{view})^{-1}$. Once $(M_{view})^{-1}$ is computed, we can simply extract the fourth column and take it as the start point of the world-space ray. See Fig. 3.19, where the world-space ray's start point, named WS_Start, is set to **EYE**.

[Note: Inverse rotation]

As presented in Section 2.2.2, a rotation matrix is composed of orthonormal vectors. Consider multiplying a 3D rotation matrix R with its transpose R^T:

$$
\begin{aligned}
RR^T &= \begin{pmatrix} u_x & u_y & u_z \\ v_x & v_y & v_z \\ n_x & n_y & n_z \end{pmatrix} \begin{pmatrix} u_x & v_x & n_x \\ u_y & v_y & n_y \\ u_z & v_z & n_z \end{pmatrix} \\
&= \begin{pmatrix} u \cdot u & u \cdot v & u \cdot n \\ v \cdot u & v \cdot v & v \cdot n \\ n \cdot u & n \cdot v & n \cdot n \end{pmatrix} \\
&= \begin{pmatrix} 1 & 0 & 0 \\ 0 & 1 & 0 \\ 0 & 0 & 1 \end{pmatrix}
\end{aligned}
$$

As $RR^T = I$, R^T is R's inverse, i.e., $R^{-1} = R^T$.

[Note: Code for computing the world-space ray]

This note presents the function Pick that converts the screen-space cursor position, denoted by (X_s,Y_s) which corresponds to (x_s, y_s) in the main text, into the world-space ray, represented by the start point WS_Start and the direction vector WS_Direc.

The first four statements of the function compute CS_Direc, the camera-space ray's direction vector presented in Equation (3.8). The start point of the camera-space ray is not computed because it is 'incorrectly' assumed to be (0,0,0).

The inverse view transform $(M_{view})^{-1}$ computed in Equation (3.9) is denoted by M_view_Inv. Its fourth column is assigned to WS_Start. The last three statements define the vector in Equation (3.10).

```
void Pick( VECTOR3* WS_Start, VECTOR3* WS_Direc,
           MATRIX4X4* M_view_Inv, MATRIX4X4* M_proj,
           int ViewportW, int ViewportH,
           int X_s, int Y_s )
{
  VECTOR3 CS_Direc;
  CS_Direc.x = (((2.0f*X_s)/ViewportW)-1)/M_proj->_11;
  CS_Direc.y = -(((2.0f*Y_s)/ViewportH)-1)/M_proj->_22;
  CS_Direc.z = -1.0f;

  WS_Start->x = M_view_Inv->_14;
  WS_Start->y = M_view_Inv->_24;
  WS_Start->z = M_view_Inv->_34;

  WS_Direc->x = CS_Direc.x*M_view_Inv->_11
              + CS_Direc.y*M_view_Inv->_12
              + CS_Direc.z*M_view_Inv->_13;
  WS_Direc->y = CS_Direc.x*M_view_Inv->_21
              + CS_Direc.y*M_view_Inv->_22
              + CS_Direc.z*M_view_Inv->_23;
  WS_Direc->z = CS_Direc.x*M_view_Inv->_31
              + CS_Direc.y*M_view_Inv->_32
              + CS_Direc.z*M_view_Inv->_33;
}
```

3.7.2 Ray-object Intersection Test

Once the world-space ray is computed, we need to find out which object it hits *first* on its way from WS_Start along the direction of WS_Direc. To do this, we go through the objects in the scene and collect the objects intersected by the ray.

How can we determine if the ray intersects an object represented in a polygon mesh? In principle, we have to perform the ray intersection test with *every* triangle of the object. It would be costly. A faster but less accurate method is to approximate a polygon mesh with a *bounding volume* (BV) that completely contains the polygon mesh, and then do the ray-BV intersection test.

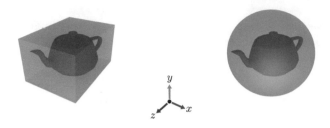

Fig. 3.20: The most popular bounding volumes are the AABB and the bounding sphere.

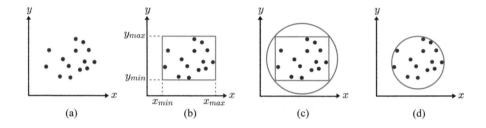

Fig. 3.21: AABB and bounding sphere construction. (a) Input vertices. (b) A 2D AABB is described by (x_{min}, x_{max}) and (y_{min}, y_{max}). (c) A poor-fit bounding sphere. (d) A tighter bounding sphere.

The geometry of a BV is usually much simpler than that of the input polygon mesh. Fig. 3.20 shows two popular BVs: *axis-aligned bounding box* (AABB) and *bounding sphere*. An AABB is represented by the extents along the principal axes, i.e., (x_{min}, x_{max}), (y_{min}, y_{max}), and (z_{min}, z_{max}). A bounding sphere is represented by its center and radius.

Fig. 3.21 shows in 2D space how to construct AABB and bounding sphere. The AABB is the simplest BV to create. Its extents are initialized by the coordinates of a vertex in the input polygon mesh. Then, the remaining vertices are visited one at a time to update the extents. Fig. 3.21-(a) and -(b) show the vertices of a polygon mesh and its AABB, respectively.

A brute-force method to create a bounding sphere is to use the AABB. The center and diagonal of the AABB determine the center and diameter of the bounding sphere, respectively. Fig. 3.21-(c) shows the bounding sphere constructed from the AABB of Fig. 3.21-(b). It encompasses the AABB. However, such an AABB-based bounding sphere is often too large and may not tightly bound the polygon mesh. Fig. 3.21-(d) shows a tight bounding sphere. There are many algorithms to create a tight or an optimal bounding sphere.

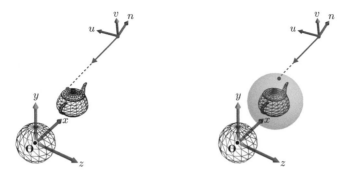

Fig. 3.22: Ray-triangle intersection test (shown in the left) produces an accurate result but would be costly especially if the number of triangles is large. Ray-sphere intersection test (shown in the right) is fast but may produce an inaccurate result. Compare two intersection points colored in red.

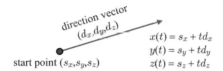

Fig. 3.23: A 3D ray is represented as a parametric equation.

This section uses the bounding sphere for ray intersection test. Fig. 3.22 compares the results of ray-triangle test and ray-sphere test. (From now on, the bounding sphere will be simply called sphere. Do not be confused with the sphere object centered at the origin.)

A ray can be represented in a *parametric equation* of t:

$$p(t) = s + td \tag{3.12}$$

where s is the start point (WS_Start in our example), and d is the direction vector (WS_Direc in our example). See Fig. 3.23. A 3D ray is defined as follows:

$$p(t) = \begin{pmatrix} x(t) \\ y(t) \\ z(t) \end{pmatrix} = \begin{pmatrix} s_x + td_x \\ s_y + td_y \\ s_z + td_z \end{pmatrix} \tag{3.13}$$

Parameter t is 0 at the start point and is 1 at the end of the ray.

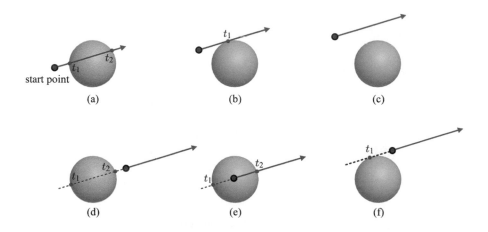

Fig. 3.24: Intersections between the ray and bounding sphere. (a) Two roots are positive, and t_1 is the parameter at the first intersection. (b) The double root t_1 is positive, and the ray is tangent to the sphere. (c) The ray does not hit the sphere, and there is no real root. (d) Two roots are negative and are discarded. (e) The root t_1 is negative and is discarded. In contrast, t_2 is positive and can be accepted or discarded depending on applications because the ray travels from the inside to the outside. (f) The double root t_1 is negative and is discarded.

If a sphere is centered at (C_x, C_y, C_z) and has radius r, it is described by the following implicit function:

$$(x - C_x)^2 + (y - C_y)^2 + (z - C_z)^2 = r^2 \qquad (3.14)$$

Let us insert $x(t)$, $y(t)$, and $z(t)$ of Equation (3.13) into x, y, and z of Equation (3.14), respectively. Then, we obtain a quadratic equation of the following form:

$$at^2 + bt + c = 0 \qquad (3.15)$$

Solving Equation (3.15) for parameter t amounts to finding the roots by the quadratic formula:

$$t = \frac{-b \pm \sqrt{b^2 - 4ac}}{2a} \qquad (3.16)$$

The roots are the parameters at the intersection points between the ray and the sphere.

In Equation (3.16), the expression underneath the square root sign is the *discriminant*. If it is positive, we have two distinct roots, t_1 and t_2, both of which are real numbers. Fig. 3.24-(a) shows its geometric interpretation, i.e., the ray intersects the sphere at t_1 and t_2. Inserting the parameters

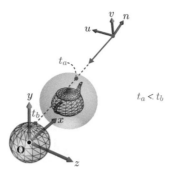

Fig. 3.25: Two objects are independently tested for ray intersection. The ray is found to hit both of the bounding spheres. Then, the teapot is chosen because its intersection point is closer to the start point of the ray.

into Equation (3.13), we obtain the 3D points at the intersections. If the discriminant is zero, we have a distinct real root, called a double root. It implies that, as shown in Fig. 3.24-(b), the ray is tangent to the sphere. If the discriminant is negative, there are no real roots. Its geometric interpretation is illustrated in Fig. 3.24-(c).

In Fig. 3.24-(a) and -(b), the roots are positive. However, we may have negative roots when the ray intersects the sphere in its opposite direction. Three possible cases are illustrated in Fig. 3.24-(d), -(e), and -(f). The negative roots are all discarded, and we consider only the positive roots. When we have two positive roots for a sphere, we take the smaller, e.g., t_1 in Fig. 3.24-(a).

From all bounding spheres in the scene, such positive ts are collected. The bounding sphere hit *first* by the ray is the one with the *smallest* t. Fig. 3.25 shows that both of the bounding spheres are hit by the ray, but t_a is smaller than t_b. Consequently, the teapot is selected as the first-hit object.

In the previous subsection, we assumed the start point of the camera-space ray to be the origin. It was an incorrect assumption because the ray starts from the view frustum's near plane. It is time to correct the assumption.

Consider the camera-space ray in Fig. 3.26-(a). It is represented in a parametric equation of t. Obviously, t is 0 at the origin, and is 1 at the ray's end. The ray's end is defined by the direction vector. As presented in Equation (3.8), the z-coordinate of the direction vector is -1. Recall that the near plane's z-coordinate is $-n$. Therefore, if the ray is extended to intersect the near plane, t at the intersection point becomes n. Similarly, t at the far plane is f. Using these observations, the incorrect assumption can be simply remedied by imposing a *range constraint*: The *first* hit occurs at the smallest

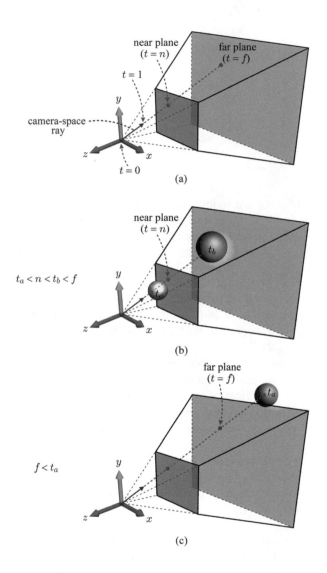

Fig. 3.26: Range constraint for object picking. (a) If an object is intersected by the ray and the intersection point is located within the view frustum, t at the intersection is within the range of $[n, f]$. (b) The intersection point located between the origin and the near plane is discarded because its t is out of the range $[n, f]$. (c) Similarly, the intersection point behind the far plane is also discarded.

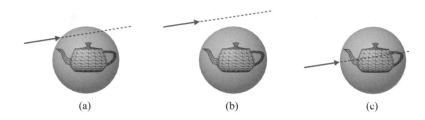

Fig. 3.27: Ray-sphere intersection test for preprocessing. (a) The ray intersects the bounding sphere, but does not intersect the mesh. (b) The ray does not intersect the sphere, and the ray-triangle test is not invoked at all. (c) The ray intersects both the bounding sphere and the mesh.

t that is "within the range of $[n,f]$." In Fig. 3.26-(b), the small ball with t_a is discarded by the range constraint, and the large ball with t_b is picked. Fig. 3.26-(c) shows another example, where the only intersection point is out of the range $[n,f]$, and no object is picked.

A ray may not intersect a polygon mesh even though it intersects its bounding sphere. See Fig. 3.27-(a). If accurate results are required, we have to resort to the ray-triangle intersection test. Even when we run the ray-triangle test, the ray-sphere test is used at the preprocessing step. If the ray does not intersect the sphere, the ray is guaranteed not to intersect the polygon mesh. See Fig. 3.27-(b). Through a simple preprocessing, time-consuming iterations of the ray-triangle test can be avoided. If the ray intersects a polygon mesh, the ray always intersects its bounding sphere, as shown in Fig. 3.27-(c), and the preprocessing step safely directs us to the ray-triangle tests.

When every triangle of a mesh is tested for intersection with the ray, multiple intersections can be found. Then, we choose the point with the smallest positive t. For algorithms of ray-triangle intersection test, ray intersection tests with other bounding volumes (such as AABB), and various acceleration techniques, readers are referred to [8], which is an excellent reference.

Exercises

1. A viewport's corners are located at $(10,20,1)$ and $(100,200,2)$.

   (a) Compute the reflection matrix for the viewport transform.

   (b) Compute the scaling matrix.

   (c) Compute the translation matrix.

2. Consider the following screen-space triangle. Each vertex is associated with $\{R, G, B, z\}$. Compute R and z for the fragment at (5,6).

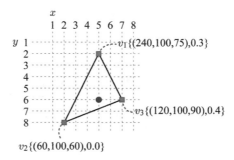

3. Let us compute the camera-space ray's start point $(x_c, y_c, -n)$ in Fig. 3.18 using a different way.

   (a) Apply the *inverse* viewport transform to (x_s, y_s), and compute the ray's start point in NDC of the clip space.

   (b) Using the fact that the result in (a) is identical to the point in Equation (3.4), compute x_c and y_c.

Chapter 4

Fragment Processing and Output Merging

The per-fragment attributes produced by the rasterizer may include a depth, a normal vector, a set of RGB colors, and a set of texture coordinates. Using these data, the fragment program determines the color of each fragment. The fragment processing stage has the strongest impact on the quality of the final image and has employed a variety of algorithms. The algorithms largely focus on lighting and texturing.

Lighting is presented in Chapter 5. Texturing is so important that three chapters (Chapters 8, 9 and 10) are devoted to it. In Section 4.1, the bare basics of texturing will be presented, which would be enough to make the readers understand what the fragment processing stage does.

Section 4.2 presents the last stage of the rendering pipeline, output merging, which is another hard-wired stage. Section 4.3 discusses the topic of z-culling. Even though z-culling is implemented in the rasterization stage, it is presented here because it requires understanding of the output merging stage.

4.1 Texturing

The simplest among the various texturing methods is *image texturing*. It may be considered as pasting or wrapping an image onto an object's surface. Fig. 4.1-(a) shows a 2D photo image pasted to an area of the teapot surface.

4.1.1 Texture Coordinates

An individual entity of a texture is called a *texel* (texture element), to distinguish it from the pixel (picture element) in the color buffer. A texture is usually represented as a 2D array of texels. See Fig. 4.1-(b). Each texel has a unique address, i.e., 2D array index. For example, the address of the upper-left corner texel in Fig. 4.1-(b) is (0,0), and its neighbor on the right-hand side has the address (1,0).

Texturing requires the *correspondences* between the texture and the object surface to be textured. In other words, for a surface point p, we should be

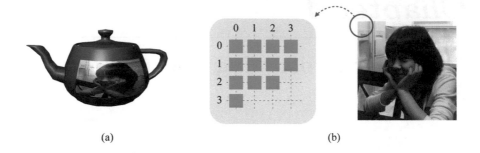

(a)   (b)

Fig. 4.1:   Image texturing. (a) An image is pasted to a part of the curved surface. (b) An image texture is an array of color texels.

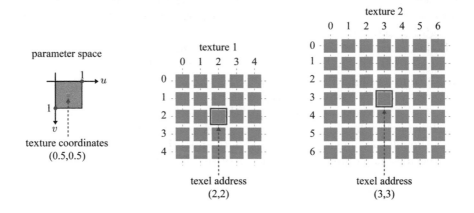

Fig. 4.2:   Using the normalized texture coordinates (u, v) allows different textures to be accessed and different texels to be fetched.

able to find a location q in the texture space such that the texel at q can be retrieved and then applied to p. In a polygon mesh, such correspondences are usually established at the vertices.

For a vertex of a polygon mesh, we could assign a texel address. However, it would then cause many problems. Above all, the mesh would be tightly coupled with a specific texture. A generic scheme is needed to avoid such coupling. It is customary to use *normalized* coordinates (u, v), where the parameters u and v range from 0 to 1. The (u, v) coordinates are named *texture coordinates*. They are independent of specific textures and are distinguished from texel addresses. As illustrated in Fig. 4.2, for example, the texture coordinates (0.5,0.5) are mapped to the texel address (2,2) in texture 1, but to (3,3) in texture 2.

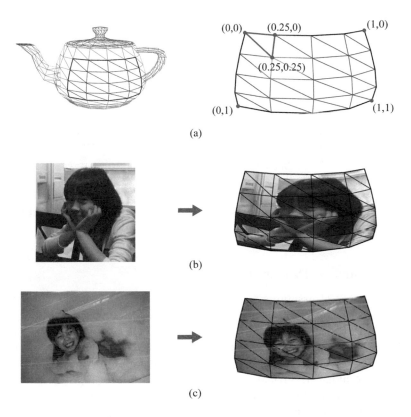

Fig. 4.3: Texture coordinates and image texturing. (a) Texture coordinates are assigned to the vertices of a patch in a polygon mesh. (b) The patch is textured with an image. (c) Using the same texture coordinates, the patch is textured with another image of a different resolution.

Fig. 4.3-(a) shows a patch of the teapot's surface. It consists of 25 vertices, and all vertices are assigned texture coordinates. (The figure shows only six among them.) Fig. 4.3-(b) and -(c) show that two images of different resolutions can be pasted to the patch without changing the texture coordinates.

Direct3D and OpenGL adopt different parameter spaces for texture coordinates. See Fig. 4.4. In Direct3D, the v-axis runs downward, but it runs upward in OpenGL. As a result, the texture coordinates (u, v) reference different locations of an image in Direct3D and OpenGL. If a textured polygon mesh is ported between Direct3D to OpenGL, the v-coordinate should be converted into $(1 - v)$ for every vertex, in order to fetch the same texel from the image texture. The conversion is so simple that, depending on the context, this book will freely choose between the two parameter spaces, but will be somewhat biased in favor of the Direct3D convention.

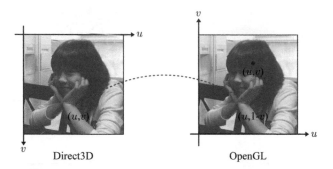

Fig. 4.4: If a textured model is transferred between Direct3D and OpenGL, the v-coordinate should be converted into $(1 - v)$.

4.1.2   Surface Parameterization

The process of assigning texture coordinates to the vertices of a polygon mesh is called *surface parameterization* or simply *parameterization*. In general, parameterization requires *unfolding* a 3D surface onto a 2D planar domain. For some 3D surfaces, parameterization is straightforward. For example, parameterizing a cylindrical surface is conceptually equivalent to cutting the surface along a vertical seam and then flattening it. See Fig. 4.5-(a). Given such an unfolded 2D mesh, (u, v) coordinates can be assigned to each vertex by mapping the rectangular mesh into a unit square with the uv-ranges of [0,1]. In the figure, the texture coordinates for four vertices are given as examples.

Unless a patch is a developable surface such as cylinder or cone, parameterizing the patch incurs distortion, e.g., the relative edge lengths of the 3D polygon mesh are not preserved in the 2D domain. This problem has been well studied in computer graphics, and many parameterization techniques have been proposed aiming at minimizing the distortion [10]. Graphics packages such as 3ds Max also provide parameterization tools, which are based on a combination of automatic and manual procedures. Fig. 4.5-(b) shows the parameterized mesh of the soldier's head.

One way to decrease the parameterization error is to subdivide the surface into a number of patches and then unfold each patch. Once a patch is parameterized, the artist draws an image for the parameterized patch. An image for a patch is often called a *chart*. Fig. 4.6-(a) shows the chart for the head mesh. Multiple charts are usually packed and arranged in a texture, which is often called an *atlas*. Fig. 4.6-(b) shows the atlas for the whole body of the soldier.

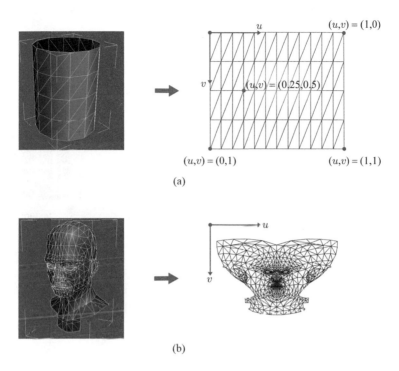

Fig. 4.5: Surface parameterization. (a) It is easy to parameterize a developable surfaces such as a cylinder. (b) Most 3D surfaces cannot avoid distortion during parameterization, but well-designed parameterization algorithms keep the distortion minimized.

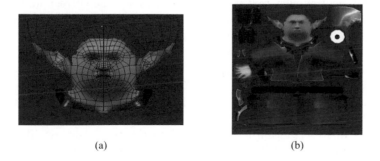

Fig. 4.6: Chart and atlas. (a) The entire 3D mesh is often subdivided into a set of smaller patches, and each patch is parameterized. The image texture for a patch is called a chart. (b) An atlas is a collection of charts.

4.1.3   Texture Coordinates to Texel Address

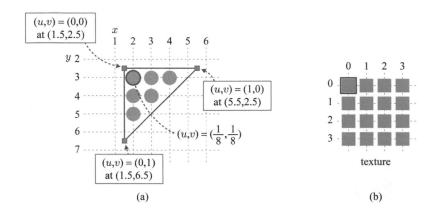

(a)   (b)

Fig. 4.7:   Computing texel addresses. (a) The scan conversion algorithm computes per-fragment texture coordinates. (b) The texel address is computed from the texture coordinates, and a texel at the address is read.

The per-vertex texture coordinates are interpolated for the screen-space fragments by the rasterizer. Consider an example shown in Fig. 4.7. The vertices of the triangle have the texture coordinates, (0,0), (0,1) and (1,0). The scan conversion algorithm presented in Chapter 3 interpolates them, along the edges first and then along the scan lines. When the scan conversion algorithm is completed, each fragment is assigned the interpolated (u, v) coordinates. For example, the upper-left fragment's texture coordinates will be $(\frac{1}{8}, \frac{1}{8})$.

Given the per-fragment texture coordinates (u, v), the corresponding texel address is automatically computed by the graphics API at run time. Direct3D performs the following computations to map (u, v) to the texel address (t_x, t_y):

$$t_x = (u \times s_x) - 0.5$$
$$t_y = (v \times s_y) - 0.5 \qquad (4.1)$$

where $s_x \times s_y$ denotes the texture resolution. See Fig. 4.7-(b). The texture's resolution is 4×4, i.e., $s_x = s_y = 4$. Then, according to Equation (4.1), the texture coordinates $(\frac{1}{8}, \frac{1}{8})$ will be mapped to the texel address (0,0). The texel at the address (0,0) is fetched and is used to determine the fragment color. In the simplest case, the fragment color can be set to the texel color. Chapter 8 presents how the texel color contributes to the final color of the fragment.

Unlike the contrived example in Fig. 4.7, the texel address computed in Equation (4.1) is generally not in integer coordinates, but in floating-point

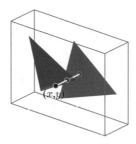

Fig. 4.8: Two triangles in the viewport compete for a pixel. The pixel will be taken by the blue triangle.

coordinates. Then, the texels *around* the texel address need to be *filtered*. This issue is also discussed in Chapter 8.

4.2 Output Merging

We have almost reached the end of the rendering pipeline. The final stage is hard-wired and is called output merging. The output of the fragment program is often called the RGBAZ fragment, which implies that a fragment has not only the RGB color but also 'A' (or alpha, representing the opacity) and 'Z' (representing the depth) values. Using the alpha and depth values, the fragment competes or combines with the pixel stored in the color buffer.

4.2.1 Z-buffering

Fig. 4.8 shows two triangles in the viewport. The pixel located at (x, y) will be colored in blue because the blue triangle is *closer* to the camera than the red triangle. Such decision is made using the *z-buffer* (also called *depth buffer*), and the algorithm using the z-buffer is called the *z-buffering* (or *depth buffering*).

The z-buffer has the same resolution as the color buffer and records the z-values of the pixels currently stored in the color buffer. When a fragment located at (x, y) is passed from the fragment program, its z-value is compared with the z-buffer value at (x, y). If the fragment has a smaller z-value, its color and z-value are used to update the color buffer and z-buffer at (x, y), respectively. Otherwise, the fragment is judged to lie behind the pixel and therefore invisible. It is discarded.

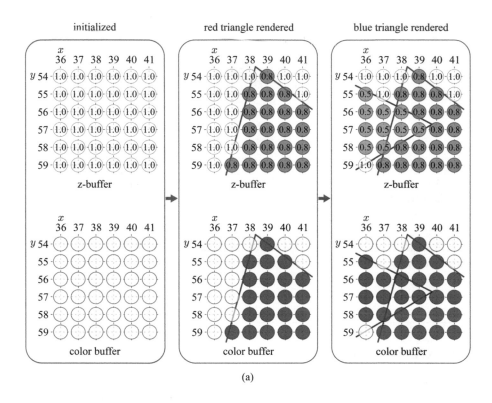

Fig. 4.9: Z-buffering visualization. (a) Rendering order is red to blue triangles.

Fig. 4.9-(a) illustrates how the z-buffer and color buffer are updated when we process the red triangle first and then the blue one shown in Fig. 4.8. Suppose that the z-range in the screen space is set to $[0.0,1.0]$. Then, the z-buffer is initialized to the largest z-value, 1.0. On the other hand, the color buffer is initialized to the background color, white, in the example.

For simplicity, the triangles are assumed to be parallel to the xy-plane of the screen space, and the blue and red triangles are located at z-locations 0.5 and 0.8, respectively. Shown in the middle of Fig. 4.9-(a) is the result of processing the red triangle. Shown in the right of Fig. 4.9-(a) is the result of processing the blue triangle. The color-buffer pixels located at (38,56), (38,57) and (39,57) are changed from red to blue. The same locations in the z-buffer are also updated.

Fig. 4.9-(b) shows the case where the processing order is reversed. Observe that, when rendering is completed, the z-buffer and the color buffer contain the same information as those in Fig. 4.9-(a). In principle, the z-buffering

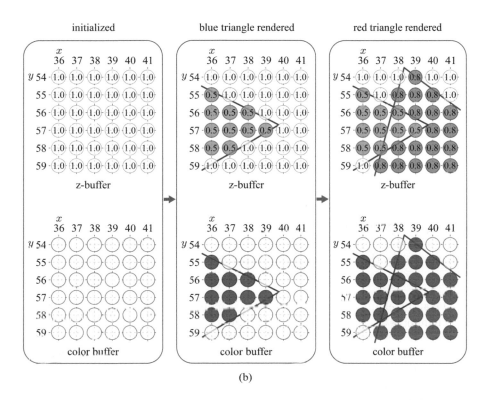

Fig. 4.9: Z-buffering visualization (*continued*). (b) Rendering order is blue to red triangles. The rendering result is the same as (a).

algorithm allows the primitives to be processed in an arbitrary order. It is one of the key features making the algorithm so popular. However, primitive ordering is important in several aspects and will be discussed in the rest of this chapter.

4.2.2 Alpha Blending

In the previous subsection, all surfaces are implicitly assumed to be opaque so that, when two surface points compete for a pixel position, one point fully occludes the other. However, some surfaces may be translucent (partially transparent). Suppose that the current fragment has a smaller depth than the pixel in the color buffer and is translucent. Then, the pixel should show through the fragment. This is achieved by *blending* the fragment color with the pixel color. The process uses the alpha value (often called *alpha channel*) of the fragment and is named *alpha blending*.

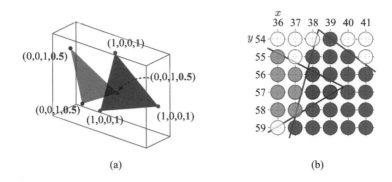

(a)   (b)

Fig. 4.10:   Alpha blending example. (a) The per-vertex alpha attributes of the blue triangle indicate that it is translucent, whereas the red triangle is opaque. (b) In the color buffer, three pixels have the blended colors.

The alpha channel typically contains as many bits as a color channel. If the red channel is assigned 8 bits, for example, the alpha channel may be assigned 8 bits, leading to 32-bit RGBA color. With 8 bits, the alpha channel can represent 256 levels of opacity. For the opacity representation, the normalized range [0,1] is preferred to the integer range [0,255]. The minimum value 0 denotes "fully transparent," and the maximum value 1 denotes "fully opaque."

A typical blending equation is described as follows:

$$c = \alpha c_f + (1 - \alpha)c_p \tag{4.2}$$

where c is the blended color, α represents the fragment's opacity, c_f is the fragment color, and c_p is the pixel color. If α is 0, for example, the fragment is fully transparent and is invisible. If α is 0.5, c will be the average of the fragment and pixel colors. The effect of Equation (4.2) is often described by placing a translucent fragment 'over' a pixel and is called an *over* operator.

Assume that, in Fig. 4.10-(a), all vertices of the blue triangle have the RGBA color, (0,0,1,0.5), and those of the red triangle have (1,0,0,1). The scan conversion algorithm interpolates the RGB channels and the alpha channel in the same manner. Therefore, all fragments of the blue triangle will be assigned (0,0,1,0.5), and those of the red triangle will be (1,0,0,1).

Suppose that the rendering order is red to blue triangles. Then, as illustrated in Fig. 4.10-(b), the blue fragment is blended with the red pixel at the positions of (38,56), (38,57) and (39,57) in the color buffer. The blended RGB color will be (0.5,0,0.5). The z-buffer values at those positions are replaced by the depth values of the blue fragments.

Recall that, as discussed in the previous subsection, the z-buffering algorithm is independent of the order of processing the primitives. However, translucent primitives cannot be rendered in an arbitrary order. They must be processed in *back-to-front* order after all opaque primitives are rendered. For this purpose, the translucent objects should be *sorted*.

Unfortunately, sorting triangles is not an easy problem. The view direction may change frame by frame, and sorting based on the view direction should be done in real time. The more triangles we have, the more computational overhead we encounter.

A variety of algorithms for handling translucent objects have been studied. In an order-independent algorithm [11], for example, the translucent objects need not be sorted. The evolving GPU enables such algorithms to be implemented in real time. However, the algorithms are not a standard component of the rendering pipeline. They are not yet implemented at the output merging stage, but are executed by the fragment program.

4.3 Z-culling

The depth test using the z-buffer is done after the fragment processing stage. When the z-value of the fragment is greater than the z-buffered value, the fragment is determined to be occluded and thus discarded. This shows a lack of efficiency because the expensive computation done by the fragment program is in vain.

Before entering the fragment processing stage, a fragment can be culled if its depth is known to be greater than the z-buffered value. Then, expensive computations including various texturing works are not executed for the culled fragment. This process is called *z-culling* and may lead to significant increase in performance. It is a hard-wired procedure located in the rasterizer.

4.3.1 Tile-based Culling

The z-culling algorithm maintains a table of *tiles* that cover the z-buffer, or equivalently the screen. A tile is composed of $n \times n$ pixels and stores z_{max}^{tile} information, which records the maximum (the deepest) among the z-values of the $n \times n$ pixels. Fig. 4.11-(a) shows an 8×8-resolution tile example, where z_{max}^{tile} is 0.7.

Consider a simple example shown in Fig. 4.11-(b), where a triangle falls into a tile. We can compute the minimum z-value of the triangle, z_{min}^{tri}, from its three vertices. If $z_{max}^{tile} < z_{min}^{tri}$, i.e., the closest point of the triangle is deeper than the deepest pixel of the tile, the triangle is determined to be fully occluded, and no fragment of the triangle has a chance to enter the fragment processing stage. It is the case in Fig. 4.11.

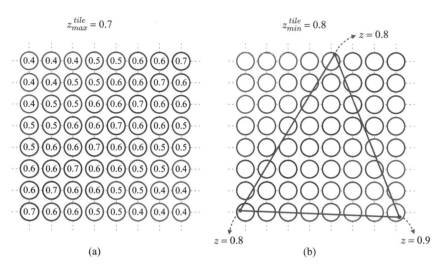

(a)   (b)

Fig. 4.11: Tile-based culling. (a) In the 8×8-resolution tile, each value represents the depth stored in the z-buffer. The deepest among the 64 pixels is 0.7. (b) The minimum z-value of the triangle is 0.8.

Fig. 4.12-(a) shows 20 instances of a single object aligned along the view direction. Fig. 4.12-(b) shows the rendering result. The first object occludes most of triangles of the other objects. In this example, z-culling can bring a great amount of performance increase if the triangles are sorted in *front-to-back* order. Sorting triangles in real time is not easy. Therefore, per-object sorting is often adopted and produces satisfactory results. When 20 objects in Fig. 4.12 are sorted front-to-back along the view direction, the overall frame rate becomes multiple times faster than an arbitrary-order rendering.

The problem of rendering invisible pixels is often referred to as *overdraw*. More specifically, it measures the number of fragments passing the depth test divided by the total number of pixels in the screen. The smaller the overdraw is, the more efficient the rendering system is. In an ideal system where no to-be-occluded fragment enters the fragment processing stage, the overdraw will be 1. Front-to-back ordering coupled with z-culling plays a key role in reducing the overdraw.

There are some tricky issues in the front-to-back ordering. Recall that, as presented in Section 1.2.2, the triangles are often reordered to increase the post-transform cache performance. Unfortunately, there is no static order of triangles that would lead to the front-to-back rendering from all possible view directions. Recently, there have been efforts aiming at both increasing the vertex cache locality and decreasing the overdraw [6]. The basic idea is to divide an object into a number of triangle clusters, determine what clusters are more likely to occlude others when viewed from a number of view directions,

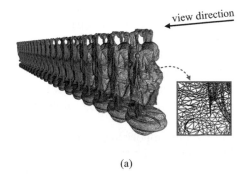

(a) (b)

Fig. 4.12: Rendering a scene of aligned objects with z-culling. (a) Twenty instances of Buddha are aligned along the view direction. (b) When the objects are front-to-back ordered, the rendering performance is significantly increased with z-culling. (The Buddha model is provided by the Stanford University Computer Graphics Laboratory.)

and finally compute a view-independent static order of clusters. This order serves the purpose of reducing the overdraw. The vertices in each cluster are reordered for increasing the vertex cache performance.

In contemporary GPUs, z-culling is automatically enabled whenever possible[1]. After analyzing the fragment program, however, the GPU often disables z-culling. Let us see an example. Suppose that the fragment program modifies the depth of the current fragment at its own. Then, the system based on z-culling will be collapsed because z-culling works using the depth information of the current fragment. In this case, z-culling is automatically disabled. See [12, 13] for other cases where z-culling is disabled. To ensure that an application takes advantage of the z-culling capabilities, readers need to understand when z-culling is disabled or when it may underperform. It can be said that z-culling is becoming less transparent to programmers.

4.3.2 Application: Pre-Z Pass

If a scene is complex enough, it may be worth adopting the *pre-Z pass* or *early-Z pass* technique which takes full advantage of the z-culling capabilities. It is a *two-pass algorithm*, i.e., rendering is invoked twice. The first pass

---

[1] NVIDIA GeForce 6 series and later GPUs support coarse-grained z-culling, named ZCULL, and GeForce 8 series and later GPUs support fine-grained z-culling, named EarlyZ [12]. The tile size used for ZCULL is larger than that of EarlyZ. ZCULL and EarlyZ are implemented by separate hardware. ZCULL is performed prior to EarlyZ, i.e., the fragments surviving ZCULL are tested by EarlyZ. In AMD Radeon series, ZCULL is named Hierarchical Z, and Hierarchical Z and EarlyZ are collectively called HyperZ.

renders the scene with no lighting and no texturing. The color buffer is not filled, but the z-buffer is filled with the depths of the visible surfaces of the scene, i.e., the surfaces closest to the viewer.

With the scene depths laid out in the z-buffer, the second pass renders the scene with full lighting and texturing. Then, z-culling discards the fragments that are occluded by the visible surfaces, and the overdraw approaches 1 at the second pass. It is a great performance gain if the fragment program performs expensive computations.

For the scene shown in Fig. 4.12, the pre-Z pass algorithm even with back-to-front ordered objects outperforms the single-pass front-to-back rendering. (If we sort the objects in front-to-back order for the first pass, z-buffer writes are reduced and the performance is slightly increased.) Another technique related with the pre-Z pass algorithm will be presented in Section 10.5.

Exercises

1. Consider five triangles competing for a pixel position. They have distinct depth values at the pixel position. If the triangles are processed in random order, how many times would the z-buffer be updated on average for the pixel position?

2. You have three surface points competing for a pixel position. Their RGBA colors and z-coordinates are given as follows: $\{(1,0,0,0.5),0.25\}$, $\{(0,1,0,0.5),0.5\}$, and $\{(0,0,1,1),0.75\}$. They are processed in back-to-front order. Compute the final color of the pixel.

3. Consider the crossing translucent polygons shown below. They occlude one another in a cycle.

   (a) Assume that the rendering order is in red, green, and blue triangles, and sketch the result of rendering.

   (b) What problem do you find? How would you resolve the problem?

4. Fog is often used to enhance the realism of the outdoor scenes and can be described by the following blending equation:

$$c = fc_f + (1 - f)c_o$$

where c is the fogged color, f represents the fog factor which increases with the distance from the viewer, c_f is the fog color, and c_o is the fragment color of the object. A simplest implementation is a *linear fog*. It starts from the near plane and ends at the far plane of the view frustum such that the object located at the near plane is clearly visible but the object at the far plane is completely fogged and invisible. Define the fog factor f as a function of the near plane's depth (N) and the far plane's depth (F).

Chapter 5

Illumination and Shaders

Illumination or *lighting* refers to the techniques handling the interaction between light sources and objects. The lighting models are often divided into two categories: *local illumination* and *global illumination*. In general, the local illumination model considers only *direct lighting*. The illumination of a surface depends solely on the properties of the surface and the light sources. In the real world, however, every surface receives light *indirectly*. Even though light sources are invisible from a particular point of the scene, light can be transferred to the point through reflections or refractions from other surfaces of the scene. The global illumination model considers the scene objects as potential indirect light sources.

Unfortunately, the cost for global illumination is often too high to permit interactivity. Consequently, local illumination has been dominant in games so as to cope with the real-time constraints. The rasterization-based architecture of the GPU is suitable for local illumination. On the other hand, the special effects industry has adopted global illumination models for generating photorealistic visual effects, which are usually produced off-line on the CPU. It may often take several minutes or hours to generate an image.

Many efforts have been reported on direct implementation of the global illumination algorithms in GPU. However, the full global illumination algorithms are not quite at the point where commercial games can use them for real-time rendering of complex scenes. The mainstream in real-time graphics is to *approximate* the global illumination effects or to *pre-compute* global illumination and use the result at run time.

This chapter presents a well-known local illumination model and shows how it is programmed in GPU. The global illumination algorithms are briefly sketched at the end of the chapter, and then various efforts to approximate or pre-compute them are presented in Chapter 10.

5.1 Phong Lighting Model

For rendering a surface illuminated by a light source, we need to represent the *irradiance* measured at the surface and the outgoing *radiance* reaching the camera. The relationship between them is described by BRDF (bidirectional

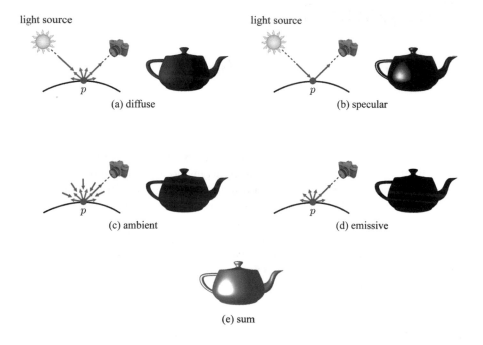

(a) diffuse

(b) specular

(c) ambient

(d) emissive

(e) sum

Fig. 5.1: Light incident on p is illustrated in blue, and reflected light is in orange color. Outgoing radiance reaching the camera is illustrated in red.

reflectance distribution function) [14]. A simplified BRDF was proposed by Phong [15].

The Phong model is a local illumination technique. Before 2001, the graphics hardware was not programmable, but a fixed-function rendering pipeline. The lighting models adopted for the fixed-function pipelines were slight variations of the Phong model. The local illumination model is physically incorrect, and so is the Phong model. Therefore, the rendering result is not photorealistic and can be easily recognized as computer-generated.

Lighting is one of the elements influenced the most by GPU evolution, and the state of the art in real-time lighting has been gradually moving away from the classic implementation of the Phong lighting model. Especially, programmability in GPU enables us to extend the local illumination model and implement a variety of more physically correct algorithms.

Nonetheless, the Phong model is still widely adopted in commercial games and lays foundations of various advanced lighting techniques. This section introduces the principle of the Phong model, and Chapter 10 shows how it has been extended toward global illumination.

In the Phong model, the perceived color of a surface point is defined by four terms named *diffuse*, *specular*, *ambient*, and *emissive*. The diffuse and

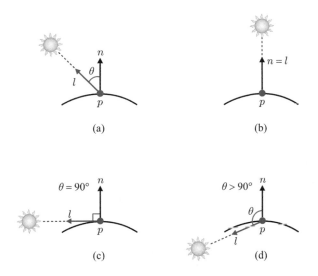

Fig. 5.2: Diffuse reflection. (a) The amount of light incident on p is defined by $max(n \cdot l, 0)$. (b) When $n = l$, the incident light reaches the maximum amount. (c) When $\theta = 90°$, it is zero. (d) When $\theta > 90°$, it is also zero.

specular terms deal with the light ray directly coming from the light source to the surface point to be lit, whereas the ambient term accounts for indirect lighting. The emissive term applies for the object emitting light itself. Fig. 5.1 illustrates the four terms and their sum. The following subsections present the four terms in order.

5.1.1 Diffuse Reflection

For lighting computation, it is necessary to specify the light source types. Frequently used are the point, area, spot, and directional light sources. The simplest among them is the directional light source, which is assumed to be considerably distant from the scene. The sun is a good example. This section considers only the directional light.

The diffuse term is based on the *Lambert's law*, which states that reflections from ideally diffuse surfaces (called Lambertian surfaces) are scattered with equal intensity in *all* directions, as illustrated in Fig. 5.1-(a). Therefore, the amount of perceived reflection is independent of the view direction and is just proportional to the amount of incoming light. See Fig. 5.2-(a). The light source is considerably distant, and consequently the *light vector l* that connects the surface point p and the light source is constant for a scene[1]. (Note that, for computational efficiency, l is defined to be opposite to the direction the light actually travels.) The *incident angle* θ of light at p is between l and the surface normal n. If θ becomes smaller, p receives more light. Assuming l and n are normalized, the dot product of n and l is used to measure the amount of incident light:

$$n \cdot l \qquad\qquad (5.1)$$

When $\theta = 0$, i.e., $n = l$, $n \cdot l$ equals 1, and therefore p receives the maximum amount of light (Fig. 5.2-(b)). When $\theta = 90°$, $n \cdot l$ equals 0, and p receives no light (Fig. 5.2-(c)). Note that, when $\theta > 90°$, p does not receive any light (Fig. 5.2-(d)). Therefore, the amount of incident light should be zero, but $n \cdot l$ becomes negative. To resolve this problem, $n \cdot l$ in Equation (5.1) is extended to the following:

$$max(n \cdot l, 0) \qquad\qquad (5.2)$$

Note that $max(n \cdot l, 0)$ determines only the 'amount' of incident light. The perceived 'color' of the surface point p is defined as follows:

$$s_d \otimes m_d \qquad\qquad (5.3)$$

where s_d is the RGB color of the light source, m_d is the *diffuse reflectance* of the object material, and $\otimes$ represents the component-wise multiplication. (In our notations, s denotes the light source, and m denotes the material.) Suppose that s_d is (1,1,0), i.e., the light source's color is yellow. If m_d is (1,1,1), for example, the diffuse color term $s_d \otimes m_d$ is (1,1,0), i.e., the yellow light is reflected as is. If m_d is (0,1,1), however, the diffuse color term becomes (0,1,0), i.e., the red component of the light source is absorbed by the material, and only the green component is reflected.

The diffuse reflection term of the Phong model is defined by combining Equations (5.2) and (5.3):

$$max(n \cdot l, 0)s_d \otimes m_d \qquad\qquad (5.4)$$

Fig. 5.1-(a) shows the teapot rendered only with the diffuse term.

5.1.2 Specular Reflection

The specular term is used to make a surface look shiny via *highlights*, and it requires *view vector* and *reflection vector* in addition to the light vector l. The normalized view vector, denoted by v in Fig. 5.3-(a), connects the surface point p and the camera position. (Note that v is defined to be opposite to the view direction.) On the other hand, the light vector l is reflected at p to define the reflection vector r.

---

[1]In contrast, a point light source is located at a specific position in the 3D scene. If a point light is used, l is not constant, but varies across a surface. Further, the distance to the light source has to be considered.

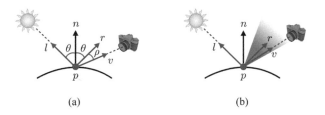

(a)   (b)

Fig. 5.3: Specular reflection. (a) Reflected light vector and view vector are denoted by r and v, respectively. (b) If v falls into the conceptual cone of the reflected vectors centered around r, a highlight is visible to the camera.

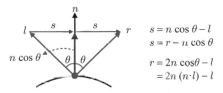

$$s = n \cos \theta - l$$
$$s = r - n \cos \theta$$

$$r = 2n \cos\theta - l$$
$$= 2n \, (n \cdot l) - l$$

Fig. 5.4: Computing reflection vector in the context of lighting.

Let us compute r. In Fig. 5.4, the incident angle θ of l with respect to n is equal to the reflection angle of r. The two right triangles in the figure share the side represented by the vector $n\cos\theta$. Consider the base s of the triangle at the left-hand side. It connects l and $n\cos\theta$, and is defined as

$$n\cos\theta - l \qquad (5.5)$$

The base of the triangle at the right-hand side is also s and is defined as

$$r - n\cos\theta \qquad (5.6)$$

Equations (5.5) and (5.6) should be identical, and therefore we can derive r as follows:

$$r = 2n\cos\theta - l$$

As $n \cdot l = \cos\theta$, r is rephrased as follows:

$$r = 2n(n \cdot l) - l \qquad (5.7)$$

In the context of lighting, l is assumed to be a unit vector, and therefore r is also a unit vector.

Return to Fig. 5.3-(a), and consider the angle ρ between r and v. For a perfectly shiny surface, the highlight at p is visible to the camera only when

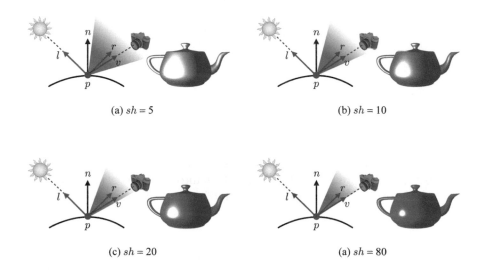

(a) $sh = 5$ (b) $sh = 10$

(c) $sh = 20$ (a) $sh = 80$

Fig. 5.5: Consider the term $(r \cdot v)^{sh}$ that approximates the amount of perceived highlight. In the figure, both r and v are fixed. As sh increases, the highlight falls off more sharply, and consequently the camera perceives less highlight at p. Accordingly, the highlighted area on the teapot surface becomes smaller.

$\rho = 0$. For a surface that is not perfectly shiny, the maximum highlight occurs when $\rho = 0$ but decreases rapidly as ρ increases. Fig. 5.3-(b) illustrates the cone of the reflected light rays, the axis of which is r. If v is located within the cone, the highlight is visible to the camera. The rapid decrease of highlights within the cone is often approximated by

$$(r \cdot v)^{sh} \tag{5.8}$$

where sh represents the *shininess* (smoothness) of the surface. When $r = v$, $(r \cdot v)^{sh} = 1$, regardless of the value sh, and the maximum highlight is visible to the camera. When $r \neq v$, the highlight is less likely to be visible as sh increases.

Fig. 5.5 illustrates that, as sh increases, the cone of the reflected light rays becomes smaller, and the highlights are more focused on the object surface. For a perfectly shiny surface, the value of sh is ∞ such that the highlight at p is visible to the camera only when $\rho = 0$.

The specular term is defined as

$$(max(r \cdot v, 0))^{sh} s_s \otimes m_s \tag{5.9}$$

where s_s is the RGB color of the specular light, and m_s is the *specular reflectance* of the object material. The *max* function is needed for the same reason taken for the diffuse reflection term. In general, s_s is equal to s_d used in Equation (5.4). Unlike m_d, m_s is usually a gray-scale value rather than an RGB color. It enables the highlight on the surface to end up being the color of the light source. (Imagine a white light shining on a red-colored metallic object. Most of the object surfaces would appear red, but the highlight would be white.) Fig. 5.1-(b) shows the teapot rendered only with the specular term.

5.1.3   Ambient Reflection

The ambient light describes the light reflected from the various objects in the scene, i.e., it accounts for *indirect lighting*. The ambient light has bounced around in the scene and arrives at a surface point from *all* directions, rather than along a particular direction. As a consequence, reflections from the surface point are also scattered with equal intensity in all directions. These facts imply that the amount of ambient light incident on a surface point is independent of the surface orientation, and the amount of perceived reflection is independent of the view direction. Therefore, the ambient reflection term is simply defined as follows:

$$s_a \otimes m_a \qquad (5.10)$$

where s_a is the RGB color of the ambient light, and m_a is the *ambient reflectance* of the object material. Fig. 5.1-(c) shows the teapot rendered only with the ambient term. The rendering result simply looks like a 2D object because there is no difference in shade across the teapot's surface.

The ambient term approximates the inter-reflection of real-world lighting and enables us to see into shadowy corners of the scene that are not directly lit by light sources. For example, in Fig. 5.1-(a) and -(b), the lower-right part of the teapot is completely dark because it is not directly lit. In contrast, the same part of the teapot in Fig. 5.1-(c) is slightly illuminated. However, the ambient term presented in Equation (5.10) is too simple to capture the subtleties of real-world indirect lighting. Section 10.4 presents a technique to make the ambient reflection more realistic.

5.1.4   Emissive Light

The emissive term describes the amount of light emitted by a surface itself. It is simply an RGB color value and is denoted by m_e. Fig. 5.1-(d) shows the teapot rendered only with the emissive term. (The object has little emissive color.) The rendering result looks like 2D as in the case of the ambient reflection. Note that, in the local illumination model, an emissive object per se is not a light source, and it does not illuminate the other objects in the scene.

The Phong model sums the four terms to determine the surface color:

$$max(n \cdot l, 0)s_d \otimes m_d + (max(r \cdot v, 0))^{sh} s_s \otimes m_s + s_a \otimes m_a + m_e \qquad (5.11)$$

Fig. 5.1-(e) shows the result of adding the four terms. If an object does not emit light, the emissive term m_e is simply deleted. If an object is close to a Lambertian surface, the RGB components of m_d are large and those of m_s are small. In order to describe a shiny metallic object, m_s should be made large.

5.2   Shaders and Shading Languages

There has been a tremendous increase in GPU performance. The GPU has a massively parallel architecture such that hundreds of fine-grained cores independently operate on vertices and fragments. On the other hand, the GPU that used to be a fixed-function processor has evolved into a programmable processor augmented with some special-purpose fixed-function stages. In fact, the term GPU standing for graphics processing unit implies programmable chips, like the term CPU for central processing unit.

5.2.1   Vertex and Fragment Shaders

Shading refers to depicting depth perception in 3D objects by varying levels of lightness. In computer graphics, the lightness is computed using a lighting model. An executable program running on the GPU is called a *shader* in the sense that its main job is shading.

Fig. 5.6:   The vertex and fragment shaders are written for the programmable stages of the rendering pipeline.

Fig. 5.6 is basically a copy of Fig. 2.1 and shows that the first shader in the rendering pipeline is the *vertex shader* (also known as *vertex program*). The input and output of a vertex shader are structures containing the vertex data such as position, normal, color, texture coordinates, etc. The vertex shader runs once for each vertex. Each vertex is processed independently of the others. Therefore the parallel architecture of GPU is well suited for processing a large number of vertices simultaneously.

The vertices output by the vertex shader are assembled into primitives (such as triangles), and the hard-wired *rasterizer* produces the fragments which fill in the primitives. Then, the *fragment shader*[2] (also known as *fragment program*) runs once for each fragment and calculates its color.

5.2.2 High-Level Shading Language*

If you are not interested in shader programming or have no experience in high-level language programming, you can skip this subsection, Section 5.3.1, and Section 5.3.3. Otherwise, you are encouraged not to do so. They are easy to follow.

A few languages have been developed for shader programming. They include High Level Shading Language (HLSL) [16] developed by Microsoft for use with the Direct3D API, and Cg (C for graphics) [17] developed by NVIDIA. HLSL and Cg are very similar because Microsoft and NVIDIA have worked in close collaboration for developing the shading languages. Another popular language is GLSL (OpenGL Shading Language) developed for use with the OpenGL API [2].

All of HLSL, Cg, and GLSL are C-like languages, and therefore programmers with experiences in C do not have difficulties in understanding their data types, operations, and control flow. However, the shading languages work on GPUs, the goal and architecture of which are different from those of CPUs. The differences shape the shading languages in a distinct way.

Once you understand either HLSL, Cg, or GLSL, there would be little challenge in programming a shader in the other languages. This section presents the minimal syntax of HLSL, which can serve as a foundation for understanding the shader examples given in this book. Readers are referred to [16] for more on HLSL.

In addition to the basic types such as `float`, HLSL supports vectors up to four elements and matrices up to 4×4 elements. For example, `float4` and `float2x3` define a four-element vector and a 2×3-element matrix, respectively, where each element is a `float` value.

In a shader, functions can be either top-level or intrinsic. The vertex or fragment shader itself is a top-level function and may call intrinsic functions, which include the user-defined functions and the standard library functions. An example of a frequently used library function is `mul()`, which can be used for matrix-matrix, matrix-vector, and vector-matrix multiplications.

---

[2]Recall that, in Direct3D, the word *pixel* is used for both fragment and pixel. Consequently, Direct3D calls the fragment shader *pixel shader*. It is a misnomer because the shader processes a fragment, not a pixel. The processed fragment competes or combines with the pixel in the color buffer to update the pixel's color.

Shaders accept two kinds of input data. One is the *uniform data* that remain constant for multiple executions of a shader, and the other is the *varying data* that are unique to each execution of a shader. The uniform input for a vertex shader may include the world, view, and projection transforms. It is either provided as a global variable or specified with the keyword `uniform` in the parameter list. In contrast, the position and texture coordinates of each vertex can be provided as the varying input.

```
float4x4 WorldViewProj;

void VS_TransformVertex(float4 Pos : POSITION,
                        float2 Tex : TEXCOORD0,
                    out float4 oPos : POSITION,
                    out float2 oTex : TEXCOORD0)
{
  oPos = mul(WorldViewProj, Pos);
  oTex = Tex;
}
```

Shown above is a simple vertex shader, which transforms the object-space vertex into the clip space. The world, view, and projection transforms are combined into a single matrix `WorldViewProj`. It is the uniform input provided as a global variable. The vertex shader takes as varying inputs the vertex position (`Pos`) and texture coordinates (`Tex`). All varying inputs must have associated *semantic labels* such as `POSITION` and `TEXCOORD0`. The semantics can be assigned by two methods: (1) Appending a colon and the semantic label to the parameter declaration. (2) Defining a structure with semantics assigned to the structure members. (The above sample code takes the first method. The second method will be presented soon.) In a typical model used in games, multiple textures are used, and they are enumerated using `TEXCOORD0`, `TEXCOORD1`, etc.

The output data can be described using the keyword `out` if the data are included in the parameter list, as shown above. Otherwise, the return value of a shader is automatically taken as the output. (This will be presented soon.) The above vertex shader produces two elements as output: The clip-space vertex that is the result of applying `WorldViewProj` to the object-space vertex `Pos`, and the texture coordinates that are simply copied from the input.

All outputs must have associated semantic labels. A shader provides output data to the next stage of the rendering pipeline, and the output semantics are used to specify how the data should be linked to the inputs of the next stage. For example, the output semantic `POSITION` represents the clip-space position of the transformed vertex that is fed to the rasterizer. Note that the input and output vertices use the same semantic label `POSITION` for different meanings.

5.3 Lighting in the Pipeline

As presented in Section 2.3, lighting can be computed per vertex. It is *per-vertex lighting*. In contemporary real-time graphics, however, lighting is usually computed by the fragment shader. It is *per-fragment lighting*. Section 5.3.1 presents per-vertex lighting in HLSL, and Section 5.3.2 discusses its drawbacks. Then, Section 5.3.3 presents the HLSL programs for per-fragment lighting. For simplicity, both of the lighting methods implement the Phong model presented in Equation (5.11).

5.3.1 Per-vertex Lighting in HLSL*

In the box shown below, VSInput is the input structure for the vertex shader. It consists of vertex position and normal defined in the object space. The output of the vertex shader is another structure VSOutput, which consists of clip-space position of the vertex and its color.

```
struct VSInput {
  float3 Pos : POSITION;    // object-space position
  float3 Nor : NORMAL;      // object-space normal
};

struct VSOutput {
  float4 Pos : POSITION;    // clip-space position
  float4 Color : COLOR;     // vertex color
};
```

The boxes shown below and at the next page contain the global variables and the vertex shader. For simplicity, suppose that the world is composed of a single object. Let us then take the object space as the world space such that no world transform is needed. The view transform is combined with the projection transform to make a single 4×4 matrix named ViewProj. It is used to transform the input vertex from the world space to the clip space. The other global variables specify the properties of the light source and the object material.

```
float3    Eye;          // eye position
float4x4  ViewProj;     // view+projection transform
```

```
float3    Light;         // light vector
float3    SourceDiff;    // s_d
float3    SourceSpec;    // s_s
float3    SourceAmb;     // s_a

float3    MaterialDiff;  // m_d
float3    MaterialSpec;  // m_s
float     MaterialSh;    // sh
float3    MaterialAmb;   // m_a
float3    MaterialEmi;   // m_e
```

```
VSOutput VS_PhongPerVertex(VSInput vInput) {
  VSOutput vOutput;

  vOutput.Pos = mul(ViewProj, float4(vInput.Pos, 1));

  // Diffuse
  float Diffuse = max(dot(vInput.Nor, Light), 0.0f);
  float3 PhongD = Diffuse * SourceDiff * MaterialDiff;

  // Specular
  float3 Refl = 2.0f*vInput.Nor*dot(vInput.Nor, Light)
              - Light;
  float3 View = normalize(Eye - vInput.Pos);
  float Specular = pow(max(dot(Refl, View), 0.0f),
                       MaterialSh);
  if (Diffuse <= 0.0f) Specular = 0.0f;
  float3 PhongS = Specular * SourceSpec * MaterialSpec;

  // Ambient
  float3 PhongA = SourceAmb * MaterialAmb;

  // Emissive
  float3 PhongE = MaterialEmi;

  // Sum
  vOutput.Color = float4(PhongD+PhongS+PhongA+PhongE, 1.0f);

  return vOutput;
}
```

The vertex shader is a straight implementation of the Phong model. It invokes several intrinsic functions: `max(a,b)` for taking the larger between two input parameters `a` and `b`, `normalize(v)` for making `v` a unit vector, `pow(a,b)` for raising `a` to the power `b`, and `dot(a,b)` for dot product of two vectors `a` and `b`.

The color values computed for the vertices are interpolated by the rasterizer. A fragment with an interpolated color enters the fragment shader. The fragment shader shown below simply outputs the input color. The input semantic `COLOR` of the fragment shader implies the fragment color interpolated by the rasterizer.

```
float4 FS_PhongPerVertex(float4 Color : COLOR) : COLOR {
    return Color;
}
```

5.3.2 Per-vertex Lighting vs. Per-fragment Lighting

Per-vertex lighting often produces unpleasant results. Consider an ideally smooth sphere and a point p on its surface. Fig. 5.7-(a) shows a polygon mesh representation of the sphere, where p is located at a vertex and is associated with vertex normal n. Suppose that the view vector v is identical to the reflection vector r. Then, the maximum highlight will be perceived at p. The rendering result in Fig. 5.7-(a) shows the captured highlight.

Suppose that the sphere is now modeled in a low-resolution mesh. See Fig. 5.7-(b). The 'to-be-highlighted' point p is not located at any vertex of the mesh. Assume the sphere is a shiny metallic object, and its shininess parameter sh is large. In the cross-section illustration, the vertices closest to p are denoted by p_1 and p_2, but they do not have highlights due to the large shininess parameter. The colors of p_1 and p_2 are computed through per-vertex lighting and then interpolated. Consequently, the highlight is not captured at or around p in the rendering result.

Such a problem of per-vertex lighting can be overcome by employing per-fragment lighting, which is often called a normal interpolation shading. The vertex shader does not compute the vertex color, but simply passes the vertex normal to the rasterizer. The rasterizer interpolates the vertex normals and assigns an interpolated normal to each fragment. Then, the fragment shader computes the fragment color using the interpolated normal.

The cross-section illustration in Fig. 5.7-(c) shows three fragments between p_1 and p_2. They have normals computed by interpolating the vertex normals, n_1 and n_2. Consider the fragment denoted by p_m. Its normal n_m is likely to be similar to n in Fig. 5.7-(a). Then, p_m will be highlighted by per-fragment lighting, and we have the rendering result shown in the figure.

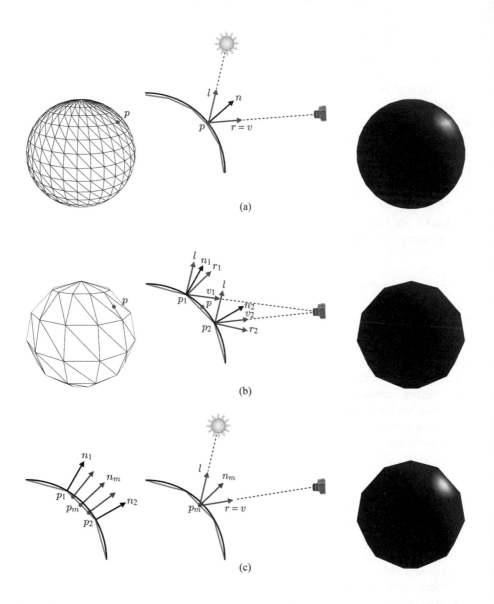

(a)

(b)

(c)

Fig. 5.7: Highlights in per-vertex lighting and per-fragment lighting. (a) A point p of an ideally smooth surface is located at a vertex of a fine mesh. It is highlighted through per-vertex lighting. (b) A coarse mesh is used, where p is not located at a vertex any longer. When the mesh is rendered by per-vertex lighting, the highlight is missing. (c) In per-fragment lighting, the fragment p_m is highlighted using the interpolated normal n_m. The fragments around p_m are also highlighted.

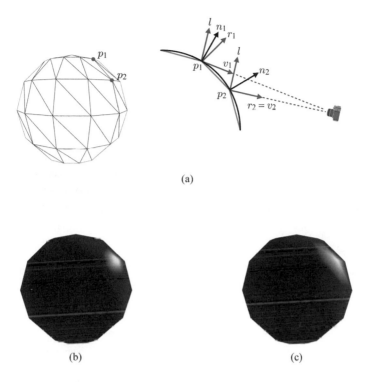

(a)

(b)   (c)

Fig. 5.8:   Highlights in a coarse polygon mesh. (a) The camera has moved, and the highlight is captured at p_2. (b) Per-fragment lighting produces a high-light focused around p_2. (c) Per-vertex lighting produces a wider highlight.

Now suppose that, as illustrated in Fig. 5.8-(a), the camera has moved and perceives the maximum highlight at p_2. Fig. 5.8-(b) shows the result of per-fragment lighting. Compare the image with that of Fig. 5.7-(c). The highlight is floating around the sphere's surface, but its area does not significantly change.

Fig. 5.8-(c) shows the result of per-vertex lighting performed with the same model and the same camera position. Observe that per-vertex lighting produces a wider highlight. It is because the vertex colors are *evenly* interpolated across the triangles. Worse still, imagine a sequence of animated frames, where the image of Fig. 5.8-(c) follows that of Fig. 5.7-(b). A wide highlight would appear abruptly.

In general, the results of per-fragment lighting are superior to those of per-vertex lighting because per-fragment lighting enables finer control over the final image. This is why per-vertex lighting is rarely used in contemporary games.

5.3.3   Per-fragment Lighting in HLSL*

In the shader implementation of per-fragment lighting, the vertex shader input is identical to VSInput used for per-vertex lighting. However, the vertex shader output (VSOutput) and the fragment shader input (FSInput) are changed, as shown below. The same global variables (such as ViewProj) defined for per-vertex lighting will be used.

```
struct VSOutput {
  float4 Pos : POSITION;        // clip-space position
  float3 WPos : TEXCOORD0;      // world-space position
  float3 Nor : TEXCOORD1;       // world-space normal
};

struct FSInput {
  float3 WPos : TEXCOORD0;      // world-space position
  float3 Nor : TEXCOORD1;       // world-space normal
};
```

```
VSOutput VS_PhongPerFragment(VSInput vInput) {
  VSOutput vOutput;

  vOutput.Pos = mul(ViewProj, float4(vInput.Pos, 1));
  vOutput.WPos = vInput.Pos;
  vOutput.Nor = vInput.Nor;

  return vOutput;
}
```

First of all, the vertex shader computes the clip-space vertex position. It is the required task for every vertex shader. Then, the vertex shader outputs the world-space position and normal of each vertex to the rasterizer as if they were texture coordinates. They are interpolated across each polygon, and the world-space position and normal "of each fragment" are input to the fragment shader.

Shown in the next page is the fragment shader. First of all, it normalizes the interpolated normal (fInput.Nor) passed from the rasterizer. Even though the per-vertex normals are unit vectors, the per-fragment normals generated by interpolating the per-vertex normals are not unit vectors in general. They should be made into unit vectors because every normal used for lighting is assumed to be a unit vector. Not surprisingly, the rest of the fragment shader is actually identical to the vertex shader for per-vertex lighting.

```
float4 FS_PhongPerFragment(FSInput fInput) : COLOR {

    // Normalizing the interpolated normal vector
    float3 Nor = normalize(fInput.Nor);

    // Diffuse
    float Diffuse = max(dot(Nor, Light), 0.0f);
    float3 PhongD = Diffuse * SourceDiff * MaterialDiff;

    // Specular
    float3 Refl = 2.0f*Nor*dot(Nor, Light)
                - Light;
    float3 View = normalize(Eye - fInput.WPos);
    float Specular = pow(max(dot(Refl, View), 0.0f),
                          MaterialSh);
    if (Diffuse <= 0.0f) Specular = 0.0f;
    float3 PhongS = Specular * SourceSpec * MaterialSpec;

    // Ambient
    float3 PhongA = SourceAmb * MaterialAmb;

    // Emissive
    float3 PhongE = MaterialEmi;

    // Sum
    return float4(PhongD+PhongS+PhongA+PhongE, 1.0f);
}
```

5.4   Global Illumination

This section presents two well-known algorithms for global illumination, *ray tracing* [18] and *radiosity* [19]. In the history of computer graphics, they were the first algorithms proposed for global illumination and are still widely used. Detailed discussions on global illumination are beyond the scope of this book. This section presents the skeletons of ray tracing and radiosity algorithms. Interested readers are referred to the standard textbooks [20, 21].

5.4.1   Ray Tracing

Recall that the view frustum is taken as a pencil of projection lines converging on the camera. Let us fix the number of projection lines to the resolution of the final image such that a projection line determines the color of a pixel. See Fig. 5.9-(a), which illustrates the projection lines composing an 8×6-resolution image. (Only the projection lines at the upper and right edges are illustrated.) In the ray tracing algorithm, the view frustum is not processed by the projection transform. Instead, a ray is shot along the opposite direction of each projection line and is traced to determine the color brought by the projection line. The ray is called *primary ray*.

The primary ray may not hit any object in the scene. Then, the default or background color is taken as the pixel color for the ray. If the primary ray intersects an object, first of all it is tested if the intersection point is in shadow. For that purpose, a *secondary ray* named a *shadow ray* is cast toward each light source. See Fig. 5.9-(b), where the shadow ray s_1 is shot from the intersection point p_1. If s_1 hits another object on the way to the light source, p_1 is determined to be in shadow, and the direct contributions from the light source to p_1 are ignored. (This is the case in the example.) If s_1 hits the light source, direct lighting is computed at p_1.

In addition to the shadow ray, two more secondary rays are fired from p_1: *reflection ray* (r_1) and *refraction ray* (t_1). The primary ray incident on p_1 is reflected with respect to p_1's normal n_1 to define the reflection ray r_1. Equation (5.7) in Section 5.1.2 presented how to compute the reflection vector using the light vector and the surface normal. Similarly, the reflection ray r_i is computed as follows:

$$r_i = I_i - 2n_i(n_i \cdot I_i) \tag{5.12}$$

where I_i is the primary ray incident on p_i.

The refraction ray is often called a transmitted ray and is spawned if p_1 is not opaque. Calculation of the refraction ray t_i is presented in [Note: Refraction vector].

Ray tracing is a recursive algorithm. Each of the secondary rays $(r_1$ and $t_1)$ is recursively traced as if it were another primary ray, and it is tested against all objects inhabiting the scene. Then, the colors computed through the rays are added to the color computed using the shadow ray s_1. In Fig. 5.9-(b), r_1 hits p_2 of an opaque object, and a shadow ray (s_2) and a reflection ray (r_2) are spawned. No refraction ray is spawned. In contrast, t_1 hits p_3 that is translucent, and three secondary rays $(s_3, r_3,$ and $t_3)$ are spawned.

The recursive structure of the ray tracing algorithm conceptually generates a *ray tree*, shown in Fig. 5.9-(c). The ray tree is expanded until the reflection/refraction rays leave the scene without hitting any object or a predetermined recursion level is reached.

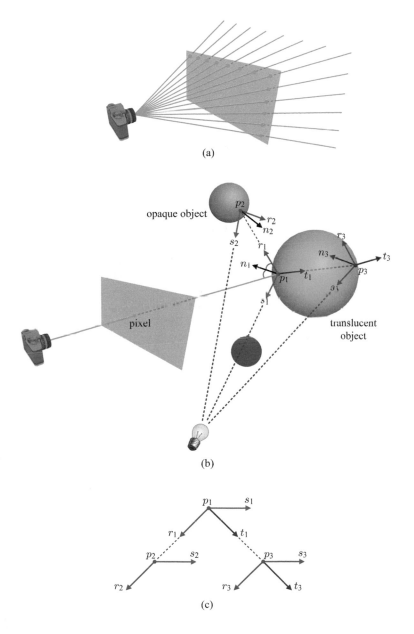

Fig. 5.9: Recursive ray tracing. (a) The projection lines converging on the camera determine the pixel colors. (b) For a primary ray, up to three secondary rays are spawned. (In this illustration, a point light source is used instead of a directional light source.) (c) The rays are structured in a tree.

[Note: Refraction vector]

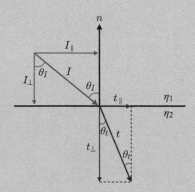

Fig. 5.10:   Computing the refraction vector using Snell's law.

Calculating the refraction vector t starts with Snell's law:

$$\eta_1 \sin \theta_I = \eta_2 \sin \theta_t \tag{5.13}$$

where η_i is the *refractive index* of medium i (e.g., 1.0 for a vacuum, 1.33 for water, etc.), θ_I is the incident angle, and θ_t is the refraction angle. See Fig. 5.10. The incident vector I, normal vector n, and refraction vector t are assumed to be unit vectors. The incident vector I can be decomposed into a tangential component $I_{\parallel}$ and a normal component $I_{\perp}$.

$$I = I_{\parallel} + I_{\perp} \tag{5.14}$$

Similar decomposition can be made for the refraction vector:

$$t = t_{\parallel} + t_{\perp} \tag{5.15}$$

Then, we have the following:

$$\begin{aligned} \sin \theta_I &= \frac{\|I_{\parallel}\|}{\|I\|} = \|I_{\parallel}\| \\ \sin \theta_t &= \frac{\|t_{\parallel}\|}{\|t\|} = \|t_{\parallel}\| \end{aligned} \tag{5.16}$$

Equation (5.13) can be rephrased using Equation (5.16):

$$\|t_{\parallel}\| = \frac{\eta_1}{\eta_2}\|I_{\parallel}\| \tag{5.17}$$

Because the directions of $t_{\parallel}$ and $I_{\parallel}$ are identical, Equation (5.17) can be converted into

$$t_{\parallel} = \frac{\eta_1}{\eta_2}I_{\parallel} \tag{5.18}$$

$I_\perp$ and n have the opposite directions, and their relation is described as

$$I_\perp = -n \cos \theta_I \qquad (5.19)$$

Then, using Equations (5.14) and (5.19), $t_\parallel$ in Equation (5.18) is rephrased:

$$\begin{aligned}
t_\parallel &= \tfrac{\eta_1}{\eta_2} I_\parallel \\
&= \tfrac{\eta_1}{\eta_2}(I - I_\perp) \\
&= \tfrac{\eta_1}{\eta_2}(I + n \cos \theta_I) \\
&= \tfrac{\eta_1}{\eta_2}(I - n(n \cdot I))
\end{aligned} \qquad (5.20)$$

Now let us compute $t_\perp$. As $t_\perp$ and n have the opposite directions, their relation is described as follows:

$$\begin{aligned}
t_\perp &= -n\cos\theta_t \\
&= -n\sqrt{1 - \sin^2 \theta_t}
\end{aligned} \qquad (5.21)$$

The Snell's law presented in Equation (5.13) leads to the following:

$$\begin{aligned}
\sin^2 \theta_t &= (\tfrac{\eta_1}{\eta_2})^2 \sin^2 \theta_I \\
&= (\tfrac{\eta_1}{\eta_2})^2(1 - \cos^2 \theta_I) \\
&= (\tfrac{\eta_1}{\eta_2})^2(1 - (n \cdot I)^2)
\end{aligned} \qquad (5.22)$$

Equation (5.21) can be rephrased using Equation (5.22):

$$\begin{aligned}
t_\perp &= -n\sqrt{1 - \sin^2 \theta_t} \\
&= -n\sqrt{1 - (\tfrac{\eta_1}{\eta_2})^2(1 - (n \cdot I)^2)}
\end{aligned} \qquad (5.23)$$

The refraction vector t is obtained by summing $t_\parallel$ in Equation (5.20) and $t_\perp$ in Equation (5.23):

$$\begin{aligned}
t &= t_\parallel + t_\perp \\
&= \tfrac{\eta_1}{\eta_2}(I - n(n \cdot I)) - n\sqrt{1 - (\tfrac{\eta_1}{\eta_2})^2(1 - (n \cdot I)^2)} \\
&= \tfrac{\eta_1}{\eta_2}I - n(\tfrac{\eta_1}{\eta_2}(n \cdot I) + \sqrt{1 - (\tfrac{\eta_1}{\eta_2})^2(1 - (n \cdot I)^2)})
\end{aligned} \qquad (5.24)$$

5.4.2 Radiosity

Radiosity algorithm simulates bounced light between *diffuse surfaces*. Light hitting a surface is reflected back to the environment, and each surface of the environment works itself as a light source. The radiosity algorithm does not distinguish light sources from the objects to be lit by the light sources.

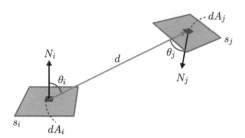

Fig. 5.11: The fraction of energy leaving one surface and arriving at another is described by the form factor. It can be determined by considering the geometry of the scene.

Radiosity of a surface is defined to be the rate at which light leaves the surface. To illuminate a scene through radiosity, all surfaces of the scene are subdivided into so-called *patches*. A patch could be a polygon of the scene, for example. Then, the *form factors* among all the patches are computed. The form factor describes the fraction of light that leaves one patch and arrives at another. It depends on the distance and the relative orientation between the patches, and can be intuitively understood as a coefficient describing how much the patches can see each other.

Consider two patches s_i and s_j shown in Fig. 5.11, each with the differential area dA and the surface normal N. The form factor f_{ij} is defined as follows:

$$\alpha_{ij}\frac{cos\theta_i cos\theta_j}{\pi d^2} \tag{5.25}$$

where α_{ij} denotes the visibility between dA_i and dA_j, d is the vector connecting dA_i and dA_j, θ_i is the angle between N_i and d, and θ_j is the angle between N_j and $-d$. If dA_i and dA_j are visible from each other, α_{ij} is 1. Otherwise, it is 0.

Equation (5.25) represents a point-to-point form factor. In principle, it should be integrated in order to compute the form factor between the patches s_i and s_j. Assuming the radiosities are constant over the extent of a patch, computing the patch-to-patch form factor is reduced to computing a point-to-patch form factor. Consider a representative point p of all points on patch s_i. (It would be the center of s_i.) The form factor between p and s_j can be calculated using the *hemisphere* placed at p, as shown in Fig. 5.12-(a). Its axis N is the surface normal at p. Suppose that patch s_j is fully visible from p. It is projected onto the hemisphere surface and then is projected onto the base of the hemisphere. The form factor is defined to be the area projected on the hemisphere's base divided by the base area. This process was proposed by a German engineer Wilhelm Nusselt and is called the Nusselt analog.

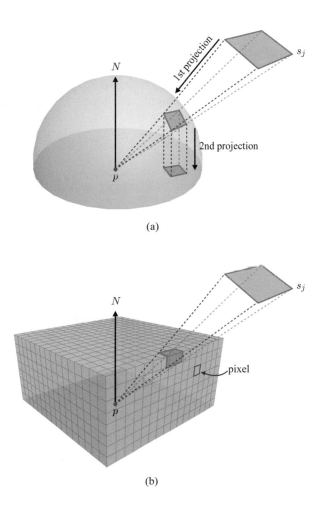

(a)

(b)

Fig. 5.12: Form factor computation. (a) Nusselt analog using a hemisphere. (b) Rasterization using a hemicube. (The form factors depend solely on the geometry of the scene. For a static scene, they are computed only once, and can be reused, for example, as the lighting and material attributes are altered.)

The radiosity of a patch is the sum of the rate at which the patch itself emits light and the rate at which it reflects light. Then, we have the following equation:

$$B_i = E_i + r_i \sum_{j=1}^{n} B_j f_{ij} \qquad (5.26)$$

where B_i and B_j are the radiosities of patches i and j, respectively, E_i is the initial radiosity of patch i, r_i is the reflectance of patch i, and f_{ij} is the form factor. E_i is non-zero only for the light sources. $\sum_{j=1}^{n} B_j f_{ij}$ describes the *irradiance* (incoming light). Rearranging the terms in Equation (5.26) leads to the following:

$$B_i - r_i \sum_{j=1}^{n} B_j f_{ij} = E_i \qquad (5.27)$$

When Equation (5.27) is considered for every patch in the scene, we obtain the following:

$$
\begin{pmatrix}
1 - r_1 f_{11} & -r_1 f_{12} & \cdots & -r_1 f_{1n} \\
-r_2 f_{21} & 1 - r_2 f_{22} & \cdots & -r_2 f_{2n} \\
\vdots & \vdots & \ddots & \vdots \\
-r_n f_{n1} & -r_n f_{n2} & \cdots & 1 - r_n f_{nn}
\end{pmatrix}
\begin{pmatrix}
B_1 \\ B_2 \\ \vdots \\ B_n
\end{pmatrix}
=
\begin{pmatrix}
E_1 \\ E_2 \\ \vdots \\ E_n
\end{pmatrix}
\qquad (5.28)
$$

By solving the system, the radiosity of each patch is obtained. Then, the irradiance of each patch can also be computed using Equation (5.26).

Presented so far is the conceptual sketch of the classic radiosity algorithm. A variety of optimization techniques have been developed. For example, the hemisphere is often replaced by the *hemicube*, each face of which is an array of pixels. See Fig. 5.12-(b). Each pixel has a square area, and the form factor between p and a pixel depends on the pixel's position in the hemicube. For example, the pixel located at the corner of the hemicube has a smaller form factor than the pixel centered at the top face. The per-pixel form factors can be pre-computed. Then, patch s_j is *projected* onto the faces of the hemicube. (Each of the five faces is processed independently.) The form factor between p and s_j is the sum of the form factors of the pixels covered by the projection of s_j. The hemicube enables form factor calculation to use the ordinary rendering algorithm. Further, the visibility of s_j is neatly handled using z-buffering. (Rendering onto the hemicube is considered a special instance of creating a *cube map*. Section 10.1 presents how the environment is rendered onto a cube map.)

The radiosity algorithm is too expensive to be implemented in real time. It is often run at the preprocessing stage, and the irradiance values are stored in a texture to be used at run time. The texture is named *light map*. Section 10.2.2 presents a technique utilizing the light map created by running the radiosity preprocessor.

Exercises

1. Equation (5.11) is developed assuming a directional light source.

   (a) How would you modify Equation (5.11) for handling multiple directional light sources?

   (b) How would you modify Equation (5.11) for replacing the directional light source by a point light source?

2. Note the slight difference between Equations (5.7) and (5.12). What makes the difference?

3. Consider applying ray tracing to a sphere centered at the origin with radius 2.

   (a) A ray is fired from (10,1,0) with the direction vector $(-1,0,0)$. Represent the ray in a parametric equation of t.

   (b) Using the implicit equation of the sphere and the parametric equation of the ray, compute the intersection point between the sphere and the ray.

   (c) In order to compute the reflection ray, the surface normal at the intersection is needed. How would you compute the normal in this specific example?

   (d) Compute the reflection ray.

Chapter 6

Parametric Curves and Surfaces

The representation of a 3D surface we have considered so far is limited to a polygon mesh. It has been widely used in real-time graphics, and as a matter of fact, it has been the only representation accepted by commodity graphics hardware. However, the polygon mesh is not a continuous accurate representation, but approximates a smooth surface. Such a nature reveals several problems. To list a few, its planar facets are not easy to hide in the rendered images, and we often need to control the levels of the representation detail [4]; if a high-resolution mesh is adopted to hide the polygonal nature, it may require large vertex/index buffers; editing or deforming a polygon mesh per se is a hard problem.

An alternative that suffers much less from those problems is a *parametric representation*, where a surface is defined as a function of parameters. Above all, it does not approximate the smooth surface but is a smooth surface itself. Parametric surfaces were developed in computer-aided design and manufacturing industries, and are increasingly garnering attention in the interactive graphics field especially because evolving graphics hardware begins to accept them. (This will be presented in Chapter 7.)

There exist many parametric representations describing smooth surfaces[1]. The simplest among them is the Bézier surface, which was named after Pierre Bézier, a French engineer at Renault. This chapter focuses on it. The Bézier curve forms the foundations of the Bézier surface and therefore is presented first.

6.1   Parametric Curves

A *parametric curve* is described as a function of a parameter t. A line is an instance of a curve. Section 6.1.1 starts with presenting a parameterized line segment and extends it into quadratic and cubic Bézier curves. Section 6.1.2 presents another type of parametric curve, the Hermite curve.

---

[1]There are numerous books in the area of parametric curves and surfaces. An excellent introductory book is [22].

6.1.1 Bézier Curves

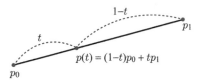

Fig. 6.1: A line segment connecting two end points is represented as a linear interpolation of the two points.

Consider a line segment bounded by two points p_0 and p_1, shown in Fig. 6.1. It can be represented in a parametric equation:

$$p(t) = (1 - t)p_0 + tp_1 \qquad (6.1)$$

where t is in the range $[0,1]$. The function $p(t)$ maps an interval of real values represented by parameter t to a continuous set of points.

Suppose that t takes a specific value. Then, $p(t)$ in Equation (6.1) is reduced to a point. It corresponds to a *linear interpolation* of p_0 and p_1, and can be described as a *weighted sum* of the two points. The line segment is divided into two parts by $p(t)$, and the weight for an end point is proportional to the length of the part "on the opposite side," i.e., the weights for p_0 and p_1 are $(1 - t)$ and t, respectively, in Fig. 6.1.

The function $p(t)$ is vector-valued, e.g., $p(t) = (x(t), y(t), z(t))$ for 3D space. When $p_0 = (x_0, y_0, z_0)$ and $p_1 = (x_1, y_1, z_1)$, linear interpolation is applied to each of the xyz-components:

$$p(t) = \begin{pmatrix} x(t) \\ y(t) \\ z(t) \end{pmatrix} = \begin{pmatrix} (1 - t)x_0 + tx_1 \\ (1 - t)y_0 + ty_1 \\ (1 - t)z_0 + tz_1 \end{pmatrix}$$

Two points define a line segment, not a general curve. For defining a curve, we need three or more points. A well-known technique for constructing a parametric curve using those points is the *de Casteljau algorithm*, named after its inventor Paul de Casteljau, a French mathematician at Citroën. It is an algorithm of recursive linear interpolations. Given three points, p_0, p_1, and p_2, the consecutive pairs are linearly interpolated:

$$p_0^1 = (1 - t)p_0 + tp_1 \qquad (6.2)$$

$$p_1^1 = (1 - t)p_1 + tp_2 \qquad (6.3)$$

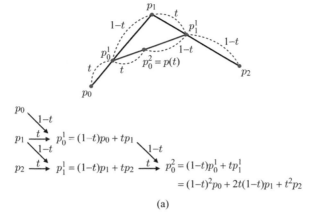

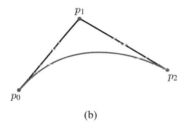

$$p_1 \xrightarrow{t} p_0^1 = (1-t)p_0 + tp_1$$

$$p_2 \xrightarrow{t} p_1^1 = (1-t)p_1 + tp_2 \xrightarrow{t} p_0^2 = (1-t)p_0^1 + tp_1^1$$
$$= (1-t)^2 p_0 + 2t(1-t)p_1 + t^2 p_2$$

(a)

(b)

Fig. 6.2: A quadratic Bézier curve is recursively defined by the de Casteljau algorithm. (a) Illustration of the de Casteljau algorithm. (b) Quadratic Bézier curve defined by three control points.

where superscript 1 denotes the first level of recursion. Then, p_0^1 and p_1^1 are linearly interpolated:

$$p_0^2 = (1-t)p_0^1 + tp_1^1 \qquad (6.4)$$

Superscript 2 denotes the second-level result. The process of recursive interpolation is illustrated in Fig. 6.2-(a).

When we insert Equations (6.2) and (6.3) into Equation (6.4), we obtain the quadratic (degree-2) Bézier curve:

$$p_0^2 = p(t)$$
$$= (1-t)^2 p_0 + 2t(1-t)p_1 + t^2 p_2 \qquad (6.5)$$

As shown in Fig. 6.2-(b), the curve interpolates the end points, p_0 (when $t = 0$) and p_2 (when $t = 1$). The curve is pulled toward p_1 but does not interpolate it. Three points, p_0, p_1, and p_2, are called *control points* in the sense that they control the shape of the curve.

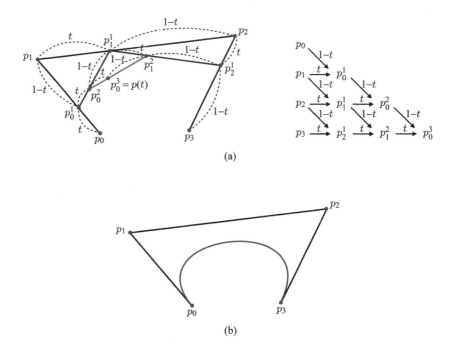

(a)

(b)

Fig. 6.3: A cubic Bézier curve is recursively defined by the de Casteljau algorithm. (a) Illustration of the de Casteljau algorithm. (b) Cubic Bézier curve defined by four control points.

The de Casteljau algorithm can be used for constructing higher-degree Bézier curves. Fig. 6.3-(a) illustrates three levels of linear interpolations for constructing a cubic (degree-3) Bézier curve. The equation of the cubic Bézier curve is derived as follows:

$$p_0^3 = p(t)$$
$$= (1-t)^3 p_0 + 3t(1-t)^2 p_1 + 3t^2(1-t)p_2 + t^3 p_3 \qquad (6.6)$$

The cubic Bézier curve has 4 control points. The curve interpolates the end points, p_0 (when $t = 0$) and p_3 (when $t = 1$). The curve is pulled toward p_1 and p_2 but does not interpolate them.

A degree-n Bézier curve requires $(n+1)$ control points. As shown in Equations (6.1), (6.5), and (6.6), the coefficient associated with a control point is a polynomial of parameter t. The coefficients are named *Bernstein polynomials*. The Bernstein polynomial for p_i in the degree-n Bézier curve is written as follows:

$$B_i^n(t) = {}_nC_i t^i (1-t)^{n-i}$$

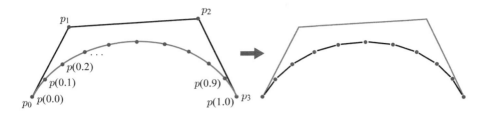

Fig. 6.4: A Bézier curve can be displayed through tessellation. This figure shows the result of uniform tessellation.

Then, the Bézier curve is described as a weighted sum of the control points:

$$p(t) = \sum_{i=0}^{n} B_i^n(t)p_i$$

The typical method to display a Bézier curve is to approximate it using a series of line segments. This process is often called *tessellation*. It *evaluates* the curve at a fixed set of parameter values and joins the evaluated points with straight lines. Fig. 6.4 shows an example of uniform tessellation, where the curve is evaluated at 11 evenly spaced values of parameter t and is approximated by 10 line segments[2].

The Bézier curve has many interesting properties, and one of them is its *affine invariance*. Suppose that a curve C needs to be affine-transformed and displayed. Then, we would have two options to implement it. One option is to evaluate C into a set of points P, and then affine-transform P. Fig. 6.5-(a) shows an example for rotation. The other option is to affine-transform the control points of C, and then evaluate the curve defined by the transformed control points. See Fig. 6.5-(b). The results are the same, but the latter is usually preferred because we need to transform a smaller number of points. Affine invariance has an influence on the design of the newest pipeline architecture presented in Chapter 7.

You may consider using a higher degree Bézier curve. For example, a quartic (degree-4) Bézier curve can be constructed using five control points. Such higher-degree curves are expensive to evaluate and often reveal undesired wiggles. However, they do not bring significant advantages. In contrast, quadratic curves have little flexibility. Therefore, cubic Bézier curves are most popularly used in the graphics field.

---

[2]Non-uniform tessellation methods are usually preferred. An example is adaptive tessellation, which adapts the tessellation factor based on the curvature.

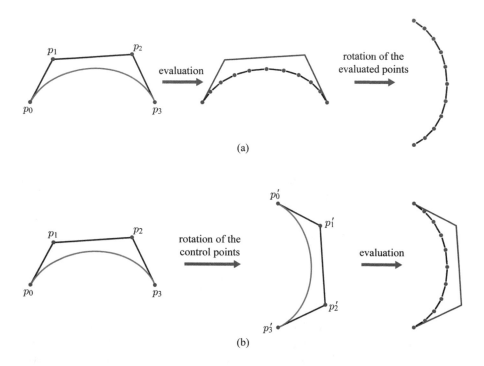

Fig. 6.5: Affine invariance. (a) Evaluation and then rotation of the evaluated points. (b) Rotation of the control points and then evaluation. The two methods produce the same result.

6.1.2   Hermite Curve and Catmull-Rom Spline

Consider the first-order derivative of the cubic Bézier curve. It can be obtained by differentiating the Bézier curve's equation with respect to t:

$$\dot{p}(t) = \frac{d}{dt}[(1-t)^3 p_0 + 3t(1-t)^2 p_1 + 3t^2(1-t)p_2 + t^3 p_3]$$
$$= -3(1-t)^2 p_0 + [3(1-t)^2 - 6t(1-t)]p_1 + [6t(1-t) - 3t^2]p_2 + 3t^2 p_3 \tag{6.7}$$

This represents the *tangent vectors* along the curve.

Consider the tangent vectors, v_0 at p_0 and v_3 at p_3, which are obtained by setting the parameter t in Equation (6.7) to 0 and 1, respectively:

$$v_0 = \dot{p}(0) = 3(p_1 - p_0) \tag{6.8}$$

$$v_3 = \dot{p}(1) = 3(p_3 - p_2) \tag{6.9}$$

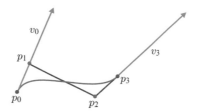

Fig. 6.6: The tangent vectors at the end points, v_0 and v_3, are defined as $3(p_1 - p_0)$ and $3(p_3 - p_2)$. Then, the curve can be defined in terms of $\{p_0, v_0, p_3, v_3\}$.

They are illustrated in Fig. 6.6. Let us rewrite Equations (6.8) and (6.9) as follows:

$$p_1 = p_0 + \frac{1}{3}v_0 \qquad (6.10)$$

$$p_2 = p_3 - \frac{1}{3}v_3 \qquad (6.11)$$

The Bernstein form of the Bézier curve in Equation (6.6) can be rewritten using Equations (6.10) and (6.11):

$$
\begin{aligned}
p(t) &= (1-t)^3 p_0 + 3t(1-t)^2 p_1 + 3t^2(1-t)p_2 + t^3 p_3 \\
&= (1-t)^3 p_0 + 3t(1-t)^2 (p_0 + \tfrac{1}{3}v_0) + 3t^2(1-t)(p_3 - \tfrac{1}{3}v_3) + t^3 p_3 \\
&= (1 - 3t^2 + 2t^3)p_0 + t(1-t)^2 v_0 + (3t^2 - 2t^3)p_3 - t^2(1-t)v_3
\end{aligned}
$$
$$(6.12)$$

Now, the curve is defined in terms of $\{p_0, v_0, p_3, v_3\}$, i.e., two end points and their tangent vectors. The curve has the same geometry as the Bézier curve defined in terms of $\{p_0, p_1, p_2, p_3\}$. This new representation is called the *Hermite curve* that was named in honor of Charles Hermite, a French mathematician.

To model a curve with many inflection points, the Bézier or Hermite curves can be concatenated to define a piecewise curve, named a *spline*. Fig. 6.7-(a) shows an example that is composed of four cubic Hermite curves. Given a list of points q_is, we can define a Hermite curve for each interval $[q_i, q_{i+1}]$. In Fig. 6.7-(a), consider two Hermite curves, c_1 defined over the interval $[q_1, q_2]$, and c_2 defined over $[q_2, q_3]$. For the spline to be globally continuous, c_1 and c_2 should share the tangent vector at q_2. The choice of the tangent vector is not unique, and several options are available. The *Catmull-Rom spline* [23] uses q_{i-1} and q_{i+1} to define the tangent vector v_i at q_i:

$$v_i = \tau(q_{i+1} - q_{i-1})$$

where τ controls how sharply the curve bends at q_i and is often set to $\frac{1}{2}$, as is the case in Fig. 6.7-(b). The Catmull-Rom spline is popularly used in games, mainly for being relatively easy to compute.

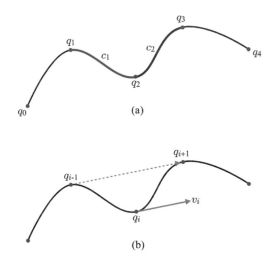

Fig. 6.7: Catmull-Rom spline. (a) A spline composed of cubic Hermite curves passes through the given points q_is. Two adjacent Hermite curves should share the tangent vector at their junction. (b) The tangent vector at q_i is parallel to the vector connecting q_{i-1} and q_{i+1}.

6.2   Application: Camera Path

The parametric curve has many applications. For example, it is often used to define a path along which an object moves. Consider the camera path shown in Fig. 6.8-(a). If the camera moves along the curve and captures the scene, the rendered images will appear dynamic even though the scene is static. Such a camera path is often defined by the Catmull-Rom spline.

Recall that viewing is specified in terms of {**EYE,AT,UP**}. The Catmull-Rom spline can be evaluated with an appropriate set of parameters to determine the camera position **EYE** moving on the path. For simplicity, the camera path in Fig. 6.8-(a) is composed of a single Hermite curve segment $p(t)$. In a simple implementation, a step size Δt may be used such that **EYE** continuously moves from $p(t)$ to $p(t + \Delta t)$ for a pre-defined time interval. In Fig. 6.8-(a), Δt is 0.1 and is traversed per second.

AT and **UP** define the camera orientation. See Fig. 6.8-(b). **AT** is set to the origin of the world space, and **UP** is set to its y-axis. Then, uvn-axes of the *camera space* are defined according to the method described in Section 2.2. Fig. 6.8-(c) shows the moving camera space, and Fig. 6.8-(d) shows the scene images captured from three sampled positions on the path.

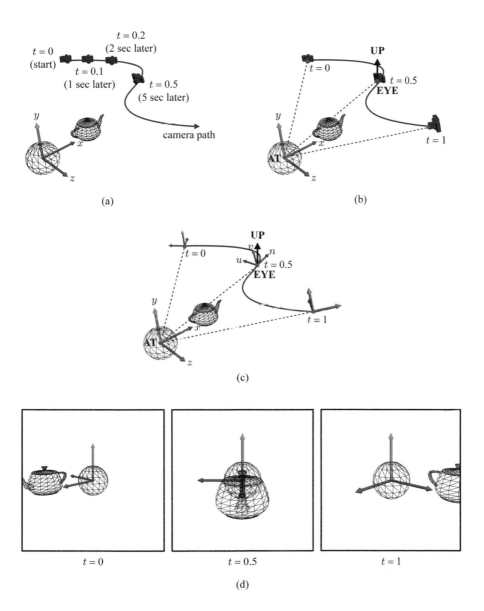

Fig. 6.8: The camera travels along a curved path and captures a static scene. (a) The path is described as a parametric curve. Each sampled point on the curve defines **EYE**. (b) **AT** and **UP** are fixed to the origin and the y-axis of the world space, respectively. (c) Given {**EYE,AT,UP**}, the camera space is defined. It is moving along the curve. (d) The scene is captured with the moving camera space.

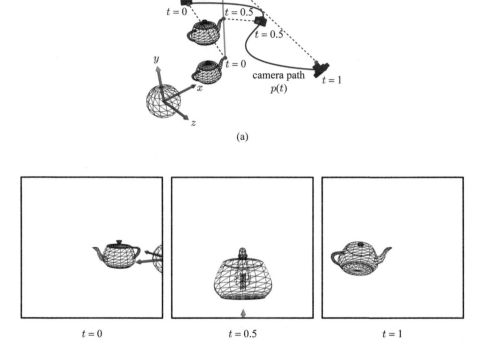

(a)

(b)

Fig. 6.9: Both **EYE** and **AT** are moving. (a) **EYE** and **AT** are computed by sampling $p(t)$ and $q(t)$, respectively. (b) The scene is captured with the moving camera space.

Suppose that the teapot is translating upward, as shown in Fig. 6.9-(a), and **AT** is set to the position of the teapot's mouth. The path of **AT** can be defined by another curve $q(t)$. For a frame, **EYE** and **AT** are computed by sampling $p(t)$ and $q(t)$, respectively. **UP** is usually set to the y-axis. Then, we have the rendering results shown in Fig. 6.9-(b) for three sampled positions of the camera.

6.3 Bézier Surfaces

The parametric curves form the foundations of the parametric surfaces. For presenting the Bézier curves, we proceeded from the line segment to the quadratic Bézier curve, and then to the cubic Bézier curve. This section follows a similar sequence: the bilinear patch, the biquadratic Bézier patch, and then the bicubic Bézier patch. (A patch refers to a finite piece of surface.) In addition, the Bézier triangle is presented at the last subsection.

6.3.1 Bilinear Patch

The simplest form of a surface patch is a *bilinear patch*. It is defined by four control points. See Fig. 6.10-(a). The control points, p_{00}, p_{01}, p_{10}, and p_{11}, are not necessarily in a plane. As shown in Fig. 6.10-(b), the patch has a rectangular domain with two parameters u and v, where the u- and v-axes run horizontally and vertically, respectively. Both u and v range from 0 to 1. A pair of u and v maps to a point $p(u, v)$ on the patch.

The process of constructing a bilinear patch can be described as a combination of linear interpolations along u and v. See Fig. 6.10-(c). The control points are first interpolated in terms of u, i.e., p_{00} and p_{01} are linearly interpolated to generate p_0^u, and p_{10} and p_{11} are linearly interpolated to generate p_1^u:

$$p_0^u = (1 - u)p_{00} + up_{01} \tag{6.13}$$

$$p_1^u = (1 - u)p_{10} + up_{11} \tag{6.14}$$

Then, p_0^u and p_1^u are linearly interpolated in terms of v to define the equation of $p(u, v)$:

$$\begin{aligned} p(u, v) &= (1 - v)p_0^u + vp_1^u \\ &= (1 - u)(1 - v)p_{00} + u(1 - v)p_{01} + (1 - u)vp_{10} + uvp_{11} \end{aligned} \tag{6.15}$$

It is a bilinear interpolation (interpolation along u, and then interpolation along v), and therefore $p(u, v)$ is named the bilinear patch.

As can be seen in Fig. 6.10-(c), p_0^u and p_1^u are connected by a line segment. Conceptually, the bilinear patch can be considered as a set of infinitely many such line segments, as illustrated in Fig. 6.10-(d). In the set, a line segment is associated with a distinct value of u and is a linear function of v.

Note that, in Equation (6.15), the coefficient for a control point works as a weight for the control point. Fig. 6.10-(e) visualizes the weights for the control points in the uv-domain. Specific values of u and v partition the domain into 4 rectangles. The weight for a control point is proportional to the area of the rectangle "on the opposite side." For example, the weight for p_{00} is $(1 - u)(1 - v)$, and that for p_{11} is uv. This is basically the same

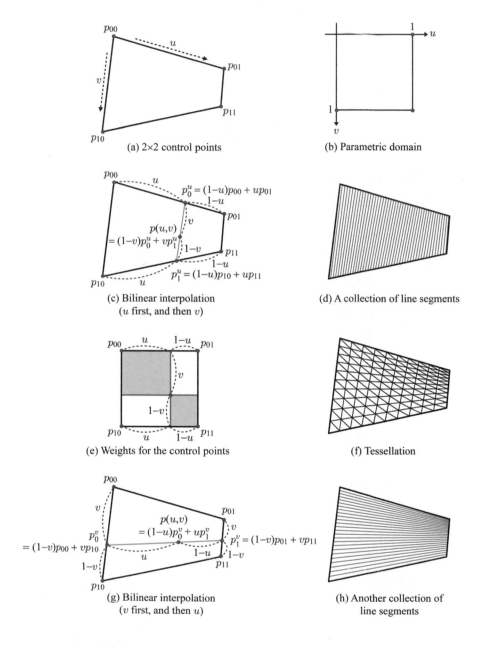

(a) 2×2 control points

(b) Parametric domain

(c) Bilinear interpolation
(*u* first, and then *v*)

(d) A collection of line segments

(e) Weights for the control points

(f) Tessellation

(g) Bilinear interpolation
(*v* first, and then *u*)

(h) Another collection of
line segments

Fig. 6.10: A bilinear patch in the *uv*-domain is defined through bilinear interpolation of four control points.

observation we made in linear interpolation of Fig. 6.1, where the weight for p_0 is $(1 - t)$, and that for p_1 is t.

In general, displaying a bilinear patch requires us to *tessellate* the patch into a triangle mesh, i.e., the bilinear patch is *evaluated* at a number of points, and the evaluated points are connected to form triangles that approximate the surface of the patch. As in the case of displaying a Bézier curve, the simplest method is uniform tessellation. It uniformly samples the uv-domain. For that purpose, nested `for` loops (one for u, and the other for v) can be used. See below.

```
foreach u in the range [0,1]
   foreach v in the range [0,1]
      Evaluate the patch using (u,v) to obtain (x,y,z)
   endforeach
endforeach
```

Simply put, the body of the nested `for` loops uses Equation (6.15) to map an instance of (u, v) to a 3D point (x, y, z) on the patch. Using such a set of evaluated points, a triangle mesh is constructed. Fig. 6.10-(f) shows the tessellation result where both u and v are uniformly sampled by 10 steps each.

The bilinear patch in Equation (6.15) can be represented in a matrix form as follows:

$$\begin{aligned}
p(u, v) &= \begin{pmatrix} 1 - v & v \end{pmatrix} \begin{pmatrix} p_{00} & p_{01} \\ p_{10} & p_{11} \end{pmatrix} \begin{pmatrix} 1 - u \\ u \end{pmatrix} \\
&= \begin{pmatrix} 1 - v & v \end{pmatrix} \begin{pmatrix} (1 - u)p_{00} + up_{01} \\ (1 - u)p_{10} + up_{11} \end{pmatrix} \\
&= (1 - u)(1 - v)p_{00} + u(1 - v)p_{01} + (1 - u)vp_{10} + uvp_{11}
\end{aligned} \tag{6.16}$$

The 2×2 matrix in the first line of Equation (6.16) corresponds to the 2×2 net of control points shown in Fig. 6.10-(a). The row and column vectors surrounding the matrix are degree-1 Bernstein polynomials in v and u, respectively. In the second line, the column vector contains p_0^u and p_1^u shown in Fig. 6.10-(c).

In Equation (6.16) and in Fig. 6.10-(c), linear interpolations are done along u first and then along v. The order can be reversed as follows:

$$\begin{aligned}
p(u, v) &= \begin{pmatrix} 1 - v & v \end{pmatrix} \begin{pmatrix} p_{00} & p_{01} \\ p_{10} & p_{11} \end{pmatrix} \begin{pmatrix} 1 - u \\ u \end{pmatrix} \\
&= \begin{pmatrix} (1 - v)p_{00} + vp_{10} & (1 - v)p_{01} + vp_{11} \end{pmatrix} \begin{pmatrix} 1 - u \\ u \end{pmatrix} \\
&= (1 - u)(1 - v)p_{00} + u(1 - v)p_{01} + (1 - u)vp_{10} + uvp_{11}
\end{aligned}$$

The bilinear interpolation using the reversed order is illustrated in Fig. 6.10-(g), where p_0^v and p_1^v are connected by a line segment. The bilinear patch can

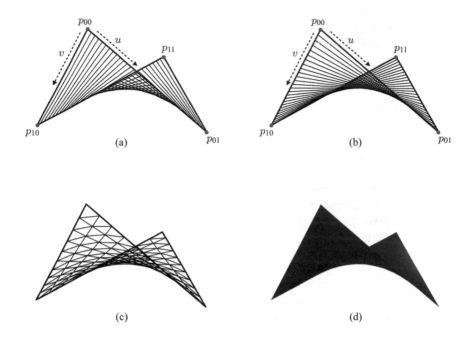

Fig. 6.11: The control points are not necessarily in a plane, and consequently the bilinear patch is not planar in general. (a) Visualized bilinear patch: Interpolation along u first, and then along v. (b) Interpolation along v first, and then along u. (c) Tessellated patch. (d) Rendering result.

then be conceptualized as a set of infinitely many line segments shown in Fig. 6.10-(h). Each line segment is a linear function of u. Note that the patch geometry is independent of the order of interpolations. The patches in Fig. 6.10-(d) and -(h) have the same surface geometry and are rendered through tessellation, e.g., using the triangle mesh in Fig. 6.10-(f). Fig. 6.11 shows another instance of the bilinear patch.

6.3.2 Biquadratic Bézier Patch

The bilinear patch requires a 2×2 net of control points. If we extend it to a 3×3 net, we obtain a *biquadratic Bézier patch*. Fig. 6.12-(a) shows a set of control points structured in a 3×3 net. The matrix form for the bilinear patch in Equation (6.16) is extended into:

$$p(u,v) = \begin{pmatrix} (1-v)^2 & 2v(1-v) & v^2 \end{pmatrix} \begin{pmatrix} p_{00} & p_{01} & p_{02} \\ p_{10} & p_{11} & p_{12} \\ p_{20} & p_{21} & p_{22} \end{pmatrix} \begin{pmatrix} (1-u)^2 \\ 2u(1-u) \\ u^2 \end{pmatrix} \quad (6.17)$$

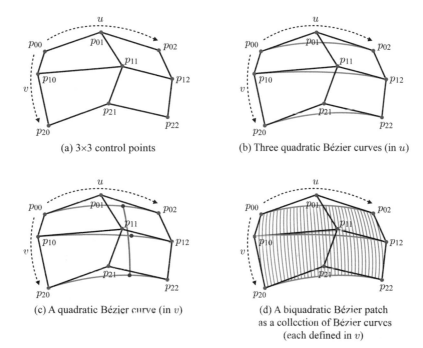

(a) 3×3 control points

(b) Three quadratic Bézier curves (in u)

(c) A quadratic Bézier curve (in v)

(d) A biquadratic Bézier patch
as a collection of Bézier curves
(each defined in v)

Fig. 6.12: Computing a biquadratic Bézier patch.

Not surprisingly, Equations (6.16) and (6.17) are quite similar. The 2×2 matrix is extended to the 3×3 matrix, which represents the 3×3 net of the control points shown in Fig. 6.12-(a). The degree-1 Bernstein polynomials are extended to degree-2 polynomials.

Fig. 6.12-(b) shows three quadratic Bézier curves, each of which is defined by a *row* of the 3×3 control point matrix. The curves are quadratic functions of parameter u. Shown below is the result of multiplying the last two matrices in Equation (6.17):

$$
\begin{aligned}
p(u,v) &= \left((1-v)^2 \ 2v(1-v) \ v^2 \right) \begin{pmatrix} p_{00} \ p_{01} \ p_{02} \\ p_{10} \ p_{11} \ p_{12} \\ p_{20} \ p_{21} \ p_{22} \end{pmatrix} \begin{pmatrix} (1-u)^2 \\ 2u(1-u) \\ u^2 \end{pmatrix} \\
&= \left((1-v)^2 \ 2v(1-v) \ v^2 \right) \begin{pmatrix} (1-u)^2 p_{00} + 2u(1-u)p_{01} + u^2 p_{02} \\ (1-u)^2 p_{10} + 2u(1-u)p_{11} + u^2 p_{12} \\ (1-u)^2 p_{20} + 2u(1-u)p_{21} + u^2 p_{22} \end{pmatrix}
\end{aligned}
$$

(6.18)

The quadratic Bézier curves in Fig. 6.12-(b) correspond to the three elements of the column vector in the second line of Equation (6.18).

Assume a specific value of u for the three quadratic Bézier curves. Then, each curve is reduced to a point. Taking the three points as control points, a

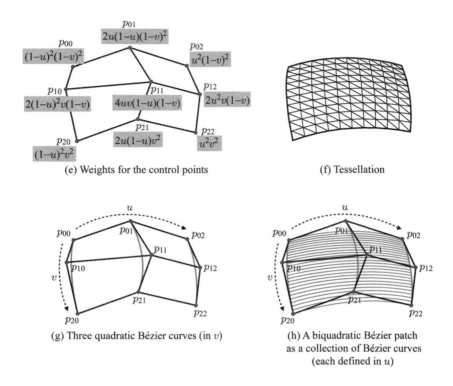

(e) Weights for the control points

(f) Tessellation

(g) Three quadratic Bézier curves (in v)

(h) A biquadratic Bézier patch as a collection of Bézier curves (each defined in u)

Fig. 6.12: Computing a biquadratic Bézier patch (*continued*).

quadratic Bézier curve (in terms of parameter v) is constructed, as shown in Fig. 6.12-(c). Then, a biquadratic Bézier patch can be conceptually taken as a set of infinitely many quadratic Bézier curves, as illustrated in Fig. 6.12-(d). One thing to note is that the left and right boundaries of the patch in Fig. 6.12-(d) are the Bézier curves constructed from $\{p_{00}, p_{10}, p_{20}\}$ and $\{p_{02}, p_{12}, p_{22}\}$, respectively.

When we complete matrix multiplications in Equation (6.18), the equation of the biquadratic Bézier patch is obtained:

$$p(u, v) = (1-u)^2(1-v)^2 p_{00} + 2u(1-u)(1-v)^2 p_{01} + u^2(1-v)^2 p_{02} +$$
$$2(1-u)^2 v(1-v) p_{10} + 4uv(1-u)(1-v) p_{11} + 2u^2 v(1-v) p_{12} +$$
$$(1-u)^2 v^2 p_{20} + 2u(1-u)v^2 p_{21} + u^2 v^2 p_{22}$$

$$(6.19)$$

The coefficient associated with a control point is a combination of the Bernstein polynomials in u and v, and works as a weight for the control point. Fig. 6.12-(e) illustrates the weights for all control points.

Rendering the patch requires the tessellation procedure, which is basically identical to the one discussed in the bilinear patch case. In the tessellator, the

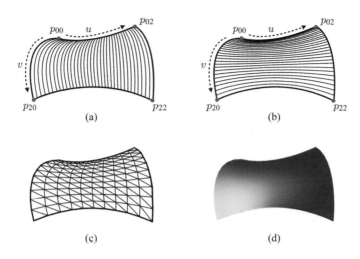

Fig. 6.13: An example of biquadratic Bézier patch. (a) Interpolation along u first, and then along v. (b) Interpolation along v first, and then along u. (c) Tessellation. (d) Rendering result.

body of the nested `for` loops may use Equation (6.19) to map each instance of (u, v) to a point (x, y, z) on the patch. Fig. 6.12-(f) shows an example of the tessellation result.

As observed in the bilinear patch, we can reverse the order of processing u and v. We can generate three quadratic Bézier curves, each of which is defined by a *column* of the 3×3 control point matrix, as shown in Fig. 6.12-(g). The curves are quadratic functions of parameter v. Then, the curves are combined in terms of u. The resulting surface is visualized in Fig. 6.12-(h), which is identical to the surface in Fig. 6.12-(d). Note that the top and bottom boundaries of the patch in Fig. 6.12-(h) are the Bézier curves constructed from $\{p_{00}, p_{01}, p_{02}\}$ and $\{p_{20}, p_{21}, p_{22}\}$, respectively. Therefore, the boundary curves of the biquadratic Bézier patch are the four quadratic Bézier curves, which are constructed from the four boundaries of the 3×3 control point net. Fig. 6.13 shows another example of biquadratic Bézier patch, a saddle-like patch.

In Fig. 6.12, the de Casteljau algorithm was completed along one parameter, and then it was applied along the other parameter. This is often called *two-stage explicit evaluation*. Fig. 6.14 shows another way of implementing the de Casteljau algorithm for constructing a biquadratic Bézier patch. We alternate interpolations along u and v. The 3×3 net of the control points is considered as a collection of four 2×2 nets. Then, a bilinear interpolation is performed per 2×2 net. For example, in Fig. 6.14, bilinear interpolation on the 2×2 net of $\{p_{00}, p_{01}, p_{10}, p_{11}\}$ produces p_{00}^1. When the four 2×2 nets are

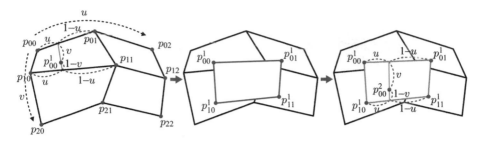

Fig. 6.14: For each 2×2 net of the control points, bilinear interpolation is performed. For the resulting 2×2 points, another bilinear interpolation is performed.

processed, we obtain p_{00}^1, p_{01}^1, p_{10}^1, and p_{11}^1:

$$
\begin{aligned}
p_{00}^1 &= (1-u)(1-v)p_{00} + u(1-v)p_{01} + (1-u)vp_{10} + uvp_{11}\\
p_{01}^1 &= (1-u)(1-v)p_{01} + u(1-v)p_{02} + (1-u)vp_{11} + uvp_{12}\\
p_{10}^1 &= (1-u)(1-v)p_{10} + u(1-v)p_{11} + (1-u)vp_{20} + uvp_{21}\\
p_{11}^1 &= (1-u)(1-v)p_{11} + u(1-v)p_{12} + (1-u)vp_{21} + uvp_{22}
\end{aligned}
\tag{6.20}
$$

Taking $\{p_{00}^1, p_{01}^1, p_{10}^1, p_{11}^1\}$ in Equation (6.20) as a new 2×2 net of control points, another step of bilinear interpolation is performed:

$$
\begin{aligned}
p_{00}^2 &= (1-u)(1-v)p_{00}^1 + u(1-v)p_{01}^1 + (1-u)vp_{10}^1 + uvp_{11}^1\\
&= (1-u)(1-v)[(1-u)(1-v)p_{00} + u(1-v)p_{01} + (1-u)vp_{10} + uvp_{11}]+\\
&\quad u(1-v)[(1-u)(1-v)p_{01} + u(1-v)p_{02} + (1-u)vp_{11} + uvp_{12}]+\\
&\quad (1-u)v[(1-u)(1-v)p_{10} + u(1-v)p_{11} + (1-u)vp_{20} + uvp_{21}]+\\
&\quad uv[(1-u)(1-v)p_{11} + u(1-v)p_{12} + (1-u)vp_{21} + uvp_{22}]\\
&= (1-u)^2(1-v)^2 p_{00} + 2u(1-u)(1-v)^2 p_{01} + u^2(1-v)^2 p_{02}+\\
&\quad 2(1-u)^2 v(1-v)p_{10} + 4uv(1-u)(1-v)p_{11} + 2u^2 v(1-v)p_{12}+\\
&\quad (1-u)^2 v^2 p_{20} + 2u(1-u)v^2 p_{21} + u^2 v^2 p_{22}
\end{aligned}
\tag{6.21}
$$

This algorithm is often called *repeated bilinear interpolations*. Note that Equation (6.21) is identical to Equation (6.19), i.e., the two-stage explicit evaluation and the repeated bilinear interpolations produce the same biquadratic Bézier patch.

6.3.3 Bicubic Bézier Patch

The bilinear patch with a 2×2 net of control points has been extended into the biquadratic Bézier patch with a 3×3 net. The extension can be continued to define the *bicubic Bézier patch* constructed on a 4×4 net of control points illustrated in Fig. 6.15-(a).

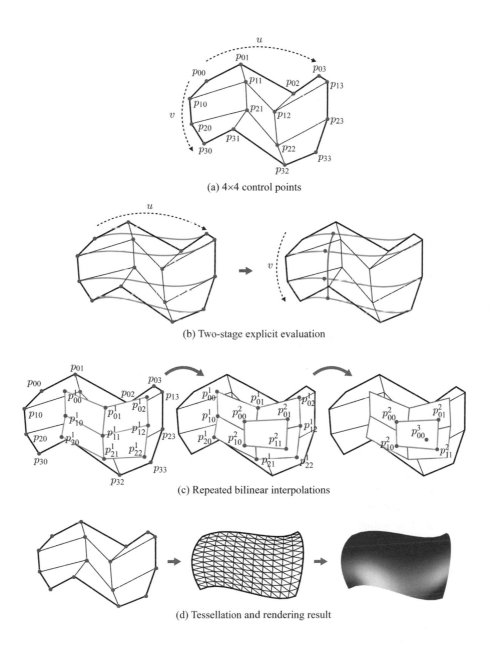

Fig. 6.15: Computing a bicubic Bézier patch.

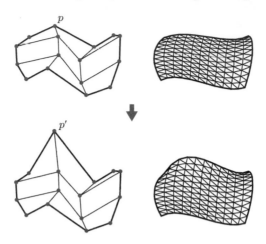

Fig. 6.16: Shape control in a Bézier patch is performed by manipulating the control points. In the figure, a control point p is moved to p', leading to a significant change of the surface geometry.

The matrix form of the bicubic Bézier patch is also obtained by extending that of the biquadratic Bézier patch in Equation (6.17):

$$
\begin{pmatrix} (1-v)^3 & 3v(1-v)^2 & 3v^2(1-v) & v^3 \end{pmatrix}
\begin{pmatrix} p_{00} & p_{01} & p_{02} & p_{03} \\ p_{10} & p_{11} & p_{12} & p_{13} \\ p_{20} & p_{21} & p_{22} & p_{23} \\ p_{30} & p_{31} & p_{32} & p_{33} \end{pmatrix}
\begin{pmatrix} (1-u)^3 \\ 3u(1-u)^2 \\ 3u^2(1-u) \\ u^3 \end{pmatrix}
$$
$$(6.22)$$

The 4×4 matrix in the middle represents the 4×4 net of the control points, and the row and column vectors surrounding the matrix are degree-3 Bernstein polynomials in v and u, respectively.

As discussed in the biquadratic patch, the de Casteljau algorithm can be implemented using either the two-stage explicit evaluation or the repeated bilinear interpolations. Fig. 6.15-(b) shows the former. Four cubic Bézier curves are constructed first (in terms of u), each using a row of the 4×4 control point matrix, and then they are combined in terms of v. In contrast, Fig. 6.15-(c) shows the repeated bilinear interpolations.

Fig. 6.15-(d) shows the results of tessellation and shading. Note that the boundary curves of the bicubic Bézier patch are the four cubic Bézier curves, which are constructed from the four boundaries of the 4×4 control point net.

Fig. 6.16 shows that moving a control point in a Bézier patch leads to a change of the surface shape. It is the beauty of the Bézier patch. We could have the same result by directly manipulating the vertices of the triangle mesh, but then we would have to move many more vertices.

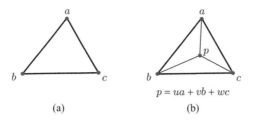

$p = ua + vb + wc$

(a)   (b)

Fig. 6.17: Degree-1 Bézier triangle and barycentric coordinates. (a) Three control points. (b) A point of the Bézier triangle is defined by the weights (u, v, w), which are called the barycentric coordinates.

6.3.4 Bézier Triangle

A Bézier triangle is a surface patch with a *triangular net* of control points. For presenting the Bézier patches with rectangular nets of control points, we followed the order of the bilinear patch, the biquadratic patch, and the bicubic patch. The Bézier triangle will be presented in the similar fashion.

Fig. 6.17-(a) shows the simplest Bézier triangle with three control points. Let us call it degree-1 Bézier triangle. Unlike the four control points of the bilinear patch, which are not necessarily in a plane, three control points of the Bézier triangle define a plane. Therefore, the degree-1 Bézier triangle is nothing but a triangle.

Like the bilinear and Bézier patches, a surface point p on the Bézier triangle is described as a *weighted sum* of the control points, as shown in Fig. 6.17-(b):

$$p = ua + vb + wc \tag{6.23}$$

where the weights, u, v, and w, are defined as follows:

$$
\begin{aligned}
u &= \frac{area(p,b,c)}{area(a,b,c)} \\
v &= \frac{area(p,c,a)}{area(a,b,c)} \\
w &= \frac{area(p,a,b)}{area(a,b,c)}
\end{aligned}
\tag{6.24}
$$

The weights (u, v, w) are called the *barycentric coordinates* of p. Obviously, $u + v + w = 1$, and therefore w can be replaced by $(1 - u - v)$.

Observe that, in Fig. 6.17-(b), the triangle is divided into three sub-triangles, and the weight given for a control point is proportional to the area of the sub-triangle "on the opposite side." This is the same feature we have found for the cases of linear interpolation (in Fig. 6.1) and bilinear interpolation (in Fig. 6.10-(e)).

[Note: Computing barycentric coordinates]

Let us compute p's barycentric coordinates (u, v, w) with respect to the triangle $\triangle abc$ shown in Fig. 6.17-(b). First of all, the 3D points, a, b, c, and p, are all projected to one of the xy-, yz-, and zx-planes of the coordinate system. Any plane can be selected for projection unless the area of the projected triangle is zero. Let us name the projected points a', b', c', and p'.

Given the vertex coordinates (x_i, y_i)s of a 2D triangle, the area of the triangle is computed as follows:

$$\frac{1}{2}\begin{vmatrix} x_0 & x_1 & x_2 \\ y_0 & y_1 & y_2 \\ 1 & 1 & 1 \end{vmatrix} \tag{6.25}$$

Using Equation (6.25), we can compute the area of $\triangle a'b'c'$ and also the areas of three sub-triangles sharing p'. Then, using Equation (6.24), we can compute the barycentric coordinates (u', v', w') of p' with respect to $\triangle a'b'c'$. The barycentric coordinates (u', v', w') are identical to (u, v, w) because the area ratio of the sub-triangles is preserved before and after the projection.

More control points are needed for defining a non-planar Bézier triangle. Fig. 6.18-(a) shows the triangular net of control points, where a control point is added to each side of the degree-1 Bézier triangle. For constructing a surface using the triangular net, *repeated barycentric interpolations* are performed, which are in spirit the same as the repeated bilinear interpolations used for constructing the biquadratic Bézier patch. At the first iteration, barycentric interpolation is performed for each of the three triangles, which are shaded in Fig. 6.18-(b):

$$\begin{aligned} p &= ua + vb + wc \\ q &= ub + vd + we \\ r &= uc + ve + wf \end{aligned} \tag{6.26}$$

At the second iteration, barycentric interpolation is performed for the triangle $\triangle pqr$, as shown in Fig. 6.18-(c):

$$s = up + vq + wr \tag{6.27}$$

When p, q, and r in Equation (6.26) are inserted into Equation (6.27), we obtain the equation of the Bézier triangle:

$$\begin{aligned} s &= up + vq + wr \\ &= u(ua + vb + wc) + v(ub + vd + we) + w(uc + ve + wf) \\ &= u^2a + 2uvb + 2uwc + v^2d + 2vwe + w^2f \end{aligned} \tag{6.28}$$

Note that the coefficient associated with a control point is a polynomial of u, v, and w, and works as a weight for the control point. Fig. 6.18-(d) illustrates the weights for the six control points.

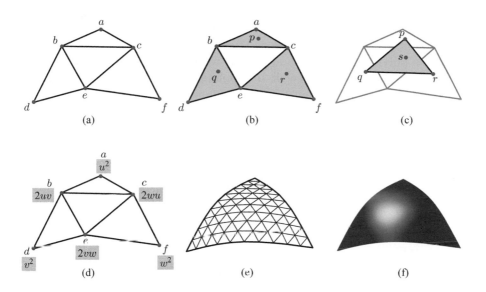

Fig. 6.18: Degree-2 Bézier triangle. (a) Triangular net of six control points. (b) Level-1 barycentric interpolations produce p, q, and r. (c) Level-2 barycentric interpolation produces s, which represents the equation of degree-2 Bézier triangle. (d) Weights for the control points. (e) Tessellated Bézier triangle. (f) Rendering result.

Rendering a Bézier triangle requires tessellation. Suppose that both u and v are sampled in the range of $[0,1]$, either uniformly or non-uniformly. Given an instance of (u, v), w is set to $(1-u-v)$. Then, Equation (6.28) is evaluated to map (u, v, w) to a point (x, y, z) on the surface. Using such a set of evaluated points, a triangle mesh can be constructed. Fig. 6.18-(e) shows the tessellation result where both u and v are uniformly sampled by 10 steps each. Fig. 6.18-(f) shows the shaded image of the Bézier triangle.

Note that, when a component of the barycentric coordinates (u, v, w) is 1, the other two components are 0s. Then, the evaluated surface point coincides with one of the corner control points. For example, if u is 1, the evaluated point becomes the control point a. Similarly, when a component of (u, v, w) is 0, the evaluated surface points form an edge of the Bézier triangle. For example, if u is 0, Equation (6.28) is reduced to $v^2 d + 2vwe + w^2 f$. It can be expressed as $(1-w)^2 d + 2w(1-w)e + w^2 f$ because $v + w = 1$. It is a quadratic Bézier curve and defines the bottom edge of the Bézier triangle shown in Fig. 6.18-(f). Observe that the bottom edge is defined solely by the control points, d, e, and f. Recall that similar features have been observed in the bilinear and Bézier patches.

Degree-3 Bézier triangle can be defined by adding one more control point per side, as shown in Fig. 6.19-(a). Note that an interior point, named e, is needed for a consistent configuration. Each control point is assigned a weight, which is a polynomial of u, v, and w. The weights can be computed through three iterations of the barycentric interpolation, which is illustrated in Fig. 6.19-(b).

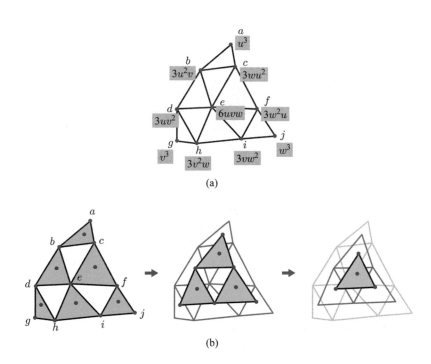

(a)

(b)

Fig. 6.19: Degree-3 Bézier triangle. (a) The triangular net is composed of 10 control points. Each control point is associated with a weight. (b) Repeated barycentric interpolations produce the equation of the Bézier triangle and the weights shown in (a).

Exercises

1. Let us construct a Bézier patch, whose degrees along u and v are two and three, respectively. You are given the following net of the control points.

$$\begin{pmatrix} p_{00} & p_{01} & p_{02} \\ p_{10} & p_{11} & p_{12} \\ p_{20} & p_{21} & p_{22} \\ p_{30} & p_{31} & p_{32} \end{pmatrix} = \begin{pmatrix} (0,0,4) & (0,3,4) & (0,6,4) \\ (3,0,0) & (3,3,0) & (3,6,0) \\ (6,0,0) & (6,3,0) & (6,6,0) \\ (5,0,4) & (5,3,4) & (5,6,4) \end{pmatrix}$$

   (a) Compute the surface point when $(u,v) = (0,1)$.

   (b) Compute the surface point when $(u,v) = (0.5, 0.5)$.

2. You are given three data points $\{(1,0),(0,1),(-1,0)\}$.

   (a) Assuming that the point $(0,1)$ is associated with the parameter 0.5, compute the quadratic Bézier curve that passes through the data points.

   (b) Compute the xy-coordinates of a point on the Bézier curve which has an associated parameter 0.75.

3. See the figure shown below. The camera is moving along the quadratic Bézier curve $p(t)$ defined by the control points, p_1, p_2, and p_3, such that **EYE** is the evaluated position on the curve $p(t)$. **AT** is moving along the linear path $q(t)$ connecting the origin and p_4. **UP** is fixed to the y-axis of the world space.

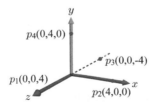

   (a) Both $p(t)$ and $q(t)$ are defined in parameter t of the range $[0,1]$. Compute the points on $p(t)$ and $q(t)$ when $t = 0.5$.

   (b) Compute the uvn-axes of the camera space when $t = 0.5$.

   (c) Compute the 4×4 translation and rotation matrices defining the view matrix when $t = 0.5$.

4. Given the following degree-2 Bézier triangle, compute the surface point where $(u, v) = (\frac{1}{3}, \frac{1}{3})$.

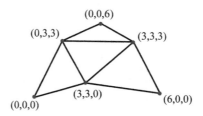

5. In the screen, we have the following triangle, each vertex of which is associated with $\{(R, G, B), z\}$.

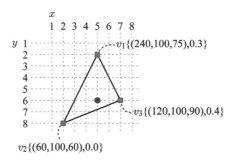

(a) Compute the barycentric coordinates of the point $(5,6)$ in terms of v_1, v_2, and v_3.

(b) Using the barycentric coordinates, compute R and z at $(5,6)$.

Chapter 7

Shader Models

GPUs have continuously evolved. The evolution can be traced in terms of the *shader models* of Direct3D. A shader model corresponds to a particular GPU architecture with distinct capabilities. Shader Model 1 started with Direct3D 8 and included assembly level and C-like instructions. In 2002, Direct3D 9 was released with Shader Model 2. Since then Direct3D 9 has been updated, and Shader Model 3 was introduced in Direct3D 9.0c released in 2004. Shader Model 4 came with Direct3D 10 in late 2006. In 2008, Shader Model 5 was announced with Direct3D 11.

As GPUs evolve, the programmable parts are getting expanded and becoming larger than the fixed-function parts. Indeed, contemporary GPUs are described as a programmable processor augmented with fixed-function units, whereas the early GPUs were characterized as additions of programmability to a fixed-function processor. The rendering pipeline discussed in the previous chapters is based on Shader Model 3, the programmable parts of which are only the vertex and fragment shaders. In Shader Models 4 and 5, we can find more programmable stages. This chapter presents the functionalities of the new stages using concrete examples.

7.1 Shader Model 4 and Geometry Shader

An obvious disadvantage of a pipeline architecture is that the performance of the entire pipeline is determined by the slowest stage, named the *bottleneck* stage. It is also the case in GPU. In Shader Model 3, the vertex and fragment shaders are separated, i.e., the instruction set of the vertex shader is different from that of the fragment shader. Suppose that, in an application, the vertex shader is complex and the fragment shader is simple. Then, the overall performance of the application depends on the performance of the vertex shader, which acts as the bottleneck of the pipeline.

Evolution of GPU has made both the vertex and fragment shaders more and more programmable, and their instruction sets can be converged. One of the key features of Shader Model 4 is a *unified shader architecture*, in which all programmable stages of the pipeline share the cores and the resources including the graphics memory.

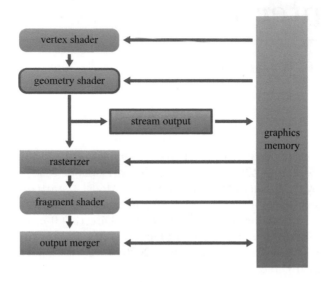

Fig. 7.1:   In Shader Model 4, a new programmable stage, called the geometry shader, and a new hard-wired stage, called the stream output, are added.

Another feature of Shader Model 4 is the addition of a new programmable stage, named the *geometry shader*. It is located between the vertex shader and the rasterizer. See Fig. 7.1. The output of the vertex shader goes to either the geometry shader if present, or the rasterizer otherwise.

The geometry shader performs per-primitive operations. Its input consists of the vertices of a primitive, i.e., three vertices of a triangle, two vertices of a line segment, or a single vertex of a point. A notable feature of the geometry shader is that it can discard the input primitive, or emit one or more new primitives.

The geometry shader redefines the GPU's role. The GPU used to be a processor that can only process the data provided by the CPU. Prior to Shader Model 4, the CPU must be invoked to fill the vertex/index buffers when new primitives are dynamically created. Now, the GPU can create or discard primitives at its own control, and therefore it can run many algorithms which were out of reach in Shader Model 3 and its ancestors. Such algorithms running solely within the GPU show improved performances because no communication with the CPU is needed.

Shader Model 4 has a new hard-wired stage, *stream output*. It enables the vertex or geometry shader to write its output directly to the graphics memory such that the output data bypass the rest of the pipeline and are iteratively processed by the vertex shader. Prior to Shader Model 4, the output of the vertex shader must pass through the rest of the pipeline and then can exit.

7.2 Application: Dynamic Particle System

A *particle system* refers to a collection of small objects named particles and is popularly used for presenting water, fire, rain, snow, smoke, dust, etc. Hundreds of GPU cores are suitable for simultaneously performing similar computations on many particles. This section presents a *dynamic* particle system, where a particle is created and destroyed at run time within the GPU using the geometry shader.

A particle system consists of two stages: simulation and rendering. The simulation stage determines the positions and velocities of the particles using physics laws, and the rendering stage renders the system using application-specific methods. Section 7.2.1 presents how to physically simulate the motions of particles. Then, Section 7.2.2 uses a representative example of particle systems, fireworks, and details how the simulation is implemented by the geometry shader. Finally, Section 7.2.3 presents how the fireworks particles are rendered.

7.2.1 Physics-based Simulation of Particles

Newton's law of motion forms the basis of *physics-based simulation*. Sir Isaac Newton put forth three laws.
• The first law: If there is no force acting on an object, the object either is at rest or moves in a constant velocity.
• The second law: A force f acting on an object produces an acceleration a related to f by "$f = ma$," where m is the mass of the object.
• The third law: When an object exerts a force f on another object, the second object exerts a force $-f$ on the first object, where f and $-f$ have an equal magnitude and opposite directions.

Among the three laws, the second law is of particular importance. In a typical implementation of physics-based simulation, the forces acting on an object of mass m are all combined to determine f, and the acceleration a is defined to be $\frac{f}{m}$. Acceleration is the time derivative of velocity and therefore can be *integrated* over a time step to obtain the change in velocity. The velocity is updated and then used for another integration to compute the change in position. The integration operations for updating the velocity and position play the key role in physics-based simulation.

Let us denote the time step by t. For the sake of simplicity, assume that acceleration a is constant during the time step t. Then, the updated velocity v is computed as follows:

$$v = v_0 + at \tag{7.1}$$

where v_0 is the initial velocity. For the time step, the position is updated by using the average of the initial velocity v_0 and the ending velocity v as follows:

$$s = s_0 + \frac{v_0 + v}{2}t \tag{7.2}$$

where s_0 and s denote the initial and updated positions, respectively.

Let us present the integration process by simulating the motion of a projectile. It may be the simplest example of physics-based simulation, but has been quite popular in games because, for example, shells and bullets fired from weapons are examples of the projectiles.

In the physics-based simulation, *gravity* is the most important and popularly used force. The law of universal gravitation defines the *acceleration of gravity*, 9.8m/s^2. It is denoted by g. An object always accelerates at the constant rate of 9.8m/s^2 due to gravity, independently of its mass. If the gravity is the only force under consideration, it is not needed to compute the acceleration a for each time step, but we can simply use g.

Let us compute the trajectory of a shell fired by a canon. For the simplicity of presentation, the time step is set to $\frac{1}{10}$ second (assuming a 10-fps animation, for example), and the acceleration of gravity g is approximated as 10m/s^2. Throughout the sequence of frames, g is applied uniformly. The 2D illustration in Fig. 7.2-(a) shows that the initial position s_0 is (5,5) and the initial velocity v_0 is (10,10). Note that g is represented by $(0, -10)$ in 2D. Velocity v_1 of the next frame is computed using Equation (7.1):

$$\begin{aligned} v_1 &= v_0 + gt \\ &= (10, 10) + (0, -10)\tfrac{1}{10} \\ &= (10, 9) \end{aligned}$$

Similarly, position s_1 of the next frame is computed using Equation (7.2):

$$\begin{aligned} s_1 &= s_0 + \tfrac{v_0 + v_1}{2}t \\ &= (5, 5) + \tfrac{(10,10)+(10,9)}{2}\tfrac{1}{10} \\ &= (6, 5.95) \end{aligned}$$

The same integration procedure computes v_2 of the following frame:

$$\begin{aligned} v_2 &= v_1 + gt \\ &= (10, 9) + (0, -10)\tfrac{1}{10} \\ &= (10, 8) \end{aligned}$$

Then, s_2 is computed:

$$\begin{aligned} s_2 &= s_1 + \tfrac{v_1 + v_2}{2}t \\ &= (6, 5.95) + \tfrac{(10,9)+(10,8)}{2}\tfrac{1}{10} \\ &= (7, 6.8) \end{aligned}$$

Fig. 7.2-(b) shows how the direction and magnitude of the velocity change over the frames, and Fig. 7.2-(c) shows the parabolic trajectory of the shell.

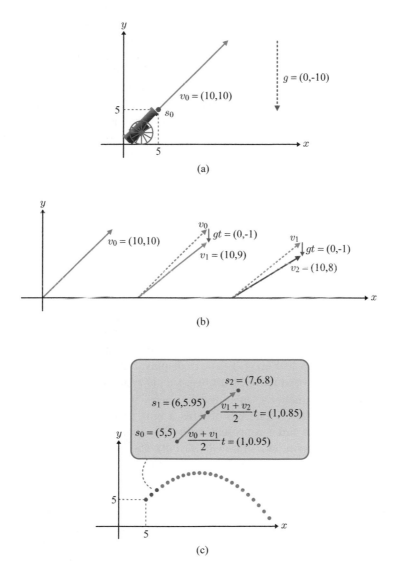

Fig. 7.2: Integration of the velocity and position of a projectile particle. (a) A particle is fired with the initial velocity v_0 and the initial position s_0. (b) The velocities of the particle are updated every frame. (c) The positions are also updated every frame, leading to the trajectory of the particle.

7.2.2 Fireworks Simulation

Fireworks is one of the simplest examples of the particle system. It can be implemented in a two-pass algorithm[1]. The first pass corresponds to the *simulation stage*. The geometry shader (GS) controls birth and death of particles and updates the live particles' states, i.e., positions and velocities. Then, the stream output (SO) stage writes the particles to the memory. The rasterizer and later stages of the pipeline do nothing in the first pass. The second pass corresponds to the *rendering stage*, and the particles stored in the memory go through the entire pipeline to be rendered.

A particle is represented as a single vertex. To give birth to a new particle, the GS creates a new vertex, determines its state, and then outputs it to the output stream. To discard a particle reaching the end of its life span, the GS simply does not write the particle to the stream.

Consider three types of particles in our fireworks example: launcher, shell, and ember. The launcher particle does not move and intermittently emits a shell particle along a randomized direction. For this purpose, the launcher uses a timer. It repeats counting down, emitting a shell when the timer reaches zero, and resetting the timer.

Fig. 7.3-(a) shows the vertex buffer initialized with the launcher particle denoted by L. The launcher is fixed at a position, and its timer is set to a pre-defined value. The vertex shader simply passes the launcher to the GS. Then, the GS decrements its timer and writes it to the memory through the SO stage. The first pass terminates. The second pass renders the vertex buffer. See the image in Fig. 7.3-(a). It displays only the launcher (colored in red). For a certain sequence of frames, this is repeated.

As soon as the launcher's timer reaches zero, a shell is emitted, and the launcher's timer is reset. The GS creates a new primitive! The shell is associated with its own timer representing its life span. Its initial velocity and position are also determined. The GS outputs the launcher and the shell to the memory. The first pass terminates. See the vertex buffer shown in Fig. 7.3-(b), which now contains the launcher and the shell denoted by S_1. The second pass renders the vertex buffer. For a certain sequence of frames, the following is repeated: The timers of the launcher and the shell are decremented, the shell's velocity and position are updated using Equations (7.1) and (7.2), respectively, and then the scene is rendered. Fig. 7.3-(b) shows a frame, where the cyan-color shell emitted by the launcher is moving upwards.

Suppose that the launcher's timer reaches zero whereas the shell's does not. Then, another shell is emitted by the launcher, and therefore the vertex buffer contains three particles, a launcher and two shells. Fig. 7.3-(c) shows the vertex buffer and the rendering result.

---

[1]In Direct3D SDK [3], a sample program named `ParticlesGS` is provided. This section presents a simplified version of `ParticlesGS`.

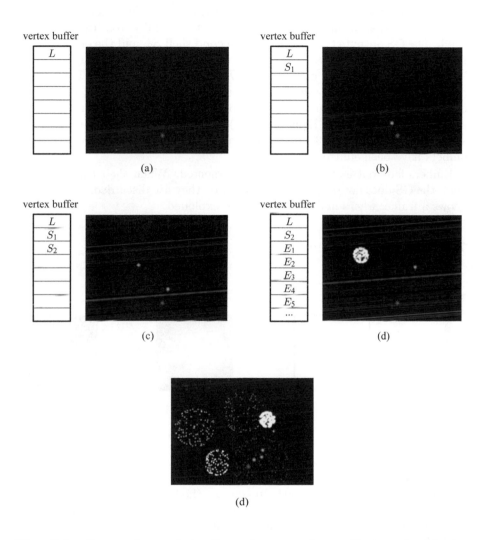

(a)   (b)

(c)   (d)

(d)

Fig. 7.3: Screen shots of the fireworks example are illustrated with the vertex buffers, where L, S, and E denote the launcher, shell, and ember particles, respectively. (a) Initially, only the launcher particle is stored in the vertex buffer. (b) The launcher has emitted a shell. (c) Another shell is emitted, and the vertex buffer contains a launcher and two shells. (d) S_1 has exploded to produce a number of embers and is removed from the vertex buffer. (e) Multiple shells have exploded. (This figure is generated using DirectX® SDK.)

When the first shell S_1 reaches the end of its life span, it explodes and emits a number of embers. The embers are assigned a timer. Their initial velocities are determined such that the embers are emitted radially from the exploding shell. The GS outputs the launcher, the second shell S_2, and the embers. The first shell S_1 is not output, i.e., it is discarded. The first pass terminates. Fig. 7.3-(d) shows the vertex buffer, where E_is denote the embers. The second pass renders the vertex buffer. For a certain sequence of frames, the timers of all particles are decremented, the velocities and positions of the shell and embers are updated using Equations (7.1) and (7.2), respectively, and then the scene is rendered. Fig. 7.3-(d) shows a frame, where a number of yellow-color embers have been emitted.

Embers fade out as their timer is decremented. When their timer reaches zero, the GS does not output the embers, i.e., they are discarded. Fig. 7.3-(e) shows a frame, where multiple shells have exploded.

7.2.3 Fireworks Rendering

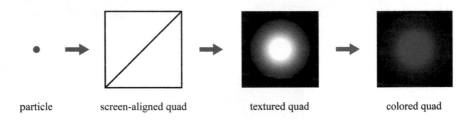

particle   screen-aligned quad   textured quad   colored quad

Fig. 7.4: A particle vertex is replaced by a quad, whose size is pre-defined. It is textured to make it look like a sphere-shaped volume. Then, the specific color of each particle is combined. In general, the black texels are made transparent so as to have the background show through. In the fireworks example, however, they are made opaque and work fine because the background is the dark sky.

Once the simulation is completed (the first pass), the particle system is rendered (the second pass). Each particle could be rendered as a point primitive, but then the rendering result may not be appealing. A better method is to use a *billboard*, which is an image-textured quad. See Fig. 7.4. Each vertex representing a particle is replaced by a quad, the gray-level texture (that is common to all types of particles) is applied to the quad, and then it is multiplied with the particle's color. The three types of particles in our example have different colors, and Fig. 7.4 shows the red-color launcher particle.

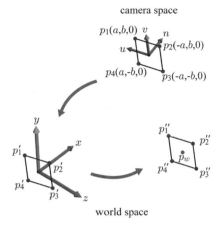

camera space

world space

Fig. 7.5: A world-space quad is obtained by transforming the pre-defined camera-space quad to the world space using the rotation part of the inverse view transform and by translating the quad to the particle position.

The billboard should always face the viewer. Otherwise, it may not be properly rendered. (The worst case is an edge-on billboard.) The billboard facing the viewer is called *screen-aligned*. Fig. 7.5 shows how the screen-aligned billboard is generated. In the camera space, a quad is pre-defined by four vectors $\{p_1, p_2, p_3, p_4\}$. As shown in the figure, they are symmetric about the origin of the camera space, and their n-coordinates are zero with respect to the uvn-axes. The quad is aligned with the uv-axes of the camera space.

Consider the *inverse* of the view transform matrix M_{view} presented in Section 2.2.2. Its upper-left 3×3 sub-matrix is a rotation that transforms a camera-space vector into the world space. When we apply the rotation to p_is, we obtain their world-space coordinates p_i's. Note that the quad defined by p_i's remains aligned with the uv-axes of the camera space whereas it is not generally aligned with the world-space basis[2].

A particle has a world-space position p_w computed at the simulation stage. When p_w is added to p_i's, we obtain the world-space points p_i''s, which define a world-space quad centered at p_w. The quad remains aligned with the uv-axes of the camera space. When the quad is rendered, it will be aligned with the xy-axes of the screen space[3].

---

[2]Recall that, as shown in Fig. 2.11, a single vector has different coordinates in two distinct bases. In Fig. 7.5, p_is represent the coordinates with respect to the camera-space basis $\{u,v,n\}$, and p_i's represent the coordinates with respect to the world-space basis $\{x,y,z\}$.

[3]The screen-aligned billboard is similar to a *sprite*, which is defined as an image texture applied to a polygon that moves around on the screen. The mouse cursor is an example of a sprite.

The geometry shader (GS) is located between the vertex shader and the rasterizer. Note that, when the primitives arrive at the rasterizer, they must be defined in the clip space. This can be ensured either by the vertex shader or by the GS. In other words, the world, view, and projection transforms, which have been performed by the vertex shader in Shader Model 3, can be done by the GS in Shader Model 4. In our fireworks example, the GS computes the world-space points p_i''s for the quad and then transforms them into the clip space.

Let us denote the clip-space points of the quad by $\{q_1,q_2,q_3,q_4\}$. The GS forms a *triangle strip* using them, i.e., $\{q_1, q_2, q_3\}$ defines a triangle, and $\{q_2, q_3, q_4\}$ defines another triangle. (See Section 1.2.2 for the triangle strip representation.) The GS creates new primitives within the pipeline! The two-triangle strip is passed to the rasterizer, and then the fragments of the quad are passed to the fragment shader, where the standard texture lookup and color combination are performed for rendering the quad.

7.3 Shader Model 5 and Tessellation

In Chapter 6, we presented the parametric surfaces. The parametric surface representation is *compact* in the sense that, for example, a fairly curved rectangular patch can be modeled as a cubic Bézier surface with just 16 control points. If the rendering pipeline accepts such a compact representation, the host CPU can send much less data, i.e., only the control points, to the GPU rendering pipeline, rather than a bulky polygon mesh approximating the smooth surface. Note that, however, the parametric surface has to be *tessellated* into a polygon mesh for rendering.

The most notable feature of Shader Model 5 is the *hardware tessellation* support. Shader Model 5 includes two new programmable stages, *hull shader* and *domain shader*, and a new hard-wired stage, *tessellator*, shown in Fig. 7.6. The goal of these stages is to enable efficient processing of smooth surfaces.

Suppose that a polygon mesh enters the rendering pipeline. In Shader Model 5, the mesh can be taken as a *control mesh* (a mesh of control points) describing a smooth surface. The first programmable stage is the vertex shader, and it can perform various animation and deformation algorithms on the control mesh. Such algorithms may be expensive, and performing the algorithms on a low-resolution control mesh significantly reduces the cost. Then, the new stages following the vertex shader can *evaluate* the control mesh to produce a high-resolution polygon mesh.

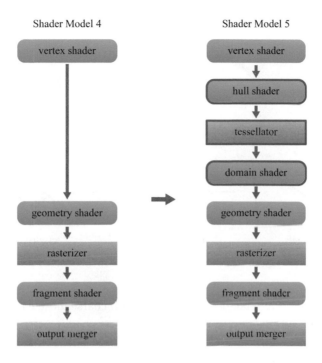

Fig. 7.6: In Shader Model 5, two programmable stages (hull shader and domain shader) and a hard-wired stage (tesellator) are newly added.

Due to the hardware tessellation capability, a variety of smooth surfaces can have direct acceleration support in Shader Model 5. The next section presents a simple application using the Bézier triangle introduced in Section 6.3.4.

7.4 Application: PN-triangles

A *PN-triangle* (standing for point-normal triangle) refers to a Bézier triangle that is derived from a triangle of a polygon mesh [24]. A PN-triangle can be tessellated into an arbitrary number of small triangles, and they replace the original triangle from which the PN-triangle is derived. See Fig. 7.7. When all triangles of the input polygon mesh are converted into PN-triangles, the input mesh can be refined into a higher-resolution mesh.

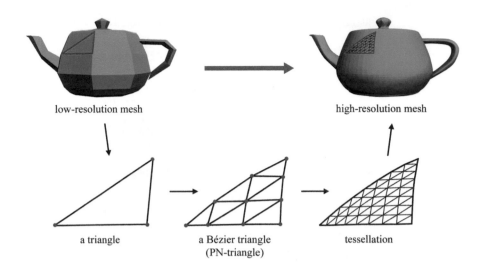

Fig. 7.7:   Using PN-triangles, a low-resolution coarse mesh can be converted into a high-resolution smooth mesh.

7.4.1   Computing Control Points

Fig. 7.8-(a) depicts a triangle t_1 extracted from a polygon mesh. Its vertex is described by (p_i, n_i), where p_i denotes the position and n_i denotes the normal. Let us convert t_1 into the degree-3 Bézier triangle shown in Fig. 7.8-(b). First of all, the corner control points of the Bézier triangle, p_{300}, p_{030}, and p_{003}, are simply set to t_1's vertices, p_1, p_2, and p_3, respectively.

The control points on each outer edge of the triangular net are defined using the vertex information (position and normal) of the corresponding edge in t_1. For example, p_{210} and p_{120} are computed using (p_1, n_1) and (p_2, n_2). Let us first compute p_{210}. Fig. 7.8-(c) shows the edge connecting p_1 and p_2. Suppose a point p_{21} on the edge, which is defined as follows:

$$p_{21} = \frac{2}{3}p_1 + \frac{1}{3}p_2$$

It will be projected onto the tangent plane at p_1 to define the mid-edge control point p_{210}. The tangent plane is perpendicular to n_1, and p_{21} is projected along the direction of n_1.

The projection is equivalent to displacing p_{21} by the vector v_{21} shown in the figure. We will compute the displacement vector v_{21}. In Fig. 7.8-(c), the vector connecting p_1 and p_{21} is defined as

$$\frac{p_2 - p_1}{3}$$

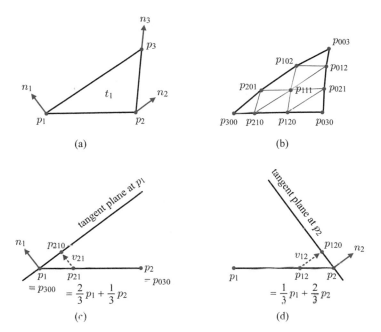

Fig. 7.8: PN-triangle generation. (a) A triangle from a polygon mesh. (b) Ten control points of degree-3 Bézier triangle are computed using (p_i, n_i)s in (a). (c) When p_{21} is displaced by v_{21}, p_{210} is obtained. (d) When p_{12} is displaced by v_{12}, p_{120} is obtained.

Let us project the vector onto n_1. As n_1 is a unit vector, the length of the projection[4] is computed as follows:

$$n_1 \cdot \frac{p_2 - p_1}{3} \tag{7.3}$$

It is a scalar value and represents the *signed length*[5]. In our example, it is negative because n_1 and $\frac{p_2 - p_1}{3}$ form an obtuse angle. To determine the displacement vector v_{21}, Equation (7.3) is negated and then multiplied with the unit vector n_1:

$$v_{21} = -(n_1 \cdot \frac{p_2 - p_1}{3})n_1 \tag{7.4}$$

---

[4]The dot product $a \cdot b$ is defined as $\|a\|\|b\|cos\theta$, where θ is the angle between a and b. When a is a unit vector, i.e., $\|a\| = 1$, $a \cdot b$ is reduced to $\|b\|cos\theta$. It is the length of b projected onto a.

[5]As $a \cdot b = \|a\|\|b\|cos\theta$, $a \cdot b$ is positive if θ is an acute angle, and is negative if θ is an obtuse angle.

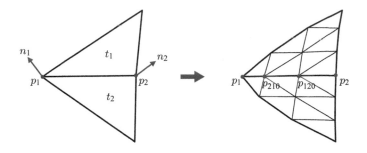

Fig. 7.9: Adjacent triangles t_1 and t_2 are converted into two PN-triangles, and they share the mid-edge control points, p_{210} and p_{120}.

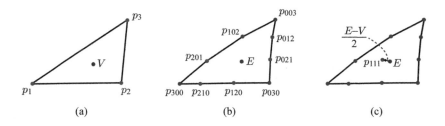

Fig. 7.10: Computing the interior control point. (a) The original vertices define V. (b) The new mid-edge control points define E. (c) E is displaced by $\frac{E-V}{2}$ to define p_{111}.

The mid-edge control point p_{210} of the Bézier triangle is obtained as follows:

$$p_{210} = p_{21} + v_{21}$$
$$= \tfrac{2}{3}p_1 + \tfrac{1}{3}p_2 - (n_1 \cdot \tfrac{p_2-p_1}{3})n_1 \qquad (7.5)$$

Fig. 7.8-(d) shows that another mid-edge control point p_{120} is obtained by displacing p_{12} using v_{12}:

$$p_{120} = p_{12} + v_{12}$$
$$= \tfrac{1}{3}p_1 + \tfrac{2}{3}p_2 - (n_2 \cdot \tfrac{p_1-p_2}{3})n_2 \qquad (7.6)$$

Observe that p_{210} in Equation (7.5) and p_{120} in Equation (7.6) are defined using only (p_1, n_1) and (p_2, n_2).

Consider triangles t_1 and t_2 shown in Fig. 7.9. They share the edge $\overline{p_1 p_2}$. When t_1 and t_2 are converted into PN-triangles, they share the mid-edge control points, p_{210} and p_{120}. It is because p_{210} and p_{120} are computed solely by the vertex information associated with $\overline{p_1 p_2}$, i.e., (p_1, n_1) and (p_2, n_2), which t_1 and t_2 share. Consequently, the high-resolution mesh produced by the two PN-triangles does not have a gap if both PN-triangles are tessellated with a uniform sampling rate. This shows that, if a watertight mesh is converted into a higher-resolution mesh using PN-triangles, the resulting mesh can be also watertight.

So far, we have computed p_{210} and p_{120}. The other four mid-edge control points, p_{201}, p_{102}, p_{012}, and p_{021}, are similarly computed. Finally, the interior control point p_{111} is computed using the position information of the other control points. See Fig. 7.10. The coordinates of the input triangle's vertices are averaged to define V:

$$V = \frac{p_1 + p_2 + p_3}{3}$$

The mid-edge control points are averaged to define E:

$$E = \frac{p_{210} + p_{120} + p_{201} + p_{102} + p_{012} + p_{021}}{6}$$

Finally, E is displaced by $\frac{E-V}{2}$ to define the interior control point p_{111}:

$$
\begin{aligned}
p_{111} &= E + \frac{E-V}{2} \\
&= \tfrac{1}{4}(p_{210} + p_{120} + p_{201} + p_{102} + p_{012} + p_{021}) - \tfrac{1}{6}(p_{300} + p_{030} + p_{003})
\end{aligned}
$$

7.4.2 Computing Control Normals

Once we compute the control points, we obtain the equation of the Bézier triangle shown in Fig. 7.11-(a). Then, as presented in Section 6.3.4, the Bézier triangle can be tessellated using a set of *uvw*-triples: The Bézier triangle's equation maps each *uvw*-triple to a surface point (x, y, z), and such evaluated points are connected into a polygon mesh. However, the vertex positions are not sufficient for rendering the polygon mesh. We need *vertex normals*.

A method for providing the vertex normals is to construct a triangular net of *control normals*. Consider the degree-2 control normal net composed of six normals, shown in Fig. 7.11-(b). (How to construct the control normal net will be presented soon.) The control normal net is evaluated in the same manner as the control point net. Simply put, a *uvw*-triple is inserted into the normal equation of Fig. 7.11-(b) to determine the vertex normal.

A single *uvw*-triple extracts a vertex position from the control point net, and a vertex normal from the control normal net. The 'degree-3' control point net (in Fig. 7.11-(a)) and the 'degree-2' control normal net (in Fig. 7.11-(b)) serve for a surface[6]. We could develop a degree-3 control normal net, but the degree-2 control normal net has proven to be sufficient.

---

[6]In fact, separation of the position and normal channels is often beneficial to the rendering pipeline, and normal mapping discussed in Chapter 9 provides a notable example.

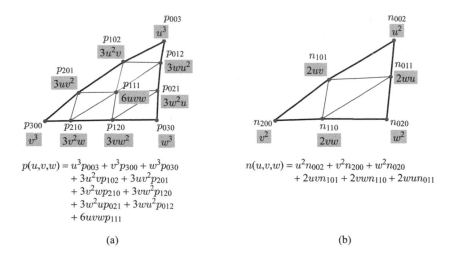

$$p(u,v,w) = u^3 p_{003} + v^3 p_{300} + w^3 p_{030}$$
$$+ 3u^2 v p_{102} + 3uv^2 p_{201}$$
$$+ 3v^2 w p_{210} + 3vw^2 p_{120}$$
$$+ 3w^2 u p_{021} + 3wu^2 p_{012}$$
$$+ 6uvw p_{111}$$

$$n(u,v,w) = u^2 n_{002} + v^2 n_{200} + w^2 n_{020}$$
$$+ 2uv n_{101} + 2vw n_{110} + 2wu n_{011}$$

(a)   (b)

Fig. 7.11: Control points and normals. (a) The control point net defines $p(u, v, w)$, which maps (u, v, w) to a vertex (x, y, z). (b) The control normal net defines $n(u, v, w)$, which maps (u, v, w) to the vertex normal at (x, y, z).

Let us now compute the control normals. As shown in Fig. 7.12-(a), the control normals located at the corners, i.e., n_{200}, n_{020}, and n_{002}, are simply set to the input vertex normals, n_1, n_2, and n_3, respectively.

The mid-edge control normals, n_{110}, n_{101}, and n_{011}, have to be determined. The average of two vertex normals of the input edge could be taken as the mid-edge control normal. See the example in Fig. 7.12-(b). The underlying surface connecting p_1 and p_2 is illustrated as a dotted curve, and the averaged normal is likely to be perpendicular to the underlying surface. However, it may often malfunction. Consider the case shown in Fig. 7.12-(c). The vertex normals, n_1 and n_2, point to the same direction, but the tangent planes at p_1 and p_2 are fairly distant. Then, the averaged normal n_{110} would be far from perpendicular to the underlying surface connecting p_1 and p_2. Instead, the normal shown in Fig. 7.12-(d) would be the correct one.

Fig. 7.12-(e) illustrates a heuristic for computing the correct normal. Suppose a plane P, which is orthogonal to the edge $\overline{p_1 p_2}$. P's normal n_P is computed as follows:

$$n_P = \frac{p_1 - p_2}{||p_1 - p_2||}$$

The end-normals n_1 and n_2 are summed to make n_{12}. Dot product of n_{12} and n_P is the length of n_{12}'s projection onto n_P. It is multiplied by $-2n_P$:

$$-2(n_{12} \cdot n_P)n_P$$

This vector is added to n_{12}, to define n'_{12}, which is the reflection of n_{12} with

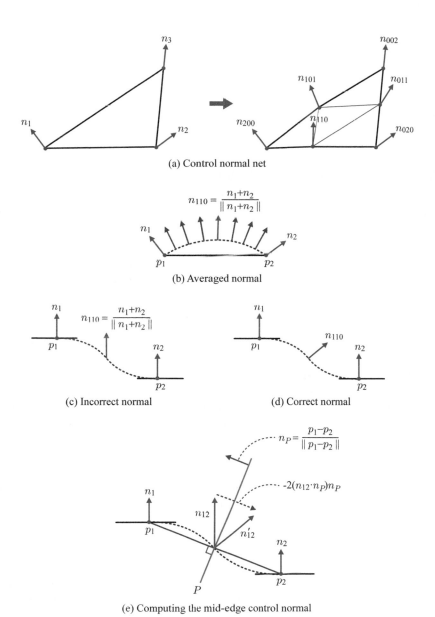

(a) Control normal net

$$n_{110} = \frac{n_1 + n_2}{\| n_1 + n_2 \|}$$

(b) Averaged normal

$$n_{110} = \frac{n_1 + n_2}{\| n_1 + n_2 \|}$$

(c) Incorrect normal

(d) Correct normal

$$n_P = \frac{p_1 - p_2}{\| p_1 - p_2 \|}$$

$$-2(n_{12} \cdot n_P)n_P$$

(e) Computing the mid-edge control normal

Fig. 7.12: Constructing a degree-2 control normal net for PN-triangle generation.

respect to P:

$$
\begin{aligned}
n'_{12} &= n_{12} - 2(n_{12} \cdot n_P)n_P \\
&= (n_1 + n_2) - 2((n_1 + n_2) \cdot \tfrac{p_1-p_2}{||p_1-p_2||}) \tfrac{p_1-p_2}{||p_1-p_2||} \\
&= (n_1 + n_2) - 2\tfrac{(n_1+n_2)\cdot(p_1-p_2)}{||p_1-p_2||^2}(p_1 - p_2) \\
&= (n_1 + n_2) - 2\tfrac{(n_1+n_2)\cdot(p_1-p_2)}{(p_1-p_2)\cdot(p_1-p_2)}(p_1 - p_2)
\end{aligned}
$$

When n'_{12} is normalized, we obtain the mid-edge control normal n_{110}. The other control normals, n_{101} and n_{011}, are similarly computed.

7.4.3 PN-triangle Tessellation

In Shader Model 5, PN-triangles can be tessellated by the new stages, i.e., the hull shader, the tessellator, and the domain shader. The input to the hull shader is generally called a *patch*. It is a new primitive type of Shader Model 5. A patch is simply a set of vertices, and the number of vertices is between 1 and 32. In the PN-triangle example, the patch input to the hull shader is simply a triangle, each vertex of which is defined by a position and a normal, as illustrated in Fig. 7.13.

In general, the hull shader converts the input patch to another patch, which is typically in a different representation. In the PN-triangle example, the hull shader implements the algorithms presented in the previous subsections. Then, the triangular nets of control points and control normals are generated. The outputs are sent to the domain shader, bypassing the tessellator.

The hull shader also determines the *tessellation factors*. These are sent to the tessellator, which generates a regular *tessellation pattern* for each patch. In the example of Fig. 7.13, each edge of the input patch is split into 8 triangle-edges.

The tessellation result is fed to the domain shader, in the form of the parametric coordinates (u, v)s. Then, the domain shader uses the coordinates to evaluate the patch passed from the hull shader. More specifically in the PN-triangle example, given the parametric coordinates (u, v), the domain shader evaluates the nets of control points and control normals using $(u, v, 1 - u - v)$ to obtain the position and normal of a vertex, respectively. The domain shader sends the complete data for the vertices to the geometry shader, or the rasterizer if no geometry shader is present.

The tessellation capability of Shader Model 5 embodies the *scalability* feature of a parametric surface, which is considered an advantage over a fixed polygon mesh representation. A parametric surface can be tessellated into an arbitrary-resolution polygon mesh. Advanced techniques such as displacement mapping (presented in Chapter 9) also benefit from the tessellation support of Shader Model 5.

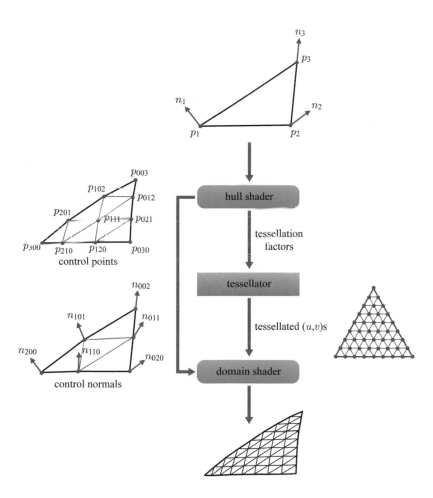

Fig. 7.13: Tessellation using the new stages introduced in Shader Model 5.

Exercises

1. Tessellation could be performed in Shader Model 4. Sketch a geometry shader algorithm that tessellates a cubic Bézier curve into a number of line segments.

2. In the fireworks example, the embers have life spans and gradually fade out. How would you implement the fade-out?

3. Suppose that, for constructing the degree-2 control normal net for PN-triangle, each mid-edge control normal is defined to be $\frac{n_1+n_2}{2}$, where n_1 and n_2 are the input vertex normals. (In this case, the mid-edge control normals are not necessarily the unit vectors.) Would the normals evaluated from the normal net be different from those evaluated from the degree-1 control normal net? Using the repeated barycentric interpolations, discuss why they are different or why not.

Chapter 8

Image Texturing

Texturing plays a key role in increasing the visual realism of the 3D scene. In general, a texture is organized in an array of texels. When the texels store color information, the texture is called an image texture. The texture dimension is not limited to 2D. For example, a 1D image texture is used for coloring a curve. Nonetheless, the main use of a texture is to store 2D image data, and this chapter focuses on 2D image texturing.

A texture may contain non-color information. For example, an array of surface normals or scene depths can be stored in a texture. These kinds of non-color textures are also crucial for enhancing the visual realism of the 3D scene. A variety of non-color texturing algorithms are presented in Chapters 9 and 10.

8.1 Texture Addressing Mode

In principle, the texture coordinates u and v are assumed to fall into the range of $[0,1]$. However, the texture coordinates outside the range can be processed by utilizing the *texture addressing mode*. Consider an image texture in Fig. 8.1-(a) and a simple polygon mesh in Fig. 8.1-(b), where the texture coordinates of three vertices are out of the range $[0,1]$. Consequently, a good many fragments of the polygons are assigned the out-of-range texture coordinates. The simplest method of handling such out-of-range texture coordinates is to assign an arbitrary color, named the *border color*, to those coordinates. Fig. 8.1-(c) shows the result obtained using gray as the border color.

Another, more popular, solution is to use the *wrap* or *repeat* mode so as to tile the texture at every integer junction. The result is shown in Fig. 8.1-(d). Note the clear boundaries between the repeated textures. If the *mirror* mode is used instead, the texture is mirrored or reflected at every integer junction, and we have smooth transition at the boundaries, as shown in Fig. 8.1-(e).

The addressing modes along the u- and v-axes can be specified independently. Fig. 8.1-(f) shows the result of setting the wrap and mirror modes to the u- and v-axes, respectively.

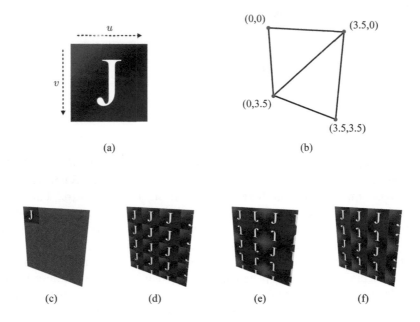

Fig. 8.1: Texture addressing modes. (a) Image texture. (b) A quad with out-of-range texture coordinates. (c) Border mode. (d) Wrap mode. (e) Mirror mode. (f) The *u*-axis follows the wrap mode whereas the *v*-axis follows the mirror mode.

[Note: Texture addressing mode in Direct3D]
A *sampler* refers to an object that can be sampled. Its representative example is a texture. In Direct3D, `Direct3DDevice9::SetSamplerState` sets the states of a texture. Its parameters include
- `D3DSAMP_ADDRESSU`
- `D3DSAMP_ADDRESSV`

The results shown in Fig. 8.1-(c), -(d), and -(e) require the parameters should be set to the following:
- `D3DTADDRESS_BORDER`
- `D3DTADDRESS_WRAP`
- `D3DTADDRESS_MIRROR`

When `D3DSAMP_ADDRESSU` is set to `D3DTADDRESS_WRAP` and `D3DSAMP_ADDRESSV` is set to `D3DTADDRESS_MIRROR`, we have the result of Fig. 8.1-(f).

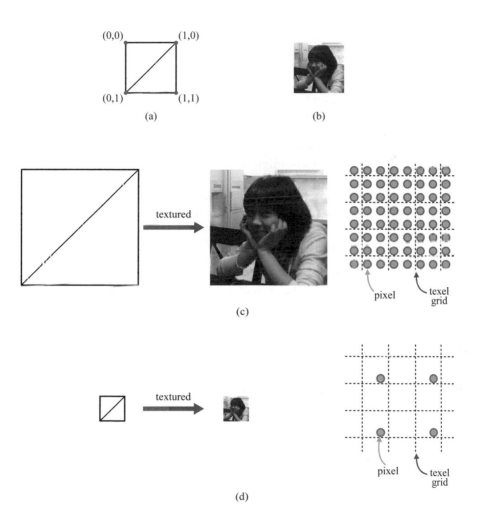

Fig. 8.2: Texture magnification and minification. (a) A quad to be textured. (b) An image texture. (c) In the magnification case, the number of pixels projected onto the texture space is greater than the number of texels. (d) In the minification case, the pixels are sparsely projected.

8.2 Texture Filtering

For a fragment located at (x, y) in the screen, its texture coordinates (u, v) are mapped to the texel address (t_x, t_y), as presented in Section 4.1.3. We say that the fragment at (x, y) is *projected* onto (t_x, t_y). In the contrived example given in Section 4.1.3, t_x and t_y were integers, and therefore the texel on the integer address was simply fetched. However, t_x and t_y are floating-point values in general, and then the texels *around* (t_x, t_y) are collected and combined to determine the texture color of the fragment. This process is called *texture filtering*.

Consider the quad shown in Fig. 8.2-(a). It is going to be textured using the image of Fig. 8.2-(b). Depending on the view, view frustum, and viewport parameters, the quad size in the screen space may vary. In Fig. 8.2-(c), the screen-space quad appears larger than the image texture, and therefore the texture is *magnified* so as to fit to the quad. Shown on the right-hand side is the texture depicted as a grid of dotted lines, where texels are located at the grid intersections. The gold dots represent the screen-space pixels[1] projected onto the texture space. There are more pixels than texels. In contrast, the screen-space quad in Fig. 8.2-(d) appears smaller than the image texture, and the texture is *minified*. As shown on the right-hand side, the pixels are sparsely projected onto the texture space.

8.2.1 Magnification

A filtering method for magnification is *nearest point sampling*. Given the 'floating-point' texel address (t_x, t_y) computed from the texture coordinates (u, v), the following rule is used to determine the 'integer' coordinates (i_x, i_y), which are nearest to (t_x, t_y):

$$(i_x, i_y) = (\lfloor t_x + 0.5 \rfloor, \lfloor t_y + 0.5 \rfloor) \qquad (8.1)$$

Fig. 8.3-(a) illustrates the nearest point sampling method and the texturing result. Observe that a block of projected pixels is mapped to a single texel. Consequently, the nearest point sampling method usually produces a blocky image. We would have a satisfying result only when the size of the texture is close to that of the screen-space primitive.

A better filtering method is *bilinear interpolation*, where four texels surrounding a projected pixel are bilinearly interpolated to determine the texture color of the pixel. See Fig. 8.3-(b). The adjacent pixels are likely to have different texture colors, and the texturing result suffers much less from the

---

[1]More precisely, they are not pixels but fragments. For a clearer comparison with *texel*, however, this chapter uses the word *pixel* instead of *fragment*.

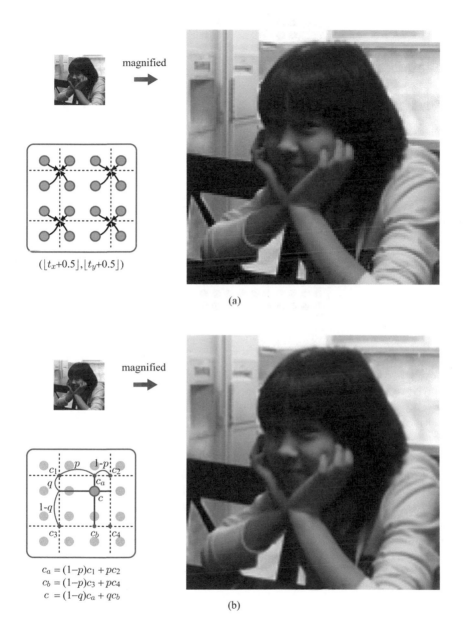

(a)

$c_a = (1-p)c_1 + pc_2$
$c_b = (1-p)c_3 + pc_4$
$c = (1-q)c_a + qc_b$

(b)

Fig. 8.3: Texture filtering for magnification. (a) A pixel takes the color of the nearest texel. (b) The colors (denoted by c_is) of four texels surrounding the projected pixel are bilinearly interpolated, using p and q which are $(t_x - \lfloor t_x \rfloor)$ and $(t_y - \lfloor t_y \rfloor)$, respectively.

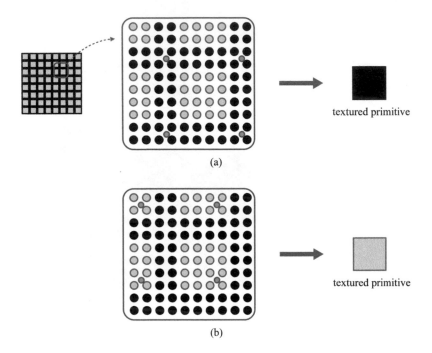

(a)

(b)

Fig. 8.4: Aliasing problems of minification. (a) If all pixels are surrounded by dark-gray texels in the checkerboard image, the textured primitive appears dark gray. (b) If all pixels are surrounded by light-gray texels, the textured primitive appears light gray.

blocky-image problem. In most cases, the texturing result obtained by bilinear interpolation shows a better quality. Further, the graphics hardware is optimized for bilinear interpolation, and the degraded performance caused by a more complex operation (bilinear interpolation) is rarely perceived. Therefore, bilinear interpolation is usually preferred to nearest point sampling.

8.2.2   Minification

Consider the checkerboard image texture shown in Fig. 8.4. Two dark-gray texel lines encompass 4×4 light-gray texel blocks both vertically and horizontally. Recall that, in the minification case, the pixels are sparsely projected onto the texture space. In the example of Fig. 8.4-(a), four pixels (depicted in gold color) are projected onto a section of the texture space. Each pixel is surrounded by the dark-gray texels and is then assigned the dark-gray color, regardless of whether nearest point sampling or bilinear interpolation is adopted for filtering. If every pixel of the screen-space primitive is surrounded

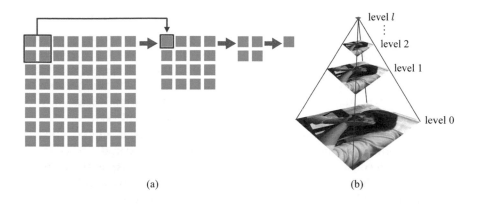

(a) (b)

Fig. 8.5: Mipmap construction. (a) The 2×2 texels are repeatedly combined into a single texel. (b) If the input texture has the resolution $2^l \times 2^l$, a pyramid of $(l + 1)$ textures is generated.

by the dark-gray texels, the textured primitive appears just dark gray. The checkerboard image is not properly textured. In contrast, the primitive appears just light gray if every projected pixel happens to be surrounded by the light-gray texels, as shown in Fig. 8.4-(b).

The above-mentioned problem is an instance of *aliasing*. It refers to a sampling error and occurs when a high-frequency signal (in our example, the checkerboard image texture of Fig. 8.4) is sampled at a lower resolution (in our example, the low-frequency pixels in Fig. 8.4). Aliasing is an ever-present problem in signal processing and computer graphics. We need an *anti-aliasing* technique for minimizing the aliasing artefact, and the next sections provide solutions in the context of texturing.

8.3 Mipmapping

Simply put, the problem observed in minification is caused by the fact that the texture is larger than the screen-space primitive. A simple solution is then to make the texture smaller such that the texture size becomes similar to the primitive size. The solution aims at *one-to-one correspondence* between pixels and texels.

8.3.1   Mipmap Construction

Consider an 8×8-resolution texture shown in Fig. 8.5-(a). It is the original texture and is *down-sampled* to a quarter size, i.e., 4×4 texture. In the simplest implementation, the colors of 2×2 neighboring texels of the original texture are averaged to determine the color of a texel in the quarter texture. Such down-sampling is repeated until a 1×1 texture is obtained, which contains the average color of the original texture in its entirety.

Given an original texture of $2^l \times 2^l$ resolution, l down-sampled textures can be generated. The original and down-sampled textures are conceptually stacked to construct a *texture pyramid* of $(l+1)$ levels, as shown in Fig. 8.5-(b). The original texture is located at level 0. The pyramid is called a *mipmap*. The prefix 'mip' is an acronym of the Latin phrase *multum in parvo*, meaning "many things in a small space."

8.3.2   Mipmap Filtering

Mipmap is by far the most popular structure used for reducing aliasing artefact in texturing. Let us now see how the mipmap is filtered. Some contrived examples would help us understand the principle. Fig. 8.6-(a) shows a minification case, where level-0 (original) texture is four times larger than the screen-space quad. Illustrated in the left of Fig. 8.6-(b) is a part of the level-0 texture, where 4×4 pixels are projected onto the area of 8×8 texels.

So far, we have regarded a pixel as a point located at the integer coordinates of the screen space. In reality, however, a pixel covers an area on the screen. For simplicity, take the area as square such that the entire screen can be considered to be tiled by an array of square pixels. Then, a pixel's projection onto the texture space is not a 'point' but an 'area' centered at the texel address (t_x, t_y). The projected area is called the *footprint* of the pixel. In Fig. 8.6-(b), the red box at the lower-right corner of level-0 texture represents a pixel's footprint that covers 2×2 texels. We do not have one-to-one correspondence between pixels and texels.

Let us move up the texture pyramid by one level to get a quarter texture. Then, as shown in Fig. 8.6-(b), the pixel's footprint covers a single texel. There is a one-to-one correspondence between pixels and texels! This is where filtering is performed. (In this contrived example, the pixel center coincides with the texel center at level 1, and therefore both nearest point sampling and bilinear interpolation return the same result.)

When a pixel footprint covers $m \times m$ texels of level-0 texture, $\log_2 m$ determines the level to visit in the mipmap structure. By convention it is called the *level of detail* and is denoted by λ. In the current example, m is the power of 2, and therefore λ is an integer. More specifically, $m = 2^1$, and $\lambda = \log_2 m = \log_2 2^1 = 1$.

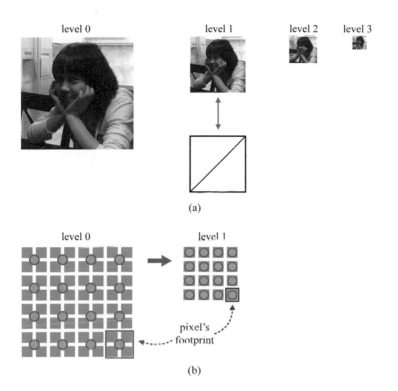

level 0   level 1   level 2   level 3

(a)

level 0   level 1

pixel's
footprint

(b)

Fig. 8.6: Mipmap filtering example. (a) The screen-space quad and level-1 texture have the same size. (b) Sixteen pixels are projected onto the area of 64 texels. A pixel's footprint covers 4 texels in the level-0 texture, but covers a single texel in the level-1 texture.

If m is not the power of 2, λ is a floating-point value. Fig. 8.7 shows an example. The pixel footprint covers 3×3 texels at the level-0 texture, and $\lambda = \log_2 3 \simeq 1.585$. Given a floating-point λ, levels $\lfloor \lambda \rfloor$ and $\lceil \lambda \rceil$ are taken as candidates. In the figure, they are levels 1 and 2. Which level to choose? An option is to take the level that is *nearest* to λ. It is computed as follows:

$$\lfloor \lambda + 0.5 \rfloor \tag{8.2}$$

Let us denote it by i_λ. In the example of Fig. 8.7-(b), i_λ is 2.

In contrast, we can choose *both* levels and then combine the filtering result from the levels. Fig. 8.7-(c) shows that bilinear interpolation is performed at each of levels 1 and 2, and then the results are linearly interpolated using the fractional part of λ (0.585 in the example). This process is called *trilinear interpolation*. (Each of levels $\lfloor \lambda \rfloor$ and $\lceil \lambda \rceil$ can be filtered using nearest point sampling, but bilinear interpolation usually produces a better result.)

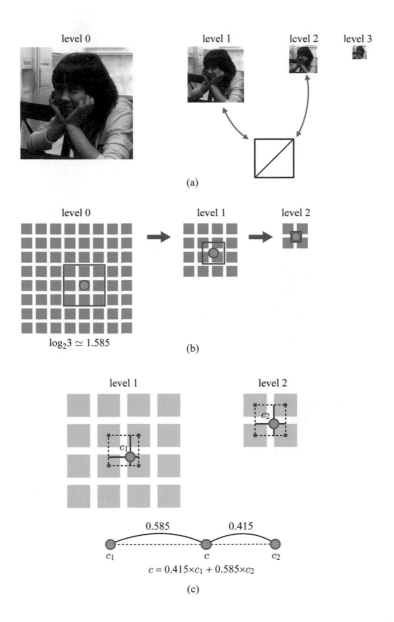

Fig. 8.7: Trilinear interpolation. (a) The screen-space quad is smaller than the level-1 texture, and is larger than the level-2 texture. (b) The level of detail λ is 1.585, and therefore levels 1 and 2 are the candidates. (c) Each level is bilinearly interpolated, and the results are linearly interpolated.

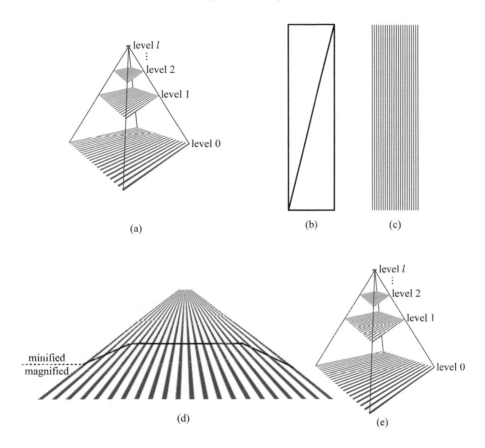

Fig. 8.8: Mipmap filtering options. (a) A mipmap constructed using a blue-stripe texture. (b) A long thin quad. (c) Mipmapping an upright quad. (d) Mipmapping an oriented quad. (e) The level-0 texture in (a) is replaced by a red-stripe texture only for a visualization purpose.

8.3.3 Options for Mipmap Filtering

Consider the mipmap shown in Fig. 8.8-(a) and the quad in Fig. 8.8-(b). When the quad is orthogonal to the view direction, the texturing result will be like Fig. 8.8-(c). On the other hand, Fig. 8.8-(d) shows a result when the quad is angled obliquely away from the viewer.

For each pixel of the screen-space primitive, it is determined whether the texture is magnified or minified. The black lines drawn in Fig. 8.8-(d) partition the textured quad into the 'magnified' and 'minified' parts. Magnification occurs at the lower part of the quad, and level-0 texture is used for texturing. In contrast, minification occurs at the upper part of the quad, and the upper levels of the mipmap may be involved.

Mipmapping is implemented in hardware, but the graphics APIs allow us to control the mipmap filtering mechanism. The major control is over magnification filter, minification filter, and mipmap level selection. For simplicity, let us abbreviate them to MAGFILTER, MINFILTER, and LEVEL, respectively.

MAGFILTER specifies how the level-0 texture is filtered for the 'magnified' part of a screen-space primitive. As discussed in Section 8.2.1, MAGFILTER has the option of nearest point sampling (which we denote by NEAREST) or bilinear interpolation (which we denote by BILINEAR).

As presented in the previous subsection, LEVEL has the option of selecting a single level (i_λ) or two levels ($\lfloor \lambda \rfloor$ and $\lceil \lambda \rceil$). Recall that i_λ is the integer that is *nearest* to λ. (In fact, Equation (8.2) for computing i_λ performs the same operation as Equation (8.1) for "nearest point sampling.") We call the option of selecting a single level NEAREST. On the other hand, if two levels are selected, the filtering results are combined through "linear interpolation," as shown in Fig. 8.7-(c). We then call the option of selecting two levels LINEAR.

The 'minified' part of a screen-space primitive is textured by selecting either i_λ or ($\lfloor \lambda \rfloor$,$\lceil \lambda \rceil$). MINFILTER specifies how the selected level is filtered. It has the same option as MAGFILTER, i.e., NEAREST or BILINEAR.

Let us iterate the options for mipmap filtering. In order to clearly present how the filtering is performed, the mipmap in Fig. 8.8-(a) is replaced by the one in Fig. 8.8-(e), where the stripe color of level 0 is changed into red.

Suppose that all of MAGFILTER, MINFILTER, and LEVEL are set to NEAREST. The quad textured with the options is shown in Fig. 8.8-(f). Because LEVEL is set to NEAREST, the textured quad has a clear boundary between the red and blue regions. The area around the boundary is where minification is done. The region right below the boundary is governed by the level-0 texture, and the region right above the boundary is by the level-1 texture. No two texture levels affect a single pixel. Note also that the stripes appear jagged over the quad because both MAGFILTER and MINFILTER are set to NEAREST.

If we change MAGFILTER into BILINEAR, we obtain the textured quad shown in Fig. 8.8-(g). See the 'magnified' part of the quad (below the black lines). The stripes appear smooth due to bilinear interpolation. In contrast, the 'minified' part is not changed because MINFILTER is still NEAREST.

If we change MINFILTER to BILINEAR, we have the textured quad shown in Fig. 8.8-(h). Bilinear interpolation is used for both magnification and minification, and texels are bilinearly interpolated at all levels of the mipmap. Consequently, all stripes of the quad appear smooth.

Let us finally change LEVEL from NEAREST to LINEAR. Then, each pixel at the 'minified' part is no longer dominated by a single mipmap level. Instead, the filtering results from two levels are linearly interpolated: Once the level of detail λ is computed for a pixel, the filtering results from levels $\lfloor \lambda \rfloor$ and $\lceil \lambda \rceil$ are linearly interpolated to determine the texture color for the pixel. The textured quad is shown in Fig. 8.8-(i). It is the result of trilinear interpolation. No clear boundary exists any longer between the red and blue regions.

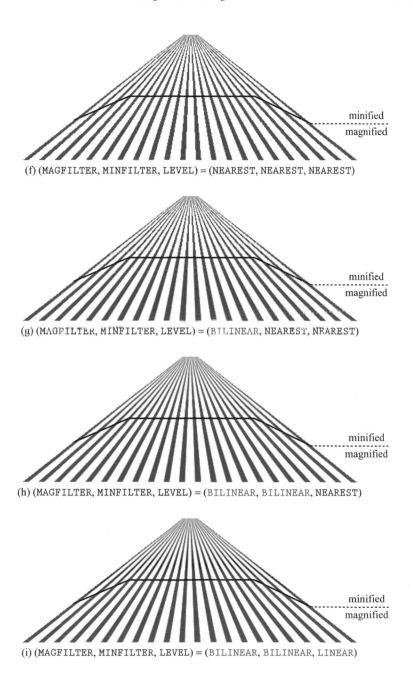

(f) (MAGFILTER, MINFILTER, LEVEL) = (NEAREST, NEAREST, NEAREST)

(g) (MAGFILTER, MINFILTER, LEVEL) = (BILINEAR, NEAREST, NEAREST)

(h) (MAGFILTER, MINFILTER, LEVEL) = (BILINEAR, BILINEAR, NEAREST)

(i) (MAGFILTER, MINFILTER, LEVEL) = (BILINEAR, BILINEAR, LINEAR)

Fig. 8.8: Mipmap filtering options (*continued*). The texturing results change as MAGFILTER, MINFILTER, and LEVEL take different options.

[Note: Direct3D texture filtering]

Recall `IDirect3DDevice9::SetSamplerState` introduced in [Note: Texture addressing mode in Direct3D] of Section 8.1. The method is used for controlling the texture filtering mode as well. It can define `D3DSAMP_MAGFILTER`, `D3DSAMP_MINFILTER`, and `D3DSAMP_MIPFILTER`, which correspond to the above-presented `MAGFILTER`, `MINFILTER`, and `LEVEL`, respectively.

`NEAREST` and `BILINEAR` used for the options of `MAGFILTER` and `MINFILTER` are implemented as `D3DTEXF_POINT` and `D3DTEXF_LINEAR`, respectively. Note that, in these cases, `D3DTEXF_LINEAR` imples bilinear interpolation. For `LEVEL`, `NEAREST` and `LINEAR` options are implemented as `D3DTEXF_POINT` and `D3DTEXF_LINEAR`, respectively.

8.4 Anisotropic Filtering

In the examples of Section 8.3.2, a pixel's footprint covers an *isotropic* (squarish) area in the texture space. However, a footprint is usually *anisotropic*. It may cover a large number of texels along one dimension but only a few along the other dimension. Further, it may have an arbitrary orientation.

The arbitrarily-shaped anisotropic footprint occurs when the primitive surface is not orthogonal to the view direction. In Fig. 8.9-(a), consider the black-boundary pixel located at the top part of the textured quad. (The pixel size is exaggerated to show that it is square.) In the texture space, the pixel's footprint would be long and narrow, as shown in Fig. 8.9-(b).

To compute the level of detail λ, traditional mipmapping algorithms often use the longest edge of the anisotropic footprint. In Fig. 8.9-(b), its length is denoted by m. Then, λ is set to $\log_2 m$. Unfortunately, filtering the mipmap with such λ is equivalent to taking the isotropic footprint, the size of which is $m \times m$, as shown in Fig. 8.9-(c). Observe that the isotropic footprint in Fig. 8.9-(c) contains blue texels whereas the anisotropic one in Fig. 8.9-(b) does not. Consequently, the textured color of the pixel will be a blend of blue and white even though it is supposed to be pure white. This explains why the top part of the textured quad is overly blurred in Fig. 8.9-(a).

The over-blurring artefact becomes serious when the textured surface is nearly edge-on. What is desired is *anisotropic filtering*, which filters only the area covered by the anisotropic footprint. It can produce the result shown in Fig. 8.9-(d), where the top part of the quad is less blurred.

Fortunately, anisotropic filtering is a standard feature of GPU and is neatly combined with mipmapping. It was first implemented in consumer-level graphics hardware in the late 1990s and has been continuously improved by hardware vendors. This section presents a simplest implementation.

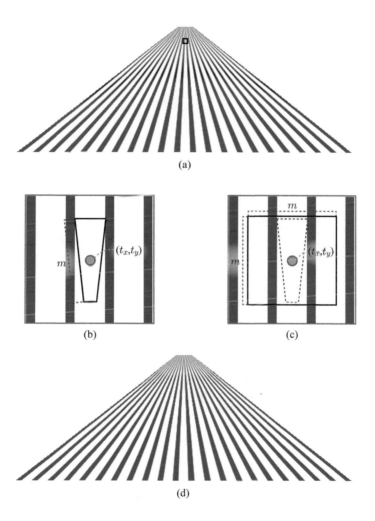

Fig. 8.9: Trilinear interpolation vs. anisotropic filtering. (a) The quad is textured using trilinear interpolation. (b) The anisotropic footprint contains only white texels. (c) The isotropic footprint contains white and blue texels. If the longest edge were used to determine λ in (b), the filtering result would be the same as that using this isotropic footprint, leading to over-blurring. (d) The quad is textured using anisotropic filtering.

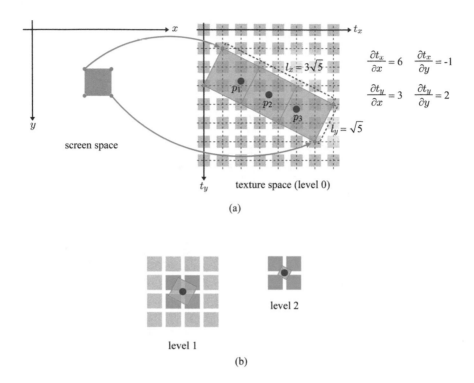

(a)

(b)

level 1

level 2

Fig. 8.10: Anisotropic filtering example. (a) The anisotropic footprint is divided into smaller isotropic footprints. (b) The level of detail λ is computed using the isotropic footprint, and directs us to levels 1 and 2. In this example, each level is filtered through bilinear interpolation.

Fig. 8.10-(a) shows a pixel in the screen space and its footprint in the texture space. (Texels are located at the grid intersections. The fraction of the texture shown in the figure contains 8×8 texels.) For the sake of simplicity, assume that the footprint is rectangular. The shorter edge's length is $\sqrt{5}$, and the longer edge's is $3\sqrt{5}$. Their ratio is three. Then, the 'anisotropic' footprint is divided into three 'isotropic' footprints. Each of the isotropic footprints is processed separately. For that purpose, a *sample point* is computed per isotropic footprint. Fig. 8.10-(a) shows three sample points, p_1, p_2, and p_3.

The edge length of the isotropic footprint, i.e., the length of the anisotropic footprint's shorter edge, determines λ. In the example, $\lambda = \log_2\sqrt{5} \simeq 1.16$. Therefore, levels 1 and 2 will be selected if LEVEL is set to LINEAR. (If the length of the anisotropic footprint's longest edge were used, levels 2 and 3 would be selected.) Each sample point is projected to levels 1 and 2. Fig. 8.10-(b) shows p_2 projected in the levels. If bilinear interpolation is adopted

 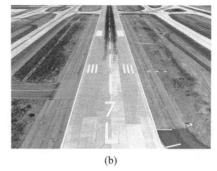

(a)   (b)

Fig. 8.11: Comparison of texturing results. (a) Trilinear interpolation, (b) Anisotropic filtering. (© 2010 Europa Technologies Gray Buildings, © 2009 CyberCity, © 2010 Google.)

as the filtering option, the 2×2 texels (colored in green) will be bilinearly interpolated for each level. The filtering results from two levels are linearly interpolated. It is *trilinear interpolation*. The results of trilinear interpolation for three sample points are averaged to return the final texture color of the pixel. [Note: Degree and axis of anisotropy] presents the algorithm in a more detail.

Return to Fig. 8.9-(d), and observe that the area of the quad affected by level-0 texture is expanded. It is because λ is determined by the length of the anisotropic footprint's shorter edge, and therefore the lower levels of the mipmap are more frequently sampled.

Fig. 8.11 compares anisotropic filtering with trilinear interpolation. The textured image created only with trilinear interpolation appears blurry toward the horizon. In contrast, the anisotropic filtering preserves the sharpness of the image texture at the area.

[Note: Degree and axis of anisotropy]

Consider four partial differentials illustrated in Fig. 8.10-(a): $\frac{\partial t_x}{\partial x}$, $\frac{\partial t_x}{\partial y}$, $\frac{\partial t_y}{\partial x}$, and $\frac{\partial t_y}{\partial y}$. Each of the differentials measures how much the texture changes with respect to the screen-space axis. A parallelogram footprint is assumed, and its width l_x and height l_y are computed as follows:

$$l_x = \sqrt{(\frac{\partial t_x}{\partial x})^2 + (\frac{\partial t_y}{\partial x})^2}$$

$$l_y = \sqrt{(\frac{\partial t_x}{\partial y})^2 + (\frac{\partial t_y}{\partial y})^2}$$

Then, the longer edge's length l_{max} and the shorter edge's l_{min} are computed using l_x and l_y:

$$l_{max} = max(l_x, l_y)$$

$$l_{min} = min(l_x, l_y)$$

In the example, $l_{max} = l_x = 3\sqrt{5}$ and $l_{min} = l_y = \sqrt{5}$.

The *degree of anisotropy* N determines how many (nearly-)isotropic footprints are produced from the original anisotropic footprint:

$$N = min(\lceil \frac{l_{max}}{l_{min}} \rceil, A_{max})$$

where A_{max} is the user-specified maximum degree of anisotropy. (In Direct3D, it corresponds to `D3DSAMP_MAXANISOTROPY` specified through `Direct3DDevice9::SetSamplerState` method.) If A_{max} is large enough, N will be three in the example. We also compute λ used to locate the mipmap levels to visit:

$$\lambda = log_2(\frac{l_{max}}{N})$$

In our example, $\lambda = log_2\sqrt{5} \simeq 1.16$, and therefore levels 1 and 2 will be selected.

When l_x is greater than l_y, as in the case of Fig. 8.10-(a), the sample points of the isotropic footprints are equally spaced along the x-dimension of the original footprint. Suppose that $\tau(t_x, t_y)$ represents a filtering function of an isotropic footprint. Then, the anisotropic filtering result is described as follows:

$$\frac{1}{N} \sum_{i=1}^{N} \tau(t_x^0 + \frac{\partial t_x}{\partial x}(\frac{i}{N+1} - \frac{1}{2}), t_y^0 + \frac{\partial t_y}{\partial x}(\frac{i}{N+1} - \frac{1}{2})) \qquad (8.3)$$

where (t_x^0, t_y^0) represent the texel address of the pixel center. In the example of Fig. 8.10, $(t_x^0, t_y^0) = (3.5, 3.5)$, three sample points at level 0 are $\{(2.0, 2.75), (3.5, 3.5), (5.0, 4.25)\}$, and τ performs trilinear interpolation for each of three points.

If l_x is smaller than l_y, ∂x in Equation (8.3) is replaced by ∂y, and we have the following equation:

$$\frac{1}{N} \sum_{i=1}^{N} \tau(t_x^0 + \frac{\partial t_x}{\partial y}(\frac{i}{N+1} - \frac{1}{2}), t_y^0 + \frac{\partial t_y}{\partial y}(\frac{i}{N+1} - \frac{1}{2}))$$

As a final note in this chapter, let us present how to combine image texturing with lighting. Suppose that the Phong model presented in Equation (5.11) is used for lighting:

$$max(n \cdot l, 0)s_d \otimes m_d + (max(r \cdot v, 0))^{sh} s_s \otimes m_s + s_a \otimes m_a + m_e$$

The diffuse reflectance m_d is set to the color fetched from the image texture. Similarly, the specular reflectance m_s can be read from another texture, which is usually a gray-scale texture, as discussed in Section 5.1.2.

Exercises

1. A pixel is projected onto an 8×8-resolution image texture. See the left-hand side of the figure shown below. The yellow rectangle is the pixel's footprint, and the red dot represents the pixel's center.

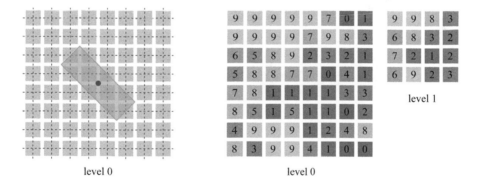

(a) Suppose that the image texture contains only gray colors. Shown at the right-hand side of the figure are the level-0 and level-1 textures in the mipmap. Construct the level-2 and level-3 textures.

(b) Suppose that trilinear interpolation is used for filtering, and the longest side of the footprint is used for selecting λ. Which levels are selected? Compute the filtering result at each level.

(c) Suppose that anisotropic filtering is used, and the shortest side of the footprint is used for selecting λ. Which levels are the candidates? Take the red dot as a sample point, and compute the filtering result at each candidate level. (Assume that each level is filtered through bilinear interpolation.)

2. Suppose that the texture coordinate u is out of the range $[0,1]$. Assuming that the texture addressing mode is *wrap*, write an equation that converts u into the range $[0,1]$.

3. Some applications such as medical imaging require 3D texturing. Consider a 3D image of $2^l \times 2^l \times 2^l$ resolution. Suppose that the 3D texture coordinates (u, v, w) are converted into the texel address (t_x, t_y, t_z).

   (a) Given a 2D image, we usually have a filtering option of nearest point sampling or bilinear interpolation. Given a 3D image, how would you extend the nearest point sampling? Write equations for the extended method.

   (b) How would you extend the bilinear interpolation method? Write equations for the extended method.

   (c) Let us construct a mipmap using the 3D image. Describe how you can down-sample the original image. What will be the size of the top image of the mipmap hierarchy? How many levels will be in the hierarchy?

Chapter 9

Bump Mapping

The use of textures is not limited to applying the material colors to the object surfaces. Non-color data can be stored in a texture. For example, many of the real-world surfaces such as brick walls have small-scale high-frequency bumpy features, and a texture can store such features.

Consider the image-textured quad shown in Fig. 9.1. The bumpy features of the brick wall are not properly exposed. If the viewpoint gets closer to the textured wall, the lack of geometric detail will be more clearly noticeable. Alternatively, we could model a highly tessellated polygon mesh with bumpy features. See Fig. 9.2. The rendering result is quite realistic. However, rendering such a high-resolution mesh requires large vertex and index buffers and incurs expensive vertex processing cost.

A way out of this dilemma is to use a low-resolution surface and represent the high-frequency geometric details in a texture. The low-resolution surface is often called a *macrostructure*, and it will be modulated by the texture. This technique is generally called *bump mapping*. (This book takes bump mapping as a general terminology, but some literature uses it in a narrow sense such that it is a synonym of normal mapping presented in Section 9.2.2.)

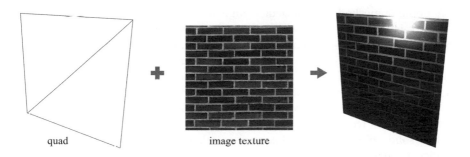

quad   image texture

Fig. 9.1: Image texturing on a simple surface does not properly present the bumpy features.

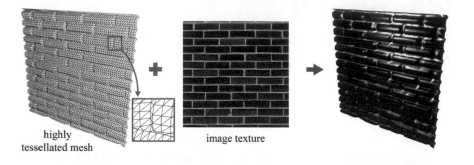

Fig. 9.2: A highly tessellated surface presents the bumpy features realistically, but it is expensive to process the huge number of vertices.

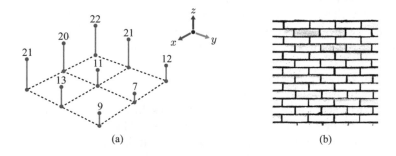

Fig. 9.3: Height map. (a) Height values are stored at regularly sampled (x, y) coordinates. (b) A height map is often visualized as a gray-scale image.

9.1 Height Field

A popular method to represent a high-frequency surface is to use a *height field*. It is a function $h(x, y)$ that returns a height or z value given (x, y) coordinates. Fig. 9.3-(a) shows an example of a discrete height field. The 2D array of height values at the regularly spaced (x, y) coordinates is stored in a texture named *height map*. The height map can be drawn in gray scales. If the height is in the range of $[0,255]$, the lowest height 0 is colored in black, and the highest 255 is colored in white. Fig. 9.3-(b) visualizes the height map that represents the brick wall's surface given in Fig. 9.2. Note that a brick with a solid color implies a flat surface whereas an unevenly colored brick implies an uneven surface.

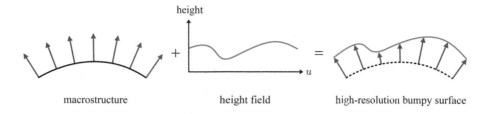

Fig. 9.4: The macrostructure surface is displaced along its normal vectors by the amounts returned by the height field function. This cross-section illustration shows only u out of the texture coordinates (u, v).

The height field represents the *displacement* of the high-frequency bumpy surface from the low-frequency macrostructure. An 'ideal' implementation of bump mapping would be to displace each surface point of the macrostructure in the direction of its surface normal by an amount returned by the height field function. The displacement amount can be fetched using the texture coordinates (u, v) associated with the point. Fig. 9.4 is extracted from J. Blinn's seminal work on bump mapping [25] and illustrates in cross section how the height field is used to displace the surface points of the macrostructure.

There are many approaches to bump mapping, and this chapter presents three among them. They process the height map in different ways. First of all, the most popular algorithm, *normal mapping*, is presented. It does not follow the ideal implementation presented in Fig. 9.4 but pre-computes a special texture, *normal map*, from the height map. At run time, the normal map is used to perturb the surface normals of the macrostructure so as to 'mimic' the geometric bumpiness. Another approach is *parallax mapping*. It takes the height map at input and runs a simplified ray tracing algorithm. Unlike normal mapping, it makes the bumps appear to block each other. Both normal mapping and parallax mapping are implemented in fragment shaders. The last algorithm presented in this chapter is *displacement mapping*, which tessellates the macrostructure and then displaces its vertices using the height map. It is closest to the ideal implementation and is emerging as an attractive algorithm due to the tessellation support in Shader Model 5. It is implemented in the domain shader with the aid of tessellator.

9.2 Normal Mapping

This section presents the procedures for creating a height map and a normal map, and then the algorithm of normal mapping.

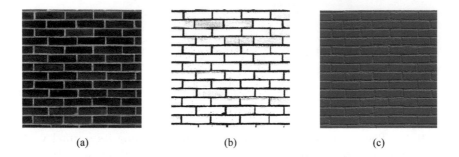

Fig. 9.5: Creation of a height map and a normal map. (a) Image texture. (b) The height map is semi-automatically constructed from the image texture. (c) The normal map is automatically constructed from the height map.

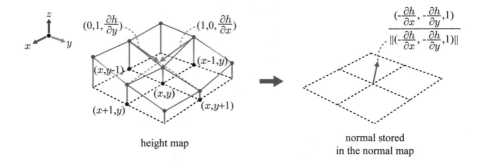

height map

normal stored
in the normal map

Fig. 9.6: The normal at a sample position of the height map is computed using the heights of its neighbors.

9.2.1   Normal Map

A gray-scale height map is usually created using 2D graphics packages. Through simple image-editing operations, the brick-wall image texture in Fig. 9.5-(a) can be converted into the height map in Fig. 9.5-(b). Not only the RGB colors are converted into gray scales, but some areas of the image are also edited. For example, the mortar between the bricks is painted in darker colors because it should be recessed. The height map has the same resolution as the image texture.

A normal map contains surface normals. It is simple to derive a normal map from a height map. Given the height map in Fig. 9.6, let us compute the surface normal at the point $(x, y, h(x,y))$. Here, h represents the discrete height function. The partial derivatives, $\frac{\partial h}{\partial x}$ and $\frac{\partial h}{\partial y}$, are needed for computing

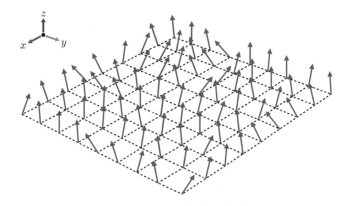

Fig. 9.7: A normal map stores normal vectors instead of color values.

the normal. They are defined by the height values stored at the four neighbors of (x,y), i.e., $\{(x+1,y),(x-1,y),(x,y+1),(x,y-1)\}$:

$$\frac{\partial h}{\partial x} = \frac{h(x+1,y) - h(x-1,y)}{2}$$

$$\frac{\partial h}{\partial y} = \frac{h(x,y+1) - h(x,y-1)}{2}$$

Then, we obtain two tangent vectors at $(x,y,h(x,y))$: $(1,0,\frac{\partial h}{\partial x})$ and $(0,1,\frac{\partial h}{\partial y})$. See Fig. 9.6. Their cross product is $(-\frac{\partial h}{\partial x}, -\frac{\partial h}{\partial y}, 1)$. It is normalized and stored as the surface normal at (x,y). The computed normals are pointing away from the height field surface. Fig. 9.7 visualizes a normal map. In general, a normal map has the same resolution as the image texture and the height map.

Presented above is a simplest algorithm. More elaborate algorithms are available, which consider more neighbors for computing the surface normal at a position of the height field. Many of 2D graphics packages such as Photoshop provide well-developed plug-ins to automatically convert a height map to a normal map.

Suppose that conventional integer RGB texture formats are used to store the surface normals. Each color component lies in the range of $[0,255]$. In contrast, each of the x-, y-, and z-coordinates of the computed normal is a floating-point value in the range of $[-1,1]$. The range conversion is needed before storing the normal (x,y,z) into the normal map:

$$R = 255(0.5x + 0.5)$$
$$G = 255(0.5y + 0.5)$$
$$B = 255(0.5z + 0.5)$$

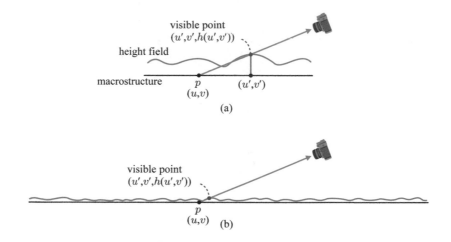

Fig. 9.8: Height field processing and its approximation (modified from [26]). (a) In principle, the point visible to the camera should be computed so that (u', v') are used for texture access. (b) The visible point is approximated to be p. Then, p's texture coordinates (u, v) are used to access both the image texture and the normal map.

Note that, as visualized in Fig. 9.7, a normal pointing away from the height field surface is generally taken as a *perturbed* instance of $(0,0,1)$. An interesting fact is that, in such a perturbed normal, the x- and y-components are usually much smaller than its z-component. Then, the dominant color of the normal map in RGB format will be blue. It can be observed in Fig. 9.5-(c).

In this section, it has been shown that the high-frequency surface detail can be recorded in a height map without requiring artists to design a highly tessellated 3D model. Instead, simple operations in an image-editing package are sufficient to create the height map. Then, a normal map is automatically created.

9.2.2 Algorithm for Normal Mapping

For now, consider the macrostructure, the height map, and the normal map as the input to the bump mapping algorithm. In our quad example, the macrostructure is composed of two triangles and four vertices. The vertices are processed by the vertex shader. Then, the macrostructure is rasterized, and the fragments are passed to the fragment shader, which would use the height map and normal map to implement bump mapping.

Suppose that the fragment shader processes p shown in Fig. 9.8-(a). Then, the surface point actually visible to the viewpoint is $(u', v', h(u', v'))$, where

$h(u', v')$ denotes the height at (u', v'). In principle, computing the visible point requires *ray tracing*, i.e., the ray connecting p and the viewpoint is traced (along the opposite direction) to compute the intersection with the height field[1]. Then, (u', v') would be used to fetch the surface normal from the normal map. The image texture would also be accessed using (u', v'). Unfortunately, it is expensive to implement ray tracing at run time[2].

Assume that, compared to the extent of the macrostructure, the height values of the height field are negligibly small, as illustrated in Fig. 9.8-(b). This may not be an unreasonable assumption for many objects such as a wide brick wall. A rough approximation can be subsequently made: The visible point is approximated to be p. Then, p's texture coordinates (u, v) can be used to access the normal map and image texture.

Such an approximate algorithm does not require the height map but takes just the normal map as input for bump mapping. The algorithm is called *normal mapping*. Suppose that the Phong model presented in Equation (5.11) is used for per-fragment lighting:

$$max(n \cdot l, 0)s_d \otimes m_d + (max(r \cdot v, 0))^{sh} s_o \otimes m_s + s_a \otimes m_a + m_e$$

In the diffuse reflection term, $max(n \cdot l, 0)s_d \otimes m_d$, n is fetched from the normal map, and m_d is fetched from the image texture. The normal map is usually filtered through bilinear interpolation.

Fig. 9.9 compares a quad rendered only with an image texture and the same quad rendered with an image texture and a normal map. Suppose that the quad lies in the xy-plane of the coordinate system. Without normal mapping, the surface normal of the quad is fixed to the z-axis unit vector $(0,0,1)$, which we denote by u_z, at every fragment. With normal mapping, the normal at a fragment is fetched from the normal map. Each normal is a 'perturbed' instance of u_z. Even for adjacent fragments, the normals fetched from the normal map may have different directions, and then the shade on the area changes rapidly and irregularly.

Normal mapping presents the *illusion* of high-frequency surface detail by combining per-fragment lighting and surface normal perturbation supplied by a normal map. This is described as an 'illusion' because it is achieved without adding or processing more geometry. By not processing a high-resolution mesh, the rendering performance is greatly increased.

---

[1]It is different from the ray tracing used for global illumination because the ray is not recursively traced. It is often called *ray casting* or *ray shooting*. However, many publications cite ray casting, ray shooting, and ray tracing interchangeably.

[2]Precisely speaking, it *was* expensive. Parallax mapping presented in Section 9.5 runs ray tracing at real time.

204   *3D Graphics for Game Programming*

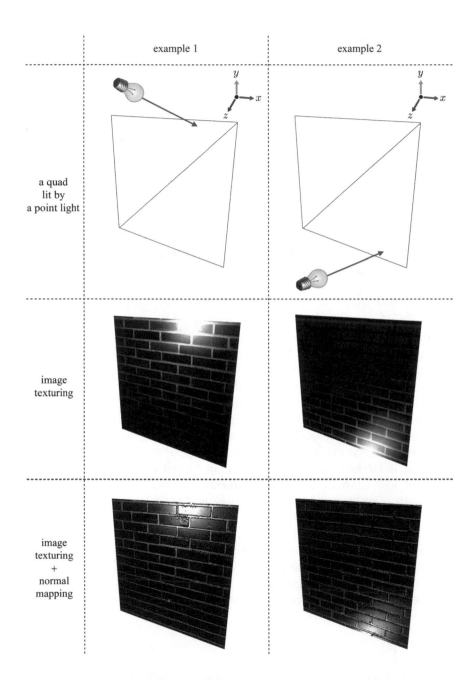

Fig. 9.9: Comparison of "image texturing only" and "image texturing combined with normal mapping."

[Note: Shaders for normal mapping]

For simplicity, suppose that the world is composed of a single object. Let us then take the object space as the world space such that no world transform is needed. In the vertex shader shown below, `ViewProj` is a combination of the view and projection transforms. The input parameter `Tex` represents the normal-map coordinates assigned per vertex. The coordinates are simply passed to the rasterizer. Assuming a point light source, the light vector (`Light`) is computed and passed to the rasterizer. Consequently, each fragment will be assigned the interpolated normal-map coordinates and the interpolated light vector.

```
void VS_main (float4 Pos : POSITION,
              float2 Tex : TEXCOORD0,   // for normal map
          out float4 oPos : POSITION,
          out float2 oTex : TEXCOORD0,
          out float3 Light : TEXCOORD1,
      uniform float3 LightPos,
      uniform float4x4 ViewProj)
{
  oPos = mul(ViewProj, Pos);
  oTex = Tex;
  Light = LightPos - Pos.xyz;
}
```

The fragment shader shown below uses the library function `tex2D()` to access the normal map. The coordinates returned by `tex2D()` are in the range of $[0,1]$, and therefore they are converted into the range of $[-1,1]$. For simplicity, the fragment shader considers only diffuse reflection and further ignores s_d and m_d in the diffuse term of the Phong model. It computes only $n \cdot l$ and returns the gray-scale color.

```
void FS_main (float2 oTex : TEXCOORD0,
              float3 Light : TEXCOORD1,
          out float4 Color : COLOR,
      uniform sampler2D NormalMap)
{
  float3 LightDir = normalize(Light);
  float3 Normal = tex2D(NormalMap, oTex).xyz;
  Normal = normalize(Normal*2.0-1.0);
  Color = dot(Normal, LightDir);
}
```

9.3   Tangent-space Normal Mapping

So far, it has been assumed that the normal map stores "perturbed instances of u_z" where u_z represents the *world-space z*-axis. However, note that, in the brick wall example of Fig. 9.9, the surface normal of the macrostructure (quad) just happens to be u_z. In general, the macrostructure is not limited to a plane, and even a plane does not generally have u_z as its surface normal.

9.3.1   Algorithm for Tangent-space Normal Mapping

Texturing is described as wrapping a texture onto an object surface. Consider the normal map shown in Fig. 9.10-(a), where the stored normals are colored in red. Imagine wrapping the normal map onto the surface of a sphere. Fig. 9.10-(b) shows the result. The surface normal at point p is denoted by n_p, and $n(u_p, v_p)$ denotes the normal fetched from the normal map using p's texture coordinates (u_p, v_p). Note that $n(u_p, v_p)$ replaces n_p. Similarly, $n(u_q, v_q)$ replaces n_q. From this example, it can be understood that the normals of the normal map should be considered as perturbed instances "of the *surface normals*," not "of u_z."

For a surface point, consider a *tangent space*, the z-axis of which corresponds to the surface normal. Fig. 9.10-(c) shows two tangent spaces, one defined for p and the other for q. The tangent spaces vary across the object surface. Assuming that a tangent space is defined for a surface point to be normal-mapped, the normal fetched from the normal map is taken as being defined in the tangent space of the point, not in the world space. In this respect, it is named the *tangent-space normal*. Fig. 9.10-(d) shows $n(u_p, v_p)$ and $n(u_q, v_q)$ defined in their own tangent spaces.

The surface normal of a polygon mesh is typically computed *per vertex* at the modeling stage. It is the vertex normal. Accordingly, the tangent space is constructed *per vertex* such that its z-axis corresponds to the vertex normal, as shown in Fig. 9.10-(e). Three orthonormal vectors define the tangent space: One is the vertex normal which we denote by N, and the other two are denoted by T (for *tangent*) and B (for *binormal*[3]). Utility functions such as D3DXComputeTangentFrameEx return the TBN vectors on each vertex of a triangle mesh. The algorithm to compute the per-vertex tangent spaces for an arbitrary triangle mesh is presented in Section 9.3.2.

---

[3]Binormal is a misnomer, and *bitangent* is a correct terminology because it is also tangent to the surface. In general, binormal is related with a curve, not with a surface: A point of a curve is associated with a single tangent vector and two normal vectors (named *normal* and *binormal*) perpendicular to each other. Following the convention in normal mapping, however, this chapter uses binormal instead of bitangent.

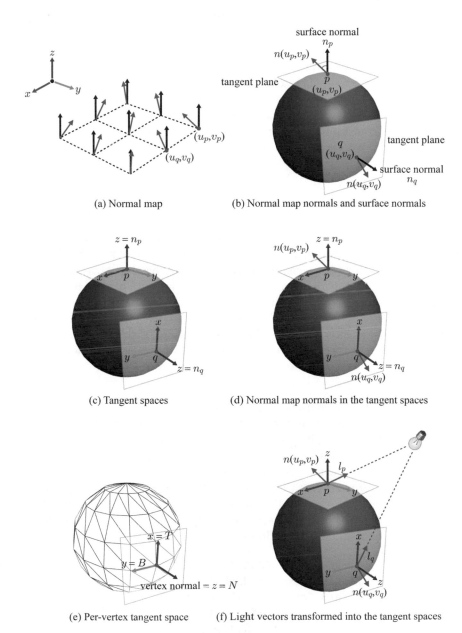

(a) Normal map

(b) Normal map normals and surface normals

(c) Tangent spaces

(d) Normal map normals in the tangent spaces

(e) Per-vertex tangent space

(f) Light vectors transformed into the tangent spaces

Fig. 9.10: Tangent spaces, tangent-space normal map, and light vectors transformed into the tangent spaces.

Now, the algorithm for tangent-space normal mapping is presented. Consider the diffuse reflection term of the Phong model, $max(n \cdot l, 0)s_d \otimes m_d$. A light source is defined in the world space, and so is the light vector l. In contrast, n fetched from the normal map is defined in the tangent space, i.e., n and l are defined in different spaces. If l is transformed into the tangent space, this inconsistency is resolved.

In general, the tangent-space basis is computed per vertex ahead of time, is stored in the vertex buffer, and is passed to the vertex shader. Then, the basis is world-transformed. Let us denote the transformed basis by $\{T,B,N\}$. Consider a 3×3 rotation matrix constructed from $\{T,B,N\}$:

$$\begin{pmatrix} T_x & T_y & T_z \\ B_x & B_y & B_z \\ N_x & N_y & N_z \end{pmatrix} \tag{9.1}$$

This is the *basis-change* matrix that can convert the world-space light vector into the tangent space. (If this is not clear, read Section 2.2.2.) In Fig. 9.10-(f), the light vector at p, denoted by l_p, is rotated by the above matrix, and consequently l_p and $n(u_p, v_p)$ are defined in the tangent space of p. Similarly, the light vector at q, l_q, is transformed into the tangent space of q.

The per-vertex tangent-space light vectors (such as l_p and l_q) are passed to the rasterizer and interpolated. Then, the fragment shader accepts the per-fragment tangent-space light vector, fetches the tangent-space normal from the normal map, and computes per-fragment lighting.

[Note: Shaders for tangent-space normal mapping]

Shown below is an extension of the vertex shader presented in [Note: Shaders for normal mapping] of Section 9.2.2. The extension is for converting the light vector into the per-vertex tangent space. For reducing the vertex buffer size, only the normal (N) and tangent (T) are stored per vertex. Then, the vertex shader computes the binormal (B) by taking the cross product of N and T, constructs the rotation matrix with $\{T,B,N\}$, and converts the light vector into the tangent space. The fragment shader for tangent-space normal mapping is the same as that of [Note: Shaders for normal mapping].

```
void VS_main (float4 Pos : POSITION,
              float3 Normal : NORMAL,
              float3 Tangent : TEXCOORD0,
              float2 Tex : TEXCOORD1, // for normal map
          out float4 oPos : POSITION,
          out float2 oTex : TEXCOORD0,
          out float3 Light : TEXCOORD1,
      uniform float3 LightPos,
      uniform float4x4 ViewProj)
```

```
{
    oPos = mul(ViewProj, Pos);
    oTex = Tex;
    Light = LightPos - Pos.xyz;
    float3 Binormal = cross(Normal, Tangent);
    float3x3 Rotation = float3x3(Tangent, Binormal, Normal);
    Light = mul(Rotation, light);
}
```

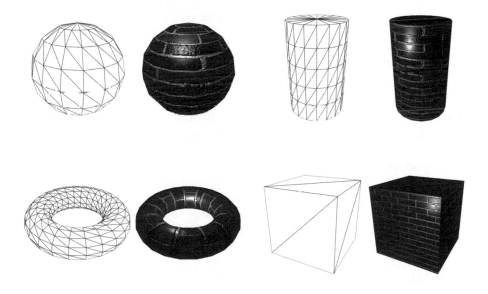

Fig. 9.11: A single pair of image texture and normal map is applied to the faces of a sphere, a cylinder, a torus, and a cube.

Fig. 9.11 shows that a single pair of the brick-wall image texture (in Fig. 9.5-(a)) and the normal map (in Fig. 9.5-(c)) can be applied to a variety of objects with arbitrary geometry. The texturing results are good, but a problem can be found. The polygonal geometry of the mesh is exposed at the silhouettes. It is unavoidable because normal mapping simply perturbs the normals during per-fragment lighting. It does not alter the geometry of the macrostructure at all.

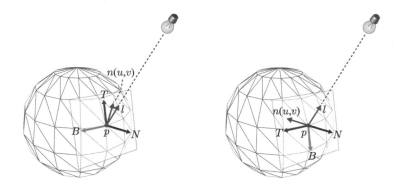

Fig. 9.12: In the different tangent spaces, the normal fetched from the normal map makes different angles with the light vector.

9.3.2 Tangent Space Computation*

Consider two tangent spaces shown in Fig. 9.12. Both of them would be considered valid because they have mutually orthogonal basis vectors and their N axes coincide with the vertex normal. Note that, however, the normal $n(u, v)$ fetched from the normal map makes different angles with l in two spaces, leading to different colors computed for p. This example shows that it is important to correctly compute T and B.

In the normal map, every normal is assumed to be defined in terms of the tangent-space basis $\{T,B,N\}$. Therefore, the T-, B-, and N-axes are respectively equivalent to the x-, y-, and z-axes illustrated in Fig. 9.10-(a). Consider triangle $\langle p_0,p_1,p_2 \rangle$ in Fig. 9.13-(a). Each vertex p_i is assigned the texture coordinates (u_i, v_i), which are used for both image texturing and normal mapping. Fig. 9.13-(b) shows the vertices *projected* into the tangent space. Note that the texture axis u is aligned with the T-axis. Similarly, the v-axis is aligned with the B-axis. Therefore, analyzing the texture coordinates (u_i, v_i)s assigned to the vertices, we can determine the directions of T and B.

Fig. 9.13-(c) shows the triangle $\langle p_0,p_1,p_2 \rangle$, together with unknown T and B. The vector connecting p_0 and p_1 is denoted by q_1, and the vector connecting p_0 and p_2 is by q_2. Then, q_1 and q_2 are defined as follows:

$$q_1 = (u_1 - u_0)T + (v_1 - v_0)B \tag{9.2}$$

$$q_2 = (u_2 - u_0)T + (v_2 - v_0)B \tag{9.3}$$

As u_is and v_is are all known, we can simply rewrite Equations (9.2) and (9.3) as follows:

$$q_1 = u_{10}T + v_{10}B \tag{9.4}$$

$$q_2 = u_{20}T + v_{20}B \tag{9.5}$$

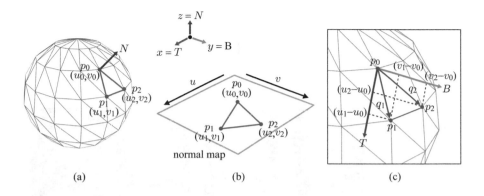

Fig. 9.13: Computing tangent space. (a) Three vertices of a triangle in the polygon mesh are associated with the texture coordinates (u_i, v_i)s. (b) The texture coordinate u_i of each vertex is defined with respect to the u-, x-, and T-axes, which are identical to each other. Similarly, v_i is defined with respect to the v-, y-, and B-axes, which are identical to each other. (c) Analysis of (u_i, v_i)s leads to the directions of the u- and v-axes, which equal the T- and B-axes, respectively.

where u_{10} abbreviates $(u_1 - u_0)$, and v_{10}, u_{20}, and v_{20} are similarly defined. We have two equations (Equations (9.4) and (9.5)) and two unknowns (T and B). More precisely, we have six equations and six unknowns because all of q_1, q_2, T, and B are 3D vectors. Let us combine Equations (9.4) and (9.5) into a linear system:

$$\begin{pmatrix} q_1 \\ q_2 \end{pmatrix} = \begin{pmatrix} u_{10} & v_{10} \\ u_{20} & v_{20} \end{pmatrix} \begin{pmatrix} T \\ B \end{pmatrix} \tag{9.6}$$

Solving the linear system, we obtain T and B.

Note that T and B obtained from Equation (9.6) are for the triangle shown in Fig. 9.13, not for vertex p_0 shared by multiple triangles. In order to compute the tangent space of p_0, the tangent vector T_i and the binormal vector B_i are computed for every triangle i sharing p_0. Then, T_is of all triangles are summed to define T'. Similarly, B' is defined.

T' and B' are not normalized and are not necessarily orthogonal to each other. Furthermore, they are not necessarily orthogonal to N. In order to convert $\{T', B', N\}$ into an orthonormal basis, the Gram-Schmidt algorithm is invoked. The orthonormal basis is the tangent-space basis for p_0. (See any linear algebra book for the Gram-Schmidt algorithm.) For the rest of this book, $\{T, B, N\}$ denotes the orthonormal basis of the per-vertex tangent space.

9.4   Authoring of Normal Map

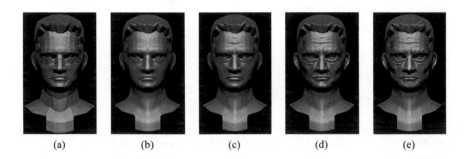

    (a)   (b)   (c)   (d)   (e)

Fig. 9.14: Sculpting. (a) shows the input low-resolution model, (b) shows a high-resolution model obtained by refining the low-resolution model, and the rest shows the results of successive sculpting operations to convert the high-resolution model in (b) to the high-frequency model in (e).

    The normal maps to be applied to planar or small-curvature surfaces can be created using a 2D graphics package, as presented earlier. However, the 2D package is not appropriate for creating a normal map for a complex surface. It is often replaced by a *sculpting tool* such as ZBrush[4]. Artists use a sculpting tool to create a high-resolution high-frequency model from a low-resolution smooth model. Then, the normal map is automatically created by the sculpting tool.

    Fig. 9.14 shows the step-by-step sculpting process. The original low-resolution model in Fig. 9.14-(a) is taken as the *macrostructure*. The high-frequency model in Fig. 9.14-(e) is taken as the *reference model*. Fig. 9.15-(a) shows the reference model overlapped with the macrostructure. (The reference model is drawn in purple-colored wireframe.) These two overlapped models are used to construct the normal map to be pasted to the macrostructure.

    First of all, the macrostructure is *parameterized* using the method presented in Section 4.1.2. Every vertex is assigned the normalized coordinates (u, v). Suppose that we want to create a normal map of resolution $s \times t$. Then, the coordinates (u, v) are multiplied by (s, t) to define the new coordinates (su, tv). Fig. 9.15-(b) shows the parameterized macrostructure, where a vertex has the coordinates (su, tv). Then, each triangle of the parameterized macrostructure

---

[4]ZBrush is a digital sculpting and painting program developed by Pixologic.

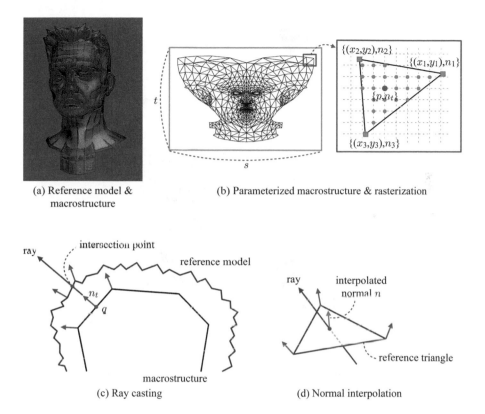

(a) Reference model &
macrostructure

(b) Parameterized macrostructure & rasterization

(c) Ray casting

(d) Normal interpolation

Fig. 9.15: Normal map creation through macrostructure parameterization and ray-triangle intersection.

is *rasterized* into a set of texels. See the magnified box in Fig. 9.15-(b). The original macrostructure is a 3D polygon mesh, and therefore a normal is associated with each vertex. The vertex normals are interpolated during rasterization such that each texel is assigned an interpolated normal. Let us denote the texel and interpolated normal by p and n_t, respectively.

Fig. 9.15-(c) illustrates in cross section a part of the 3D macrostructure overlapped with the reference model. The 3D point q corresponds to texel p. The barycentric coordinates of p with respect to the 2D triangle determine the 3D coordinates of q. A ray is cast along n_t (the interpolated normal) from q. The intersection between the ray and the reference model's triangle is computed. With respect to the reference triangle, the barycentric coordinates of the intersection point are computed. The barycentric coordinates are used to interpolate the vertex normals of the reference triangle, as shown in Fig. 9.15-(d). The interpolated normal n represents the surface normal of the

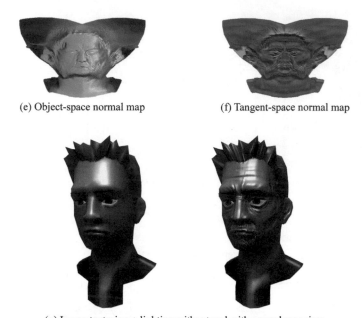

(e) Object-space normal map   (f) Tangent-space normal map

(g) Image texturing + lighting without and with normal mapping

Fig. 9.15:   Normal map creation through macrostructure parameterization and ray-triangle intersection (*continued*).

reference model. It is stored at the position of p in the normal map such that it can later be fetched using the texture coordinates (u, v).

In Fig. 9.15-(c), the macrostructure and reference model do not intersect each other. In reality, however, they usually intersect. Further, a ray may hit multiple triangles of the reference model. Fortunately, existing normal-map creation tools handle those subtleties. (There are many other normal-map creation tools besides ZBrush. They include the tools developed by NVIDIA and AMD.)

Note that the normal computed through the above process is defined in the object space. Therefore, the texture storing such normals is called an *object-space normal map*. It is drawn in Fig. 9.15-(e). The object-space normal map does not have any dominant color because the surface normals of the reference model have quite diverse directions. The object-space normals can be converted into the tangent-space normals and then stored in the normal map. It is the tangent-space normal map.

It is straightforward to convert an object-space normal into a tangent-space normal. See Fig. 9.15-(c). For each vertex of the triangle where q lies, a tangent space can be computed (using the algorithm presented in Section

Fig. 9.16: Normal mapping is used for representing highly detailed surfaces. (Image from Unreal Tournament® 3. Unreal, Unreal Tournament and Epic Games are trademarks or registered trademarks of Epic Games, Inc. All rights reserved.)

9.3.2). Then, the *TBN*-basis of q's tangent space is computed by interpolating the per-vertex *TBN*-bases. For interpolation, q's barycentric coordinates are used. The *TBN* vectors for q form the rotation matrix presented in Equation (9.1). It converts the object-space normal n into the tangent space. Fig. 9.15-(f) shows the tangent-space normal map drawn in RGB colors. The dominant color is blue, as is the case in most tangent-space normal maps.

Fig. 9.15-(g) compares the rendering results with and without normal mapping. Fig. 9.16 shows normal-mapped in-game characters. Normal mapping is ubiquitous in contemporary games.

9.5 Parallax Mapping

In normal mapping, the surface normals are perturbed for per-fragment lighting, but the height field per se is not used at run time. As a result, several problems can be observed. The problem of polygonal silhouette was already presented. Another problem is that the bumps do not appear to occlude each other, and no *motion parallax* is exhibited. (Motion parallax refers to the apparent displacement of an object relative to another object, which is caused by viewpoint change.)

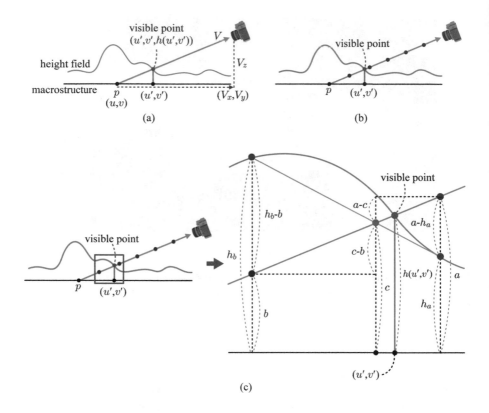

Fig. 9.17: Parallax mapping algorithm. (a) The height field is searched for the visible point. (b) Discrete ray tracing is performed using a set of sampled points. (c) Once a sample point above the height field and another below the height field are identified, root finding procedure is invoked.

Parallax mapping has been proposed as an effort to provide the parallax effect. In general, parallax mapping searches the height map for the *visible point* $(u', v', h(u', v'))$ shown in Fig. 9.17-(a). In the figure, the following can be derived using similar triangles:

$$(u', v') = (u, v) + h(u', v')(\frac{V_x}{V_z}, \frac{V_y}{V_z}) \qquad (9.7)$$

where (V_x, V_y, V_z) are the coordinates of the view vector V in the tangent space. V and (u, v) are known, and therefore (u', v') can be obtained if $h(u', v')$ is computed.

Computing $h(u', v')$ requires tracing V in its opposite direction. It is a simplified *ray tracing*[5]. In Fig. 9.17-(b), the ray connecting the current fragment p and the viewpoint is regularly sampled at discrete points. Starting from the viewpoint, each sample point is visited one by one to test if it is above or below the height field. If above, discrete ray tracing is continued. Once a point is found to be below the height field, the point and its previous sample point (that is above the height field) are selected. The visible point is located between the two sample points.

Fig. 9.17-(c) zooms in on the visible point of Fig. 9.17-(b) and denotes the heights of the selected sample points by a and b. Let h_a and h_b denote the height field values at the sample points. Then, the "height differences" at the sampled points are defined by $(a - h_a)$ and $(h_b - b)$. In Fig. 9.17-(c), the gold-color vertex with height c is shared by two triangles whose base edge lengths are $(a - h_a)$ and $(h_b - b)$. The similarity of the triangles leads to the following:

$$\frac{a - c}{a - h_a} = \frac{c - b}{h_b - b}$$

Then, c is computed as follows:

$$\frac{a(h_b - b) + b(a - h_a)}{(h_b - b) + (a - h_a)}$$

Once c is computed, it can be taken as an approximation to $h(u', v')$. Then, c replaces $h(u', v')$ in Equation (9.7), and (u', v') are determined. They are used to fetch the normal from the normal map and the color from the image texture.

However, notice that c and $h(u', v')$ are not identical in most cases. A more elaborate algorithm takes the on-the-ray point of height c as a new sample point and tests if it is above or below the height field. (In the example, it is below the height field.) Then, a new pair of sample points, where one is above and the other is below the height field, is selected. (In the example, the new pair's heights are a and c.) With the pair, the root finding procedure is repeated.

Fig. 9.18-(a) and -(b) show the results of normal mapping and parallax mapping, respectively. Note that, in Fig. 9.18-(b), some part of mortar is occluded by the bricks. Such an effect is not observed in the result of normal mapping. On the other hand, the silhouettes still reveal the low-frequency polygon mesh used for the macrostructure. Fig. 9.19 shows a parallax-mapped in-game scene.

---

[5]The evolving GPU has made it possible to implement real-time ray tracing for some limited domains, and parallax mapping is an application in such domains. Parallax mapping was first proposed by Kaneko *et al.* [27] and since then has been improved by many researchers. Parallax mapping based on ray tracing is often called *relief mapping* or *parallax occlusion mapping*.

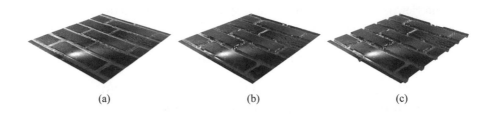

Fig. 9.18: Comparison of bump mapping results. (a) Normal mapping. (b) Parallax mapping. (c) Displacement mapping.

Fig. 9.19: Parallax mapping example. (Image from CryENGINE, Crysis and Crysis Warhead. Crytek, CryENGINE, Crysis and Crysis Warhead are registered trademarks or trademarks of Crytek GmbH in the USA, Germany and other countries. All rights reserved.)

9.6 Displacement Mapping

Unlike normal mapping and parallax mapping, where the underlying geometry of the macrostructure is not altered, *displacement mapping* tessellates the macrostructure on the fly and then displaces the vertices of the tessellated mesh using the height field. Even though displacement mapping has been widely used in off-line rendering systems such as PhotoRealistic RenderMan, it was beyond the capability of real-time applications until recently.

In Shader Model 3, no part of GPU could generate additional vertices, and therefore the macrostructure could not be tessellated. In Shader Model 4, the geometry shader can generate additional vertices on the fly. However, it is not sufficiently efficient to fully implement displacement mapping. The advent of Shader Model 5 makes displacement mapping attractive due to its hardware tessellation support. In fact, displacement mapping is one of the most distinguished applications that benefit from the new pipeline of Shader Model 5.

Fig. 9.20 illustrates the process of displacement mapping in Shader Model 5. Shown in Fig. 9.20-(a) is the macrostructure. The vertex buffer contains just nine vertices. The vertex shader processes them. Then, the macrostructure is tessellated into a high-resolution mesh shown in Fig. 9.20-(b). Using a height map, the vertices of the tessellated mesh are displaced to produce the high-frequency mesh shown in Fig. 9.20-(c). The height map is *filtered* to determine the per-vertex displacement vector. This is done by the domain shader with the aid of tessellator. Fig. 9.20-(d) shows the final rendering result with the brick-wall image textured.

Returning to Fig. 9.18, compare the result of displacement mapping with those of normal mapping and parallax mapping, and find that the silhouettes now have highly-detailed geometry. It is not surprising because the vertices at the silhouettes have been displaced in displacement mapping. Fig. 9.21 shows a displacement-mapped in-game scene.

Displacement mapping has also drawbacks. For example, it is not straightforward to set the tessellation factor to an appropriate value. The macrostructure that is highly tessellated may often take just a small fractional area in the screen. It is needed to adaptively tessellate the macrostructure at a granularity suitable for the image being rendered. Worse still, the work of displacement mapping may be in vain for some parts of the macrostructure, e.g., invisible parts. Pre-computing visibility might be needed [28].

Whereas displacement mapping is an *object-space algorithm* that operates on 3D objects, normal mapping and parallax mapping are *image-space algorithms* that operate on fragments or pixels. They are much less prone to process invisible parts of the scene, compared with the displacement mapping algorithm. Normal mapping and parallax mapping are also independent of the scene complexity.

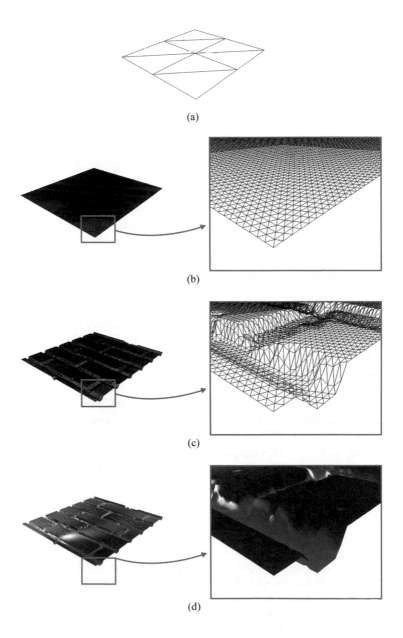

(a)

(b)

(c)

(d)

Fig. 9.20:   Displacement mapping in Shader Model 5. (a) The macrostructure is composed of eight triangles. (b) In this example, the tessellation factor is set to 63, and the macrostructure is tessellated into 47,624 triangles. (c) Displacement mapping is done using a 103×103-resolution height map. (d) The high-frequency mesh is image-textured.

(a)

(b)

(c)

Fig. 9.21: Displacement mapping example. (a) The macrostructure is drawn in white wireframe. (b) The macrostructure is tessellated and displaced. (c) The high-frequency mesh is image-textured. (This figure is generated using Heaven 2.1 based on the Unigine^{TM} engine from Unigine Corp.)

[Note: Height map and terrain rendering]

This chapter has presented the use of height map only for bump mapping. Note that, however, the height map is the most popular representation of terrain and is also frequently used for representing fluid or water surface. Fig. 9.22-(a) and -(b) respectively show a gray-scale height map and an image texture for a mountain area. A triangle mesh can be generated from a height map. Fig. 9.22-(c) shows how a height map in Fig. 9.3-(a) is converted into a triangle mesh. Fig. 9.22-(d) shows a part of triangle mesh generated from the height map of Fig. 9.22-(a). The triangle mesh can be textured and rendered, as shown in Fig. 9.22-(e).

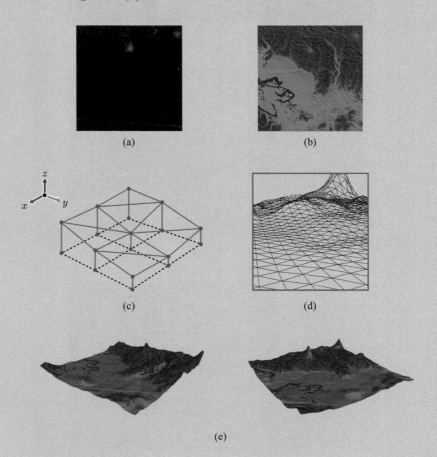

(a)

(b)

(c)

(d)

(e)

Fig. 9.22: Terrain rendering using height map and image texture. (The data were originally from the United States Geological Survey (USGS) and were processed by the authors of the paper [29].)

Exercises

1. Fig. 9.6 uses the finite difference method to compute the normal at a height field point. Describe another method that computes the normal using the surface normals of the triangles sharing the point.

2. Consider the cylinder and its parameterization shown in Fig. 4.5-(a). Suppose that the axis of the cylinder is y-axis of the coordinate system. Normal mapping is to be applied to its surface. Describe how you can compute a tangent space for each vertex (x, y, z). (You are not allowed to use any information from other vertices.)

3. The parallax mapping presented in this chapter discretely samples the ray. Such a discrete algorithm may miss some intersections. Describe why it may happen, and how you would solve or alleviate the problem.

Chapter 10

Advanced Texturing

The demand for high-quality rendering has led to the increase in computing power and programmability of GPU. Many attempts have been made to utilize the GPU power and extend the lighting functions beyond the local illumination model. As a result, a global illumination look has been increasingly added to the images generated at real time. In the algorithms developed along the trend, textures play key roles. This chapter presents a few representative algorithms that use textures for more realistic shading.

10.1 Environment Mapping

Environment mapping simulates a shiny object reflecting its surrounding environment. Fig. 10.1 shows an example. The first task for environment mapping is to capture the environment images in a texture called an *environment map*. Among several implementations, the most popular is a cubic environment map, simply referred to as a *cube map*. It consists of six square faces. Each face contains an image of the environment.

Fig. 10.1: The teapot surface reflects its surrounding environment.

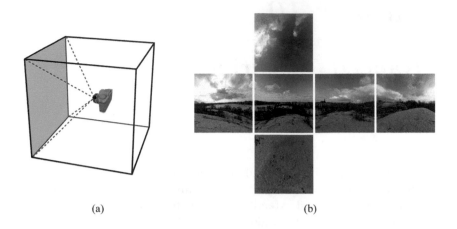

Fig. 10.2:   Cube map authoring. (a) The environment is captured or rendered along six view directions. (b) Six images are organized into a cube map. (Image courtesy of Emil Persson.)

10.1.1   Cube Mapping

Consider an imaginary cube at the center of which a camera is located, as shown in Fig. 10.2-(a). The environment can be captured onto the six faces of the cube such that each face covers a 90° field of view both vertically and horizontally. In order to build a cube map upon such a set of six images, we can use a 2D graphics package's tool, e.g., Photoshop plug-in named NVIDIA DDS Exporter[1]. Fig. 10.2-(b) shows an unfolded form of a cube map.

Fig. 10.3-(a) illustrates a cube map in cross section. Conceptually, it surrounds the object to be environment-mapped. Suppose that a surface point p reflects the environment. To determine the reflected color at p, a ray denoted by I is fired from the viewpoint toward p. It is reflected with respect to the surface normal n at p. The reflection vector R is computed as follows:

$$R = I - 2n(n \cdot I) \qquad (10.1)$$

(This is identical to Equation (5.12) presented in the section of ray tracing for global illumination.) R intersects a face of the cube map. Then, the image associated with the face is filtered to fetch the texels hit by R. They determine the reflected color at p. Environment mapping is often called a *simplified* ray tracing in the sense that only the one-bounce reflection vector (R) is traced.

Cube mapping is widely used and is supported by hardware. For example, HLSL provides a library function texCUBE(). It takes a cube map and R as

---

[1]DDS stands for DirectDraw Surface. The DDS file format was introduced with Direct3D 7 and is widely used to store textures.

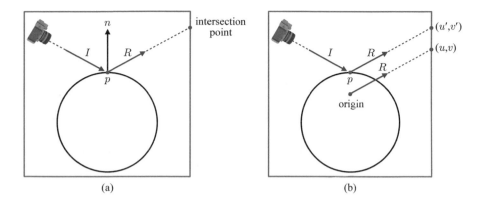

Fig. 10.3: Cube mapping. (a) The cube map (illustrated as a box) surrounds an object. A ray fired from the viewpoint is traced to determine the color reflected at p. (b) The cube map should be referenced using (u', v'), but the cube mapping algorithm uses (u, v). Only when the environment is infinitely far away, (u, v) and (u', v') will lead to the same filtering result.

input and returns an RGB color. Section 10.1.2 presents the internal mechanism of texCUBE(), i.e., how to identify the face hit by R and how to convert R into the texture coordinates (u, v) used for filtering the face's image.

Notice that R is a vector and is independent of the start point. It causes an error. See Fig. 10.3-(b). The cube map should be referenced using (u', v') returned by "the ray starting from p." However, texCUBE() actually uses "the ray starting from the origin." It returns (u, v), which are obviously different from (u', v'). Only when the environment is infinitely far away, the scene points hit by the two rays are captured at an identical texel of the cube map. Fortunately, people are fairly forgiving about the incorrectness that results when the environment is not sufficiently far away.

It is simple to implement environment mapping, and the result is fairly pleasing. Environment mapping is often taken as an effort toward global illumination, and in fact it adds a global illumination look to the images generated by a local illumination model. However, it is just a small step out of local illumination and does not sufficiently overcome its limitations. For example, the concave reflector does not reflect itself.

10.1.2 Cube Map Access*

The cube map faces are named $\{+x, -x, +y, -y, +z, -z\}$. See Fig. 10.4. The name of each face is taken from the axis pointing the face, and the remaining two axes constitute the 2D basis of the face. The coordinate system in Fig. 10.4 is left-handed.

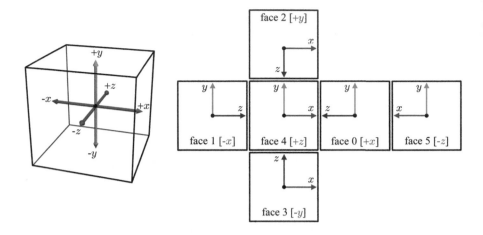

Fig. 10.4: Each face of the cube map is assigned a name and is associated with a unique 2D basis.

Once the reflection vector R is computed, the face intersected by R can be immediately identified using R's coordinate that has the largest absolute value. For example, suppose that R is $(-0.5, 0.4, -0.2)$, as shown in Fig. 10.5-(a). The x-coordinate has the largest absolute value and is negative. Therefore, face $-x$ is selected. Then, the yz-coordinates of R are divided by the absolute value of the x-coordinate to produce a 2D intersection point at face $-x$. The point hit by R has the yz-coordinates $(0.8, -0.4)$ at face $-x$.

The intersection point is then converted to the texture coordinates (u, v), following the flow shown in Fig. 10.5-(b). Note the discrepancy between the cube-face space (shown in the first picture) and the parameter space (shown in the last picture). In the cube-face space, the y- and z-axes run upward and to the right, respectively. In contrast, the u- and v-axes of the parameter space run to the right and downward, respectively. The first two steps in Fig. 10.5-(b) make the bases coincide.

In the third picture of Fig. 10.5-(b), the cube-face coordinates $(-0.4, -0.8)$ are in the range of $[-1,1]$. They have to be converted into the texture coordinates range $[0,1]$. The last step in Fig. 10.5-(b) shows the range conversion. The computed texture coordinates are $(0.3, 0.1)$. Note that the *relative* location of the original yz-coordinates $(0.8, -0.4)$ within the 2×2-sized face $-x$ is the same as that of the texture coordinates $(0.3, 0.1)$ within the 1×1-sized parameter space. The texture coordinates $(0.3, 0.1)$ are used to filter the image texture stored at face $-x$. For each of the other five faces, similar conversions are needed to obtain the texture coordinates if the face is located by the largest absolute coordinate of R.

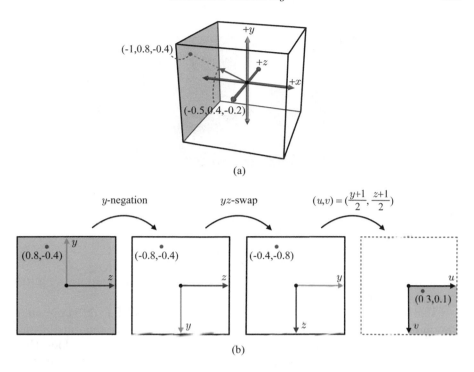

(a)

(b)

Fig. 10.5: Converting R into the texture coordinates (u, v). (a) The face intersected by R is identified, and the intersection point is computed. (b) The intersection point is converted into (u, v).

10.1.3 Dynamic Cube Mapping

A cube map is often created at a preprocessing stage. Fig. 10.2 shows an example. The images are captured by a real camera. However, a cube map can be created at run time and then immediately used for environment mapping. This technique is called dynamic cube mapping.

Note that the environment has to be rendered six times, once per cube face. Prior to Shader Model 4, the rendering pipeline should be run six times for this purpose. In Shader Model 4, however, a cube map can be created in a single pass, using the geometry shader (GS) and multiple render targets (MRT).

A *render target*[2] refers to a general off-screen buffer. MRT enables the rendering pipeline to produce images to multiple render target textures at once. In Shader Models 4, a fragment shader can write up to eight render

---

[2]It is the terminology of Direct3D and is analogous to the frame buffer object (FBO) architecture in OpenGL.

Fig. 10.6: Dynamic environment mapping is applied to the automobile surface. (Courtesy of Crash Time 3, Synetic.)

target textures simultaneously. Obviously, dynamic cube mapping requires six render targets.

Recall that the GS can emit zero or more primitives. For dynamic cube mapping, the GS replicates the incoming primitive into six separate primitives, one for a render target. For the purpose, the GS runs a `for` loop that iterates six times. At each iteration, a view matrix that is distinct per face transforms the primitive into the camera space[3]. Then, a projection matrix that is common to all faces transforms the primitive to the clip space. Each primitive is rasterized on the render target which it is assigned to.

Once a cube map is dynamically created in a single pass, the next rendering pass uses the cube map for creating environment-mapped objects. Dynamic cube mapping is an instance of two-pass rendering algorithms. (Prior to Shader Model 4, dynamic cube mapping requires seven passes in total, i.e., six passes for constructing the cube map and a pass for rendering the final scene.) Fig. 10.6 shows the snapshots of a dynamic environment-mapped object.

10.2 Light Mapping

When the scene and light sources are static, we can pre-compute part of the diffuse reflections, store the results in a texture named a *light map*, and then look up the light map at run time. This technique is called *light mapping*.

---

[3]As can be found in Fig. 10.2-(a), each face of the cube map is associated with its own **AT** and **UP** even though **EYE** is common to six faces. It implies that each face requires a distinct view transform.

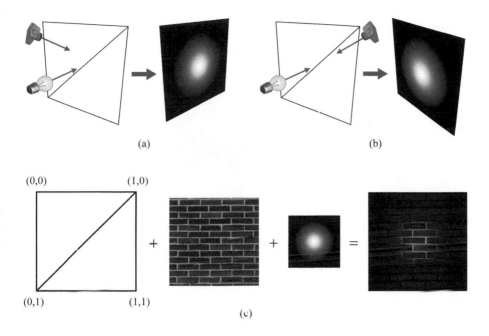

Fig. 10.7: Light mapping. (a) Both the object and the light source are static. The diffuse reflections on the object surface are captured from a viewpoint. (b) The viewpoint changes, but the diffuse reflections do not change. (c) Image texturing + light mapping.

10.2.1 Diffuse Light Mapping

Suppose that a character navigates a static environment illuminated by static light sources. Fig. 10.7-(a) shows a simple example, where a light source is fixed in front of a quad. The quad is assumed to be a Lambertian surface. Then, the reflected colors over the quad surface remain constant independently of the camera position. Fig. 10.7-(b) illustrates the quad rendered from a different viewpoint. The surface colors do not change. In rendering such a scene, light mapping increases the run-time performance.

When creating a light map, there is no real-time constraint. Therefore, we can use a lighting model that is more expensive than the one that would be used at run time. In most cases, the light map is computed using the radiosity algorithm presented in Section 5.4.2. Consequently, light-mapped scenes usually show higher quality than the ones locally illuminated. This is another advantage added to the increased run-time performance. Quake II released in 1997 was the first commercial game that used the light map.

The method for creating a light map is similar to the one for creating a normal map presented in Section 9.4. The surface to be light-mapped is

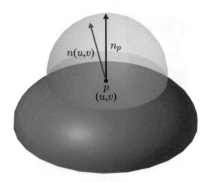

Fig. 10.8:   The normal fetched from the normal map is $n(u, v)$, but n_p is used for computing a light map.

parameterized and rasterized in a texture. For each sampled surface point corresponding to a texel, *irradiance* (incoming light) is computed. (Section 5.4.2 presented how to compute the irradiances.) The irradiance values are stored in the texture. It is the light map.

In general, the light map is combined with the image texture at run time, as illustrated in Fig. 10.7-(c). The diffuse reflectance is read from the image texture, incoming light is read from the light map, and they are multiplied to determine the diffuse reflection color. The light map is usually made much smaller than the image texture because diffuse reflection varies over a surface in a low-frequency manner.

10.2.2   Radiosity Normal Mapping*

In general, the radiosity algorithm is used for creating a light map. Recall that, as presented in Section 5.4.2, radiosity computation adopts the concept of *hemisphere*. Its orientation is defined by the surface normal n_p, as shown in Fig. 10.8. Consider combining light mapping and normal mapping. The normal $n(u, v)$ fetched from the normal map is the *perturbed* instance of n_p. If lighting were computed on the fly, $n(u, v)$ would be used. However, the light map that is going to partly replace lighting computation was created using the *unperturbed* normal n_p.

A simple solution to this discrepancy would be to use the perturbed normals stored in the normal map when the light map is created. Then, the light map would have the same resolution as the normal map. It is unnecessarily large. (Discussion on the resolution issue is presented at the end of this subsection.) Another solution has been implemented in the well-known game, Half-Life 2, leading to significant reduction of the light map resolution. It is named *radiosity normal mapping*.

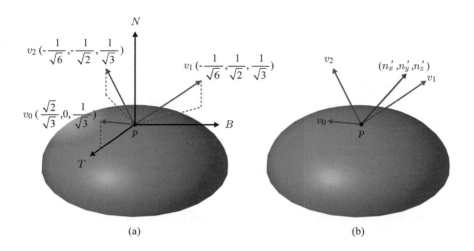

Fig. 10.9: Basis for radiosity normal mapping. (a) A new basis $\{v_0, v_1, v_2\}$ is defined. (b) The normal fetched from the normal map is transformed into the basis $\{v_0, v_1, v_2\}$.

Consider surface point p in Fig. 10.9-(a). Its tangent space is $\{p, T, B, N\}$. Three vectors, v_0, v_1, and v_2, are pre-defined in the tangent space. They are around N and evenly distributed over the space. Further, $\{v_0, v_1, v_2\}$ forms an *orthonormal basis*. Let us transform each v_i into the world space, place a hemisphere for each of them, and run the radiosity preprocessor. Then, incoming light is computed per v_i, and three different colors are computed for p. If we repeat this for all sampled points of the object surface, we obtain three light maps for the object. Each light map depends on the direction of v_i and is often called a *directional light map*.

At run time, the directional light maps are *blended*. Suppose that the normal $n(u, v)$ fetched from the normal map has the coordinates (n_x, n_y, n_z). It is a tangent-space normal and can be redefined in terms of the basis $\{v_0, v_1, v_2\}$ by the following *basis-change* (rotation) matrix:

$$\begin{pmatrix} v_0 \\ v_1 \\ v_2 \end{pmatrix} = \begin{pmatrix} \frac{\sqrt{2}}{\sqrt{3}} & 0 & \frac{1}{\sqrt{3}} \\ -\frac{1}{\sqrt{6}} & \frac{1}{\sqrt{2}} & \frac{1}{\sqrt{3}} \\ -\frac{1}{\sqrt{6}} & -\frac{1}{\sqrt{2}} & \frac{1}{\sqrt{3}} \end{pmatrix} \qquad (10.2)$$

Let (n'_x, n'_y, n'_z) denote the transformed normal. They represent the coordinates with respect to the basis $\{v_0, v_1, v_2\}$. Suppose that, for example, (n'_x, n'_y, n'_z) equal $(1,0,0)$. Then, only the light map associated with v_0 contributes to lighting at p. Another example is shown in Fig. 10.9-(b), where n'_y would be larger than n'_x and n'_z, and therefore the light map associated with v_1 would contribute more than those with v_0 and v_2.

```
float3 normal = 2.0 * normalTexel - 1.0;
float3 dp;
dp.x = saturate(dot(normal, radiosityBasis[0]));
dp.y = saturate(dot(normal, radiosityBasis[1]));
dp.z = saturate(dot(normal, radiosityBasis[2]));
dp *= dp;

float3 diffuseLighting = dp.x * lightmapColor[0]+
                         dp.y * lightmapColor[1]+
                         dp.z * lightmapColor[2];

float sum = dot(dp, float3(1.0f, 1.0f, 1.0f));
diffuseLighting /= sum;
```

The above box shows how the directional light maps are blended in practice. First of all, the normal (`normalTexel`) read from the normal map is scaled and biased. In the following statements, `radiosityBasis` represents v_is, `dot()` denotes the dot product operation, `saturate()` clamps its input to be in the range of $[0,1]^4$, and `lightmapColor` represents texels from three light maps. (For further discussions on optimization of the radiosity normal mapping algorithm, readers are referred to [30].)

Let us discuss the resolution issue in light mapping. We will find that the resolution of the directional light maps is much lower than that of the normal map. Fig. 10.10-(a) illustrates a macrostructure (in cross section) with a set of sampled points, for which the surface normals of the reference model are computed. (If this is not clear, read Section 9.4.) The normals are stored in a normal map.

Fig. 10.10-(b) shows two hemispheres used for creating the directional light maps. They are placed at sparsely sampled points, s_1 and s_2. In the cross-section view, consider only two basis vectors, leading to two directional light maps: one generated using the blue vectors (which we call 'blue map' for convenience) and the other using the red vectors (which we call 'red map').

Suppose that, in Fig. 10.10-(b), a fragment f_1 is processed at run time, and n_1 is fetched from the normal map. Then, the directional light maps are accessed to interpolate the irradiance values computed at s_1 and s_2. The blue vectors and n_1 have similar directions, and therefore the diffuse reflection at f_1 is determined mostly by the blue map. A correct color would be obtained for f_1. Similarly, when n_2 is fetched for another fragment f_2, the red map

---

[4]Note that $n(u, v)$ and v_i may form an obtuse angle. Then, their dot product becomes negative.

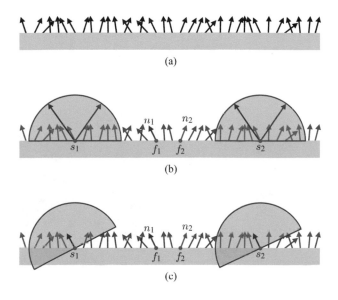

Fig. 10.10: Light map resolutions for radiosity normal mapping and traditional light mapping. (a) The macrostructure is densely sampled. The normal map stores the normals computed at the samples. (b) The directional light maps may have a lower resolution than the normal map, and therefore the macrostructure is sparsely sampled. When two fragment, f_1 and f_2, are processed at run time, the directional light maps would provide appropriate colors for both f_1 and f_2. (c) If the traditional light map has the same resolution as the directional light maps, it would provide an incorrect light color for f_2.

mostly contributes to lighting because the red vectors and n_2 have similar directions. We would obtain a correct color for f_2. This example shows that the directional light maps are allowed to have a lower resolution than the normal map.

Now suppose that the traditional light map (not the directional light maps) is created using the normal map. Let us take the same set of sparsely sampled points, $\{s_1, s_2\}$, as shown in Fig. 10.10-(c). At each sample, the irradiance is computed using the perturbed normal read from the normal map. In the current example, the normals at s_1 and s_2 happen to be similar.

Suppose that, in Fig. 10.10-(c), n_1 is fetched for f_1 at run time. Then, the color obtained by filtering the light map would be appropriate because n_1 and the perturbed normals at s_1 and s_2 have similar directions. However, n_2 fetched for f_2 is quite different from the normals used for creating the light map, and consequently an inappropriate color would be provided for f_2. In order to avoid this problem, the light map needs the same sampling rate as the normal map. It is unnecessarily high.

10.3 Shadow Mapping

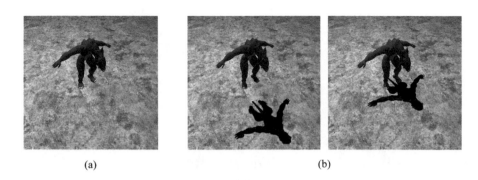

(a)   (b)

Fig. 10.11: Shadows are helpful for understanding the structure of a 3D scene. (a) Little information is provided about the spatial relationship between the character and the ground. (b) The shadows enable us to perceive the character landing at the ground.

Shadows in a rendered image increase its visual realism. They also help us understand the spatial relationships among objects in a scene, especially between the *occluders* and *receivers*. (Occluders cast shadows onto receivers.) In Fig. 10.11-(a), the relative pose of the character against the ground is not clear. In contrast, given the successive snapshots in Fig. 10.11-(b), we can easily recognize a character (occluder) landing at the ground (receiver).

Numerous shadow algorithms have been proposed for the past decades, and it is still an on-going research topic to generate realistic shadows at real time. Two main streams in shadow generation have been along the *shadow volume* algorithm proposed by F. Crow [31] and the *shadow mapping* algorithm proposed by L. Williams [32]. A shadow volume is an object-space 3D volume occluded from a light source. Every pixel is tested if it belongs to the shadow volume. In contrast, shadow mapping is a texture-based image-space technique. This section focuses on the shadow mapping algorithm and presents its essential ingredients.

A point light source generates *hard shadows*. See Fig. 10.12-(a). A surface point in the receiver is either fully lit by or fully occluded from the light source. There is a clear boundary between the fully lit region and the fully shadowed region. In contrast, an area or volumetric light source generates *soft shadows*. See Fig. 10.12-(b). The shadows are described as soft due to the *penumbra* (partially shadowed) region which is located between the

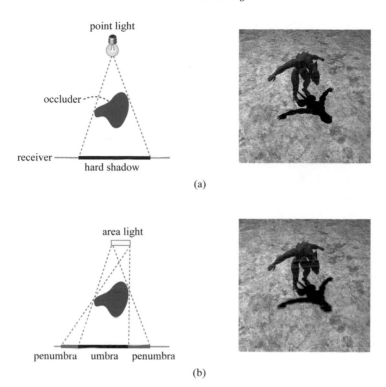

Fig. 10.12: Hard and soft shadows. (a) A surface point on the receiver is either fully lit or fully shadowed. The hard shadow has a clear boundary. (b) A surface point in the penumbra region is partially shadowed. Consequently, the shadow has a soft boundary.

umbra (fully shadowed) region and the fully lit region. A surface point in the penumbra region receives only part of the light from the light source.

Both the shadow volume and shadow mapping algorithms have been extended along many directions so as to generate soft shadows at real time [33]. However, presenting the soft shadow algorithms is beyond the scope of this book, and this section presents hard shadow generation using the shadow mapping algorithm.

10.3.1 Algorithm for Shadow Mapping

Shadow mapping algorithm goes through two rendering passes. The first pass constructs a *shadow map*, which is a *depth map* with respect to the light source. By placing the viewpoint at the light source position, the scene is rendered, and the depth values of the scene are stored in the shadow map.

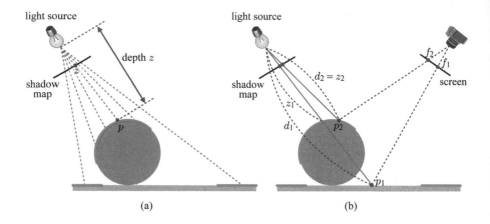

(a)   (b)

Fig. 10.13: Two-pass algorithm for shadow mapping. (a) The first pass generates a shadow map. (b) The second pass uses the shadow map to test whether a scene point is visible from the light source.

See Fig. 10.13-(a). The cyan bold lines represent the surfaces lit by the light source, i.e., visible from the light source. Consider a visible point p. The distance between p and the light source is p's depth. It is denoted by z and is stored in the shadow map. During the first pass, neither lighting nor texturing is performed, but only the depth values of the scene are recorded.

At the second pass, the scene is rendered from the camera position. In Fig. 10.13-(b), consider fragment f_1 and its world-space point p_1. The distance d_1 between p_1 and the light source is compared with the depth value z_1 of the shadow map. It is found that $d_1 > z_1$, which implies that something occludes p_1 from the light source, i.e., p_1 is not visible from the light source. Therefore, p_1 is determined to be in shadows. In contrast, consider fragment f_2 in the figure. It is found that d_2 equals z_2, i.e., p_2 is visible from the light source. Therefore, p_2 is determined to be lit.

In Fig. 10.13-(b), f_2's world-space point p_2 is assumed to coincide with a point sampled at the first pass. Unfortunately, this kind of coincidence rarely happens in reality. The scene points sampled at the second pass are usually different from the scene points sampled at the first pass.

Fig. 10.14-(a) shows a scene configuration, and Fig. 10.14-(b) shows the rendering result, where a mixture of shadowed and lit areas is generated. This artefact is called *surface acne*. Fig. 10.14-(c) explains why we have the artefact. The scene point p_1 (for fragment f_1) does not coincide with any surface point sampled at the first pass. Assume that *nearest point sampling* is adopted for filtering the shadow map. Then, z_1 will be read from the shadow map. As $d_1 > z_1$, p_1 will be determined to be shadowed. (It is incorrect.) On the other hand, consider fragment f_2 that is adjacent to f_1. The scene

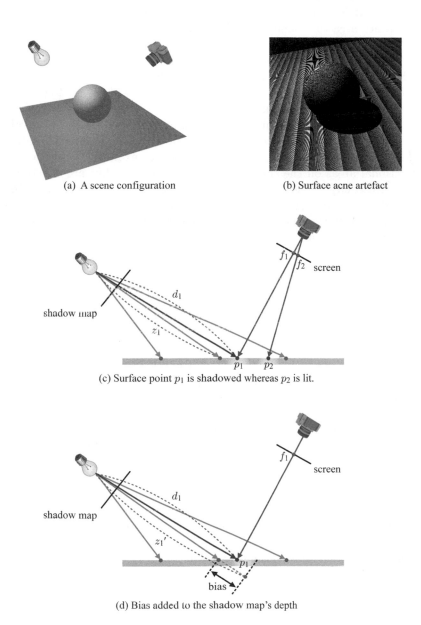

(a) A scene configuration

(b) Surface acne artefact

(c) Surface point p_1 is shadowed whereas p_2 is lit.

(d) Bias added to the shadow map's depth

Fig. 10.14: Surface acne artefact and texture resolution dependency in shadow mapping.

point for f_2 is p_2, and it will be determined to be lit through nearest point sampling. (It is correct.) Consequently, the shadowed and lit pixels coexist on a surface area that should be entirely lit.

The surface acne artefact can be avoided by moving the surface geometry away from the light source by a small amount, i.e., by adding a *bias* to the depth value read from the shadow map. In Fig. 10.14-(d), a bias value is added to z_1 to make z_1'. Then, $d_1 < z_1'$, and so p_1 will be lit. Fig. 10.14-(e) shows the result of biased shadow mapping.

It is important to appropriately determine the bias. If the bias value is too small, the surface acne artefact would not be completely eliminated but could just be reduced. Fig. 10.14-(f) shows an example, where a number of fractional areas on the sphere surface should be lit but are shadowed. In contrast, too large a bias also leads to incorrect shadows, as shown in Fig. 10.14-(g). Some areas that should be shadowed are erroneously taken as lit, and consequently the shadow appears smaller than desired. The bias value is usually fixed through a few trials[5].

Another major problem of shadow mapping is that the shadow quality is sensitive to the shadow map resolution. If the resolution of a shadow map is not high enough, multiple pixels may be mapped to a single texel of the shadow map. Fig. 10.14-(h) illustrates an example. Then, the generated shadow may appear blocky, as shown in the left image of Fig. 10.14-(i). Many algorithms have been proposed to resolve this problem. The simplest solution is to increase the shadow map resolution. Fig. 10.14-(i) shows how the shadow quality gets improved as the shadow map resolution increases. Unfortunately, this solution is expensive because the shadow map may consume a large area of the graphics memory.

Observe that Fig. 10.14-(h) is an example of the *magnification* case, presented in Section 8.2.1, where the number of pixels projected onto the texture space is greater than the number of texels. Section 8.2.1 introduced two filtering methods for magnification, nearest point sampling and bilinear interpolation, and showed that the bilinear interpolation method usually produces a better result. You might think of replacing the nearest point sampling method by the bilinear interpolation method in order to reduce the blocky shadow artefact. However, the problem is not so simple, and the bilinear interpolation method does not help. Section 10.3.3 discusses this issue in detail and presents a solution.

---

[5]The bias value can be set to a constant, or can be made proportional to the angle of the receiver to the direction of the incoming light. If the receiver is orthogonal to the light direction, the bias value can be kept small. Otherwise, it needs to be increased.

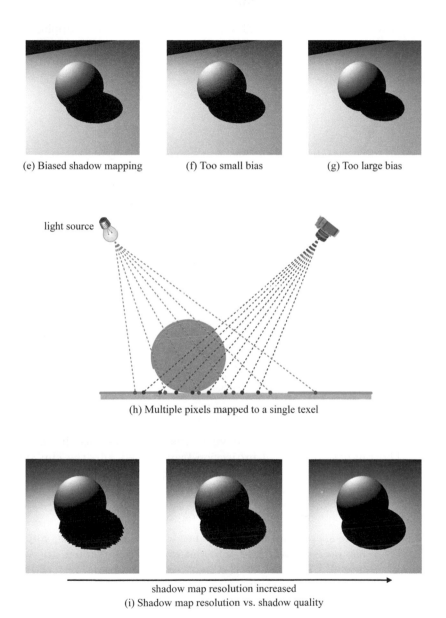

(e) Biased shadow mapping   (f) Too small bias   (g) Too large bias

light source

(h) Multiple pixels mapped to a single texel

shadow map resolution increased
(i) Shadow map resolution vs. shadow quality

Fig. 10.14: Surface acne artefact and texture resolution dependency in shadow mapping (*continued*).

10.3.2   Shader Codes for Shadow Mapping[*]

This subsection presents the full shader codes for shadow mapping algorithm. A pair of vertex and fragment shaders is given for each pass. It might not be easy to follow the shader codes. If you are not interested in the programming details, skip this subsection.

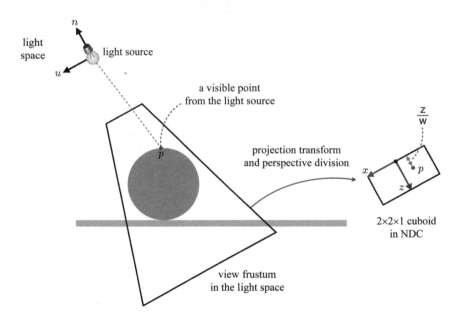

Fig. 10.15: At the first pass, the view frustum is specified in the light space. The sampled point p is projection-transformed into the clip space. Due to perspective division, p is defined in NDC within the 2×2×1 cuboid. The depth of p will be used at the second pass.

Let us detail the spaces and transforms needed for the first pass. Suppose that a vertex has been transformed into the world space through the world transform. Then, **EYE** is set to the light source position, i.e., the view parameters are specified "with respect to the light source." Consequently, the view-transformed vertices are defined in the so-called *light space*, not in the camera space. The view frustum is then specified in the light space. Shown in the left of Fig. 10.15 are the light space and the view frustum specified in it. (The light source position and $\{u, v, n\}$ axes constitute the light space. Only the u- and n-axes are illustrated in the cross-section figure.)

```
void VS_pass1 (float4 Pos : POSITION,
               out float4 oPos : POSITION,   // clip space
               out float2 oLightPos : TEXCOORD0,
           uniform float4x4 lightWVP)
{
  oPos = mul(lightWVP, Pos);
  oLightPos.xy = oPos.zw;
}

void FS_pass1 (float2 oLightPos : TEXCOORD0,
               out float4 Color : COLOR)
{
  Color = oLightPos.x/oLightPos.y;   // NDC depth z/w in [0,1]
}
```

In the above vertex shader, `lightWVP` is the combination of the world, view, and projection transforms, where the view and projection transforms are defined with respect to the light source. The vertex transformed by `lightWVP` is denoted by `oPos`. It is defined in the homogeneous clip space. The `zw`-coordinates of `oPos` are passed to the rasterizer and are interpolated. Consequently, each fragment contains the clip-space `zw`-coordinates.

The fragment shader shown above accepts the clip-space `zw`-coordinates and divides `z` by `w`. It corresponds to the *perspective division*. The result is the depth defined in NDC (normalized device coordinates) and is stored into the shadow map.

In Fig. 10.15, consider point p on the sphere surface. The right-hand side of Fig. 10.15 shows p transformed into the clip space represented in NDC. In the conceptual presentation of Section 10.3.1, the shadow map contains the world-space distances from the light source. In the implementation, the NDC depths are stored instead.

```
void VS_pass2 (float4 Pos : POSITION,
               out float4 oPos : POSITION,
               out float4 oLightPos : TEXCOORD0,
           uniform float4x4 WorldViewProj,
           uniform float4x4 lightWVP)
{
  oPos = mul(WorldViewProj, Pos);
  oLightPos = mul(lightWVP, Pos);
}
```

The second pass renders the scene from the camera's viewpoint. See the second-pass vertex shader shown in the previous page. Computing the clip-space vertex position is the required task for every vertex shader, and the first statement completes the task. Whereas oPos is defined in the clip space with respect to the camera, oLightPos is defined in the clip space with respect to the light source. Shadow mapping requires depth comparison, and oLightPos will be used for the purpose.

```
void FS_pass2 (float4 oLightPos : TEXCOORD0,
           out float4 Color : COLOR,
        uniform sampler2D shadowMap )
{
   oLightPos /= oLightPos.w; // xy in [-1,1]; z in [0,1]
   float2 Tex = oLightPos.xy*float2(0.5f,-0.5f)+0.5f;

   float pixD = oLightPos.z;
   float pixZ = tex2D(shadowMap, Tex).x;
   float bias = 1e-5;
   float visibility = (pixD > pixZ+bias) ? 0 : 1;

   Color = visibility;
}
```

See the fragment shader shown above. The xyz-coordinates of oLightPos are divided by its w-coordinate. It corresponds to the perspective division. As a result, oLightPos is now defined in NDC with respect to the light source. The second statement of the fragment shader is for obtaining the texture coordinates of the shadow map. Fig. 10.16 explicates the second statement using an example.

In the fragment shader, the fragment depth defined in NDC (with respect to the light source) is denoted by pixD, and the z-value read from the shadow map is denoted by pixZ. For depth comparison, pixZ is biased. If pixD is greater than the biased pixZ, the current fragment is determined to be shadowed. Otherwise, it is lit.

The shaders presented in this subsection are written in the context of Direct3D 9. Direct3D 10 allows direct access to the depth values of the z-buffer, and the above shaders can be made simpler. At the first pass, we do not need to explicitly store the NDC-depth values. Therefore, the second statement of the vertex shader can be deleted, and the fragment shader can be NULL. The second pass directly accesses the z-buffer for depth comparison. This leads to performance increase.

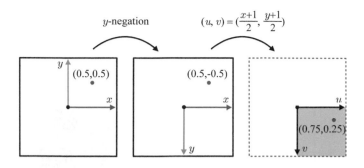

Fig. 10.16: The xy-coordinates of oLightPos are defined in the clip space represented in NDC, where the y-axis is upward. The y-axis is made downward such that it has the same direction as the v-axis of the parameter space. Then, the range $[-1,1]$ of the xy-coordinates is converted into the range $[0,1]$ of the uv-coordinates. Note that the *relative* location of the original xy-coordinates $(0.5,0.5)$ within the 2×2-sized square is the same as that of the texture coordinates $(0.75,0.25)$ within the 1×1-sized parameter space.

10.3.3 Shadow Map Filtering

Recall that, for filtering the shadow map, we assumed *nearest point sampling*. An alternative would be *bilinear interpolation*. Fig. 10.17-(a) shows a pixel p projected into the shadow map. The values of the texels surrounding p denote the depths stored in the shadow map[6]. When they are bilinearly interpolated, the result is 64. Suppose that p's depth is 50. Then, p would be determined to be lit because its depth of 50 is smaller than the interpolated depth 64.

If we chose nearest point sampling, however, p would be determined to be shadowed because the depth of the nearest point (the upper-left texel) is 10 and is smaller than p's depth 50. Depending on the filtering options, we have completely different results. Also note that the shadow quality is not improved by choosing the bilinear interpolation. A surface point is either fully lit or fully shadowed, and consequently the shadow often reveals the jagged edge shown in Fig. 10.17-(a).

A solution to this problem is to first determine the *visibilities* of a pixel with respect to the four texels, and then interpolate the visibilities. See Fig. 10.17-(b). The visibility of p with respect to the upper-left texel is 0 (shadowed) because 10 is smaller than 50. In contrast, the visibilities with respect to the other three texels are 1 (lit). The four visibility values are bilinearly

---

[6]The shadow map texels are in the range of $[0,1]$ because they are defined in NDC. In the current example, however, integer depths are used just for presentation purpose.

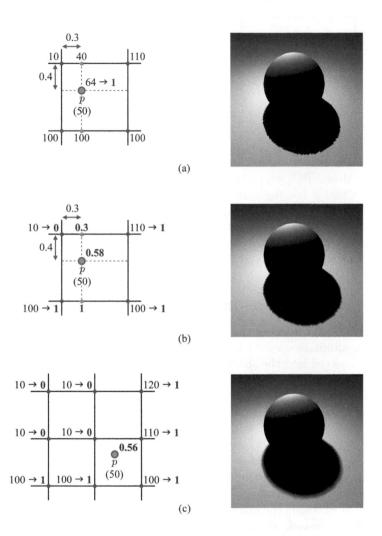

(a)

(b)

(c)

Fig. 10.17:   Shadow map filtering. (a) Bilinear interpolation does not make a meaningful difference from nearest point sampling. (b) The visibility is computed for each texel, and the visibilities are bilinearly interpolated. (c) The visibility is computed for each of nine texels, and the visibilities are averaged.

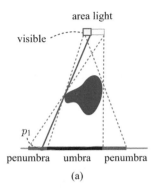
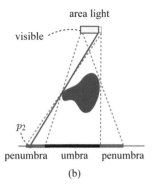

Fig. 10.18: Soft shadows in the penumbra region. (a) The part of the area light source visible from p_1 is small, and therefore p_1 is not well lit. (b) A larger part of the light source is visible from p_2, and therefore p_2 is better lit.

interpolated, and p's visibility is set to 0.58. This value is taken as the "degree of being lit." In other words, p is not restricted to the choice between "fully lit (1)" and "fully shadowed (0)," but can be assigned a degree in the range of [0,1]. As a result, the jagged edge of the shadow can be smoothed, as shown in Fig. 10.17-(b).

In general, the technique of taking multiple texels from the shadow map and blending the pixel's visibilities against the texels is named *percentage closer filtering* (PCF). Many algorithms for PCF have been proposed, and they differ in how many texels to take and how to blend the computed visibilities. Fig. 10.17-(c) shows an example, where 3×3 texels close to the projected pixel p are taken and the visibilities are simply averaged. Fig. 10.17-(c) takes more texels than Fig. 10.17-(b), and consequently the shadow edge becomes smoother. Direct3D 10 supports this method through a new function `SampleCmpLevelZero()`.

The shadow edge shown in Fig. 10.17-(c) appears *soft*. However, it is not exactly soft shadow but *anti-aliased* hard shadow. Note that soft shadows are formed by area or volumetric light sources. The PCF algorithm we have considered assumes a point light source.

As presented in Fig. 10.12-(b), soft shadows are observed at the penumbra region located between the umbra region and the fully lit region. For each surface point in the penumbra region, the "degree of being lit" can be computed by measuring how much of the area/volumetric light source is visible from the point. For example, p_1 in Fig. 10.18-(a) sees only a small portion of the area light source whereas p_2 in Fig. 10.18-(b) sees a larger portion. Consequently, p_2 will be assigned a larger degree. There are many approaches that have extended the shadow mapping algorithm to generate soft shadows, and in principle they compute how much of the area light source is visible from each surface point in the penumbra region.

Even though the shadow mapping algorithm is a step out of local illumination, it does not handle *indirect lighting*. However, the shadow map can be extended to approximate indirect lighting. It is briefly sketched in the following note.

[Note: Reflective shadow map]
Light bouncing around an environment accounts for indirect lighting. Note that *one-bounce* indirect light is caused by the surfaces visible from the light source. The shadow map stores such surfaces, and therefore its texels can be taken as "indirect light sources" that generate the one-bounce indirect lighting.

The standard shadow map (depth map) is augmented by several maps, which include the so-called *flux map*. It contains the light reflected off every surface point visible from the light source. The augmented shadow map is named a *reflective shadow map* (RSM) [34]. When a scene is rendered from the camera's viewpoint, the one-bounce indirect light incident on a surface point is approximated by summing up the illumination due to all RSM texels.

The RSM provides a rough approximation of indirect lighting. Its idea is based on the observation that, for many applications, global illumination solutions do not need to be precise, and one-bounce indirect lighting is usually sufficient. For photorealism, however, computation of multi-bounce indirect lighting is needed and remains as a major challenge in interactive computer graphics.

10.4 Ambient Occlusion

Consider the ambient term of the Phong lighting model, which accounts for indirect lighting. It assumes that the ambient light randomly bounces in the scene and arrives at a surface point from *all* directions. In reality, however, some of the directions may be occluded by the external environment. Fig. 10.19-(a) shows two surface points, p_1 and p_2. Nothing occludes the ambient light incident on p_1, but the ambient light incident on p_2 is partly occluded by the other parts of the object. *Ambient occlusion* algorithm computes how much of the ambient light is occluded, which we call the *occlusion degree*. It modulates the ambient reflection term in a lighting equation. In Fig. 10.19-(a), the occlusion degree at p_2 will be larger than that of p_1, and therefore p_2 receives less ambient light than p_1.

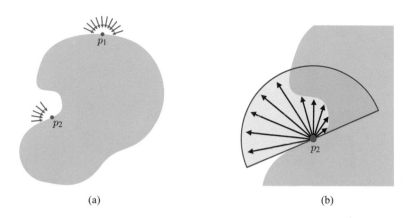

Fig. 10.19: Computing ambient occlusion. (a) The ambient light incident on a surface point can be occluded. It is the case for p_2 whereas no ambient light incident on p_1 is occluded. (b) Ray casting could be used for computing the occlusion degree.

Fig. 10.19-(b) shows a hemisphere placed at p_2. It is oriented around p_2's surface normal. The ambient light incident on p_2 is coming through the hemisphere. Imagine casting rays along the opposite directions of the incident light, i.e., from p_2 to the hemisphere surface. Some rays intersect the scene geometry. The occlusion degree is defined as the ratio between the intersected and all cast rays. Classic algorithms for computing the occlusion degree evenly sample the hemisphere surface, cast rays toward the sampled points, and count the rays intersecting the scene geometry. In the example of Fig. 10.19-(b), half of the rays intersect the scene geometry, and therefore the occlusion degree would be set to 0.5, i.e., 50% of ambient light is occluded.

Unfortunately, ray casting or tracing is an expensive operation, and the processing time depends on the scene complexity. A popular alternative is the *screen-space ambient occlusion* (SSAO) technique, which has attracted attention especially since its implementation in the well-known game, Crysis.

The key idea of SSAO is to generate a *depth map* for the scene, and consider it as the discrete approximation of the scene geometry. The Crysis implementation adopted a multi-pass rendering technique and created the depth map at the first pass. In Fig. 10.19-(c), the gold bold curves represent the visible surfaces, and their z-values are stored in the depth map.

At the second pass, a quad covering the entire screen, named a *full-screen quad*, is rendered such that a fragment of the quad corresponds to a visible surface point whose z-value is stored in the depth map. Each fragment enters the fragment shader, which then computes the occlusion degree for the visible surface point corresponding to the fragment.

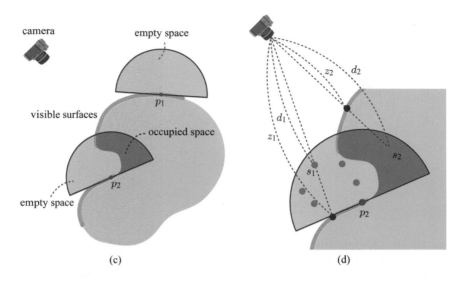

Fig. 10.19: Computing ambient occlusion (*continued*). (c) The occlusion degree could be defined using the ratio between the occupied and empty spaces. (d) Computing the ratio is approximated by the depth test using the depth map and the sampled points within the hemisphere.

In Fig. 10.19-(c), the hemisphere centered at p_2 is partitioned into the *occupied space* and the *empty space*. The occlusion degree may then be approximated as the ratio between the occupied space and the entire hemisphere space. Measuring the ratio is again approximated by using a set of sample points evenly distributed within the hemisphere. See Fig. 10.19-(d). Each sample is tested as to whether it belongs to the occupied space or the empty space. This test is implemented by comparing the sample's depth value d with the z-value stored in the depth map. For example, sample s_1 is determined to be in the empty space because its depth d_1 is smaller than z_1 in the depth map. In contrast, s_2 is determined to be in the occupied space because d_2 is greater than z_2. It is quite similar to the depth comparison performed for shadow mapping.

In the example of Fig. 10.19-(d), the occlusion degree of p_2 would be set to $\frac{3}{8}$ because three out of eight samples lose the depth test against the depth map. (It is different from 0.5, which was estimated from Fig. 10.19-(b). It is an expected discrepancy brought by different sampling methods.) For another point p_1 shown in Fig. 10.19-(c), no sample would lose the depth test, and therefore the occlusion degree would be set to zero[7].

---

[7]In the implementation of Crysis, the hemisphere is replaced by a sphere because the surface normal needed for determining the hemisphere's orientation is not available at the second

Fig. 10.20: Each row shows a polygon model, the ambient-reflected model, and the same model shaded using SSAO. (The bunny and dragon models are provided by the Stanford University Computer Graphics Laboratory.)

The occlusion degrees computed at the second pass are stored in a texture. It is passed as an input to the third pass for rendering[8]. For the ambient term $s_a \otimes m_a$ of the Phong model, the third pass determines s_a using the occlusion degree. Fig. 10.20 shows the polygon models, the shading results using only the (traditional) ambient reflection, and the results using only SSAO. Notice the change of shades across the object surface in the SSAO result.

SSAO is an image-space algorithm and is independent of the scene complexity. The rendering results produced by SSAO are usually pleasing. However, SSAO is an approximate algorithm, and it does not consider the scene geometry that is located outside the view frustum or the hemisphere. Consequently, SSAO is prone to errors. Fig. 10.21 illustrates another problem of SSAO's sampling method. Fortunately, the artefact caused by those errors is rarely perceived by the average users. Therefore, SSAO is widely accepted in shipped games. Fig. 10.22 shows an example of an in-game scene with ambient occlusion applied.

---

pass. In theory, using a sphere is incorrect because it implies that the ambient light coming from the other side of the tangent plane is considered. In practice, however, this does not cause any serious problem because, for example, we can set the occlusion degree to 0 if the number of samples winning the depth test is greater than or equal to half of the number of total samples.

[8]In the Crysis implementation, another pass postprocesses the texture containing the occlusion degrees but is not presented in this section.

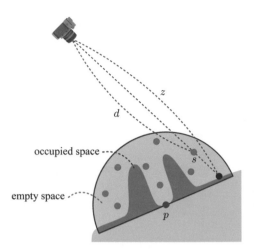

Fig. 10.21: The depth d of sample s is smaller than z stored in the depth map, and therefore s is found to be in the empty space. It implies that the ray connecting p and s does not hit any part of the scene, and the ambient light comes along the opposite direction of the ray. Obviously, it is incorrect. In this contrived example, the occlusion degree for p will be set to 0. In reality, however, the occlusion degree is much higher.

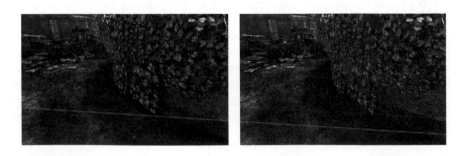

Fig. 10.22: Compare the images rendered with ambient occlusion (left) and without it (right). (Image from Gears of War® 2. Unreal, Gears of War and Epic Games are trademarks or registered trademarks of Epic Games, Inc. All rights reserved.)

10.5   Deferred Shading

So far, various types of render targets have been presented. A good example among them is the depth map used for shadow mapping and screen-space ambient occlusion (SSAO). Most contemporary games dynamically fill multiple render targets (MRT) and then combine them to create the final image. A most notable technique that extensively utilizes the MRT is *deferred shading*. This technique does not shade a fragment that will fail the depth test, i.e., shading is deferred until all "visible surfaces" of the scene are determined.

It is a multi-pass rendering algorithm and is split into *geometry pass* and *lighting passes*. At the geometry pass, various *per-pixel attributes* are computed and stored into MRT by a fragment shader. The per-pixel attributes may include texture colors, depths, and normals "of the visible surfaces."

(a) (b)

(c) (d)

Fig. 10.23:   G-buffer for deferred shading. (a) Screen-space image texture. (b) Depth map. (c) Screen-space normal map. (d) Shading computed using the G-buffer. (3D models courtesy of Tony Hayes.)

	R16	G16	B16	A16
RT0	emissive color			
RT1	normal			depth
RT2	diffuse color			AO
RT3	specular color			

Fig. 10.24: The G-buffer for StarCraft II is composed of four render targets [35]. The ambient occlusion (denoted by AO) was computed for a static scene, and will be ignored if SSAO is enabled.

Fig. 10.23-(a) shows the so-called *screen-space image texture*. Each of its texels corresponds to a screen-space pixel. Consider two adjacent texels in the texture. The color at a texel may come from an image texture for an object, whereas the color at the adjacent texel may come from a different texture for another object. Fig. 10.23-(b) is the (normalized) depth map that is visualized in gray scales. The texture shown in Fig. 10.23-(c) is named *screen-space normal map*. It contains the normals of the screen-space pixels.

The *G-buffer* stands for geometric buffer and refers to the MRT filled at the geometry pass. (The geometry pass and G-buffer are misnomers because material information as well as geometry is computed at the geometry pass and stored in the G-buffer.) The G-buffer contains all data needed for computing the colors of the screen-space pixels. It is input to the lighting passes. Note that, unlike the pre-Z pass algorithm presented in Section 4.3.2, the polygons of the scene are processed just once at the first pass, the geometry pass. Once the G-buffer is constructed, no polygon enters the pipeline for the lighting passes.

At the lighting passes, a large number of light sources can be applied to the G-buffer. All light sources are iterated. For a light source, a full-screen quad is rendered (as was done by the SSAO algorithm) such that each fragment of the quad corresponds to a pixel on the screen. The fragment shader takes the G-buffer as input, computes lighting, and determines the color of the current pixel. It is blended with the current content of the color buffer, which was computed using the previous light sources. Fig. 10.23-(d) shows the result.

Deferred shading has been successfully implemented in high-profile games. Fig. 10.24 shows the G-buffer data used in Starcraft II, where a texture has four channels, and each channel is of a 16-bit floating-point format.

Exercises

1. Consider dynamically constructing a cube map using the shaders. The scene primitives are replicated and transformed by the geometry shader. The geometry runs a `for` loop that iterates six times, and applies the view and projection transforms to the primitives per iteration.

   (a) Is the view transform distinct per iteration? Discuss why it is or why not.

   (b) Is the projection transform distinct per iteration? Discuss why it is or why not.

2. Light mapping is usually combined with image texturing, as shown in Fig. 10.7-(c).

   (a) The combination could be stored in the light map such that, at run time, the light map does not need to be combined with the image texture. What would be the disadvantages of this method?

   (b) The light mapping is often called *dark mapping* because the pixel lit by the light map is darker than the unlit texel of the image texture. Why does it happen? How would you resolve the problem?

3. A problem that could be encountered in shadow mapping is called *Peter Panning*, where shadows are disconnected from the occluder. The occluder looks as if it is floating above the shadows. When would you encounter this problem?

Chapter 11

Character Animation

In computer games, an illusion of movement is obtained by rapidly displaying a sequence of still images (frames), where the current frame is repeatedly replaced by a new one that slightly changes from the current frame. The change is made and controlled by computer animation.

In games, the most important objects to be animated are definitely the characters, especially human characters. Making a character move in a realistic way is an everlasting goal in computer animation, and a variety of techniques have been developed toward the goal. This chapter focuses on character animation and covers its fundamental algorithms upon which various state-of-the-art techniques can be built.

11.1 Keyframe Animation

In computer animation, an artist creates a sequence of motions using a modeling and animation package, and then it is played back at run time. However, the artist does not define all of the frames to be displayed. For a 30-fps animation, for example, much fewer than 30 frames are defined per second. Such frames in distinct time steps are called *keyframes*. In real-time computer animation, the *in-between frames* are automatically filled at run time. Such a keyframe-based technique originated from the traditional hand-drawn cartoon animation, where the senior key artist would draw the keyframes and the junior artist would fill the in-between frames.

The power of the keyframe animation comes from the fact that, when key data are assigned to the keyframes, they can be neatly *interpolated* to generate the in-between frames. Any data that change in the time domain can be interpolated. Typical examples include the positions, orientations, and scaling factors of the game objects. In addition, the material parameters for lighting and even texture coordinates can be interpolated.

In Fig. 11.1, the pose (position and orientation) data defined for the rectangles in `keyframe 0` and `keyframe 1` are interpolated to describe the rectangle poses in the in-between frames. (The coordinate system bound to the rectangle represents its object space.) Let the data for `keyframe 0` and `keyframe 1` be $\{\theta_0,(x_0,y_0)\}$ and $\{\theta_1,(x_1,y_1)\}$, respectively, where θ_i denotes the orienta-

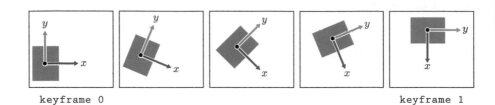

keyframe 0   keyframe 1

Fig. 11.1: The positions and orientations of the keyframes are interpolated to generate those of the in-between frames.

tion (rotation angle) and (x_i, y_i) denote the position of the rectangle's center. Consider frame t, where t is in the normalized range $[0,1]$. The pose of the rectangle in frame t is defined to be

$$\{(1-t)\theta_0 + t\theta_1, ((1-t)x_0 + tx_1, (1-t)y_0 + ty_1)\}$$

The same applies to 3D keyframe animation. Fig. 11.2-(a) shows three keyframes of the animated teapot. The teapot in **keyframe 1** is obtained by translating the teapot of **keyframe 0** along the x-axis. The pose of the teapot in **keyframe 2** is obtained by rotating and then translating the teapot of **keyframe 1**.

In Fig. 11.2-(b), the key data are presented as black dots, and linear interpolations of the data are illustrated as line segments connecting them. Let us see the orientation data shown in the left column. The teapot does not rotate between **keyframe 0** and **keyframe 1**, and therefore the three graphs remain zero in the interval. In Fig. 11.2-(a), the teapot in **keyframe 1** is first rotated about the x-axis by $90°$ and then rotated about the z-axis by $-90°$ (clockwise $90°$), leading to the orientation in **keyframe 2**. (No rotation is done about the y-axis.) Let us denote the rotation angles about the principal axes by $(\theta_x, \theta_y, \theta_z)$. In the example, $(\theta_x, \theta_y, \theta_z) = (90°, 0°, -90°)$. The three graphs of the left column in Fig. 11.2-(b) plot the rotation angles and their linear interpolation results.

Now consider translations. Let us see the position data shown in the right column. In the first graph, the x-coordinate is monotonically increasing. In contrast, the second graph shows that the y-coordinate remains zero between **keyframe 0** and **keyframe 1**, but is decreasing between **keyframe 1** and **keyframe 2**. This is compatible with Fig. 11.2-(a), where the teapot's y-coordinate in **keyframe 1** has decreased to reach the position shown in **keyframe 2**. The z-coordinate shown in the third graph is zero, implying that the teapot slides only on the xy-plane through the frames.

For creating an in-between frame at time t, the six graphs in Fig. 11.2-(b) are sampled using t to obtain the orientation $(\theta_x, \theta_y, \theta_z)$ and the position

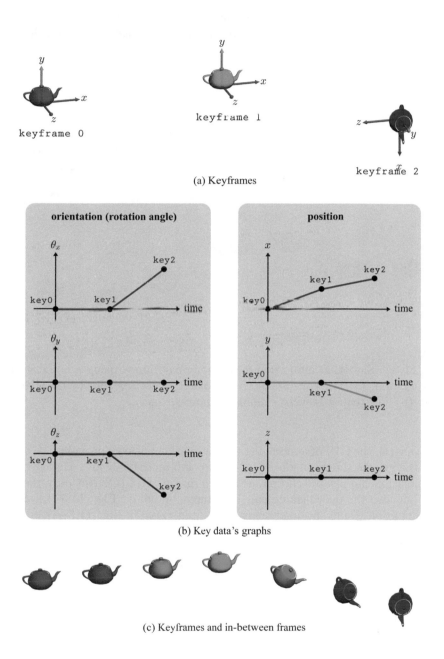

(a) Keyframes

(b) Key data's graphs

(c) Keyframes and in-between frames

Fig. 11.2: 3D keyframe animation is the extension of 2D keyframe animation. The positions and orientations of the keyframes are interpolated.

(x, y, z). With the interpolated pose data, the teapot is rendered. Fig. 11.2-(c) shows the keyframes and the in-between frames together. The colors of the teapot are also interpolated.

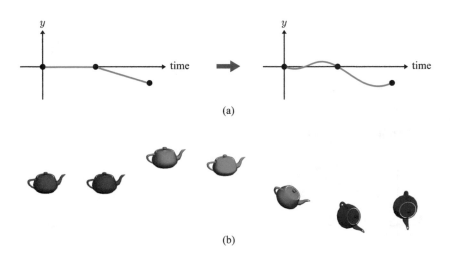

(a)

(b)

Fig. 11.3: Smoother animation may often be obtained using a higher-order interpolation. (a) The key data are interpolated by a curve, not by the straight lines. (b) The teapot traverses along a smoother path.

In general, the GUI of a modeling and animation package provides the artist with the graphs shown in Fig. 11.2-(b) for interactive editing. Higher-order interpolation can also be chosen, as shown in Fig. 11.3-(a). Not only the key data but also the curve shape can be altered by hand. Fig. 11.3-(b) shows the animation result obtained using the edited curve in Fig. 11.3-(a).

11.2 Rotation

The previous section presents interpolation of the rotation angles $(\theta_x, \theta_y, \theta_z)$. They are the *Euler angles* presented in Section 2.1.3. A problem of Euler angles is that they are not always correctly interpolated. Therefore, an alternative, named *quaternion*, is used for representing an arbitrary orientation or equivalently a rotation.

11.2.1 Interpolation of Euler Angles

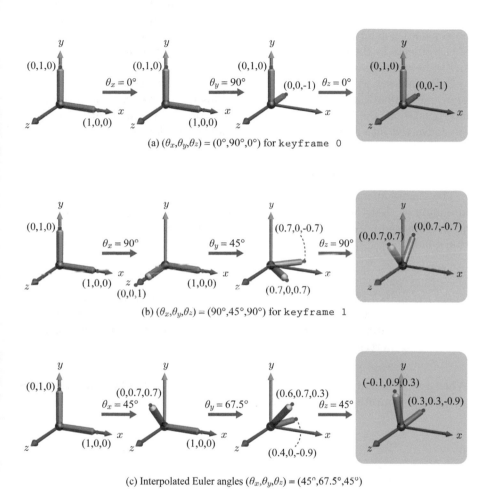

(a) $(\theta_x,\theta_y,\theta_z) = (0°,90°,0°)$ for keyframe 0

(b) $(\theta_x,\theta_y,\theta_z) = (90°,45°,90°)$ for keyframe 1

(c) Interpolated Euler angles $(\theta_x,\theta_y,\theta_z) = (45°,67.5°,45°)$

Fig. 11.4: Euler angles are widely used for representing an arbitrary orientation but are not correctly interpolated.

Euler angles $(\theta_x,\theta_y,\theta_z)$ provide an intuitive method for defining an orientation. Consider the L-shaped object in Fig. 11.4. A successive application of Euler angles is given in Fig. 11.4-(a). The resulting orientation is denoted by $(0°,90°,0°)$. The object in Fig. 11.4-(b) has the orientation of $(90°,45°,90°)$. Let us take them as the orientations of keyframe 0 and keyframe 1.

Consider an in-between frame defined when $t = 0.5$. The orientation obtained by interpolating the Euler angles is $(45°,67.5°,45°)$. Fig. 11.4-(c) shows a successive application of the interpolated Euler angles. In the resulting orientation, see the x-coordinates of the end points. They are not zero, i.e., the object does not lie in the yz-plane. It is an unexpected result because both of the objects in the keyframes lie in the yz-plane and therefore the object at any in-between frame is expected to do so.

Euler angles are not correctly interpolated and therefore are not suitable for keyframe animation. In contrast, quaternions [36] prove to be appropriately interpolated. If the Euler angles are specified for a keyframe by an artist, they are converted into a quaternion and used for interpolation.

11.2.2   Quaternion Representation

The theory of quaternion is not simple, and this subsection presents its minimum so that the readers are not discouraged from learning the beauty of quaternion. A quaternion $\mathbf{q}$ is an extended *complex number* and is represented as a quadruple:

$$(q_x, q_y, q_z, q_w) = q_x i + q_y j + q_z k + q_w$$

where (q_x, q_y, q_z) are the *imaginary part*, i, j and k are the imaginary units, and q_w is the *real part*. The imaginary part is often abbreviated to $\mathbf{q}_v$, and therefore a quaternion is denoted by $(\mathbf{q}_v, q_w)$. The imaginary units have the following properties:

$$i^2 = j^2 = k^2 = -1$$

When two different imaginary units are multiplied, the following properties of cyclic permutation are observed:

$$ij = k, ji = -k$$
$$jk = i, kj = -i$$
$$ki = j, ik = -j$$

Consider two quaternions, $\mathbf{p} = (p_x, p_y, p_z, p_w)$ and $\mathbf{q} = (q_x, q_y, q_z, q_w)$. Their multiplication is computed as follows:

$$\begin{aligned}
\mathbf{pq} &= (p_x i + p_y j + p_z k + p_w)(q_x i + q_y j + q_z k + q_w) \\
&= (p_x q_w + p_y q_z - p_z q_y + p_w q_x)i + \\
&\quad (-p_x q_z + p_y q_w + p_z q_x + p_w q_y)j + \\
&\quad (p_x q_y - p_y q_x + p_z q_w + p_w q_z)k + \\
&\quad (-p_x q_x - p_y q_y - p_z q_z + p_w q_w)
\end{aligned} \tag{11.1}$$

The *conjugate* of quaternion $\mathbf{q}$ is defined as follows:

$$\begin{aligned}
\mathbf{q}^* &= (-\mathbf{q}_v, q_w) \\
&= (-q_x, -q_y, -q_z, q_w) \\
&= -q_x i - q_y j - q_z k + q_w
\end{aligned}$$

The magnitude or norm of a quaternion is calculated in exactly the same way as is done for an ordinary vector:

$$\|\mathbf{q}\| = \sqrt{q_x^2 + q_y^2 + q_z^2 + q_w^2}$$

If $\|\mathbf{q}\| = 1$, $\mathbf{q}$ is called a *unit quaternion*.

11.2.3 Rotation Using Quaternion

Recall 2D rotation shown in Fig. 2.3. If a vector represented in (x, y) is rotated counter-clockwise by θ, the rotated vector is described as follows:

$$\begin{pmatrix} x' \\ y' \end{pmatrix} = \begin{pmatrix} \cos\theta & -\sin\theta \\ \sin\theta & \cos\theta \end{pmatrix} \begin{pmatrix} x \\ y \end{pmatrix} \tag{11.2}$$
$$= \begin{pmatrix} x\cos\theta - y\sin\theta \\ x\sin\theta + y\cos\theta \end{pmatrix}$$

Let us represent (x, y) by a complex number $x+yi$, i.e., x takes the real part and y takes the imaginary part. The complex number is denoted by $\mathbf{p}$. Given the rotation angle θ, the polar form of a unit-length complex number is defined as $\cos\theta+\sin\theta i$. Let us denote it by $\mathbf{q}$. When $\mathbf{p}$ and $\mathbf{q}$ are multiplied, we have the following result:

$$\mathbf{pq} = (x + yi)(\cos\theta + \sin\theta i) \tag{11.3}$$
$$= (x\cos\theta - y\sin\theta) + (x\sin\theta + y\cos\theta)i$$

Surprisingly, the real and imaginary parts in Equation (11.3) are identical to x' and y' in Equation (11.2), respectively.

A similar process is taken for 3D rotation. Consider rotating a 3D vector p about an axis u by an angle θ, as shown in Fig. 11.5-(a). Both the vector to be rotated and the rotation are represented in quaternions. First of all, let us represent p in a quaternion $\mathbf{p}$. The imaginary part of $\mathbf{p}$ is set to p, and the real part is set to 0:

$$\mathbf{p} = (\mathbf{p}_v, p_w) \tag{11.4}$$
$$= (p, 0)$$

The rotation axis u and rotation angle θ define another quaternion $\mathbf{q}$. For a quaternion to represent a rotation, it should have the unit length. For the purpose, the axis u is divided by its length to make a unit vector $\mathbf{u}$. Then, the polar form of a unit-length quaternion is defined as follows:

$$\mathbf{q} = (\mathbf{q}_v, q_w) \tag{11.5}$$
$$= (\sin\tfrac{\theta}{2}\mathbf{u}, \cos\tfrac{\theta}{2})$$

Finally, "rotation of p about $\mathbf{u}$ (or u) by θ" is represented as follows:

$$\mathbf{qpq}^* \tag{11.6}$$

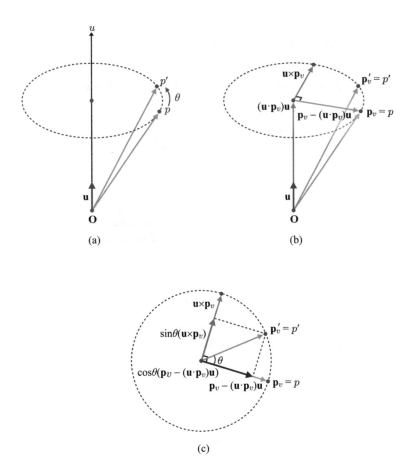

Fig. 11.5: Three-dimensional rotation. (a) Rotation of p about u by θ. (b) Two orthogonal vectors on the disk. (c) Computing vector p' using the orthogonal vectors.

The imaginary part of $\mathbf{qpq}^*$ corresponds to the rotated vector p'. Proof of Equation (11.6) is given in the following note, and an example is provided at the end of this section.

[Note: Proof of quaternion-based rotation]
 When we denote $\mathbf{p}$ and $\mathbf{q}$ by $(\mathbf{p}_v, p_w)$ and $(\mathbf{q}_v, q_w)$, respectively, $\mathbf{pq}$ in Equation (11.1) can be rewritten as follows:

$$\mathbf{pq} = (p_x q_w + p_y q_z - p_z q_y + p_w q_x)i+$$
$$(-p_x q_z + p_y q_w + p_z q_x + p_w q_y)j+$$
$$(p_x q_y - p_y q_x + p_z q_w + p_w q_z)k+ \qquad (11.7)$$
$$(-p_x q_x - p_y q_y - p_z q_z + p_w q_w)$$
$$= (\mathbf{p}_v \times \mathbf{q}_v + q_w \mathbf{p}_v + p_w \mathbf{q}_v, p_w q_w - \mathbf{p}_v \cdot \mathbf{q}_v)$$

where $\times$ represents the cross product and $\cdot$ represents the dot product.
 Using Equations (11.4), (11.5), and (11.7), $\mathbf{qpq}^*$ in Equation (11.6) is expanded as follows:

$$\begin{aligned}
\mathbf{qpq}^* &= (\mathbf{q}_v \times \mathbf{p}_v + q_w \mathbf{p}_v, -\mathbf{q}_v \cdot \mathbf{p}_v)\mathbf{q}^* \, [1]\\
&= (\mathbf{q}_v \times \mathbf{p}_v + q_w \mathbf{p}_v, -\mathbf{q}_v \cdot \mathbf{p}_v)(-\mathbf{q}_v, q_w)\\
&= ((\mathbf{q}_v \times \mathbf{p}_v + q_w \mathbf{p}_v) \times (-\mathbf{q}_v) + q_w(\mathbf{q}_v \times \mathbf{p}_v + q_w \mathbf{p}_v) + (-\mathbf{q}_v \cdot \mathbf{p}_v)(-\mathbf{q}_v),\\
&\quad (-\mathbf{q}_v \cdot \mathbf{p}_v)q_w - (\mathbf{q}_v \times \mathbf{p}_v + q_w \mathbf{p}_v) \cdot (-\mathbf{q}_v)) \, [2]\\
&= ((\mathbf{q}_v \cdot \mathbf{p}_v)\mathbf{q}_v - (\mathbf{q}_v \cdot \mathbf{q}_v)\mathbf{p}_v + 2q_w(\mathbf{q}_v \times \mathbf{p}_v) + q_w^2 \mathbf{p}_v + (\mathbf{q}_v \cdot \mathbf{p}_v)\mathbf{q}_v, 0) \, [3]\\
&= (2(\mathbf{q}_v \cdot \mathbf{p}_v)\mathbf{q}_v + (q_w^2 - \|\mathbf{q}_v\|^2)\mathbf{p}_v + 2q_w(\mathbf{q}_v \times \mathbf{p}_v), 0)\\
&= (2\sin^2\tfrac{\theta}{2}(\mathbf{u} \cdot \mathbf{p}_v)\mathbf{u} + (\cos^2\tfrac{\theta}{2} - \sin^2\tfrac{\theta}{2})\mathbf{p}_v + 2\cos\tfrac{\theta}{2}\sin\tfrac{\theta}{2}(\mathbf{u} \times \mathbf{p}_v), 0) \, [4]\\
&= ((1 - \cos\theta)(\mathbf{u} \cdot \mathbf{p}_v)\mathbf{u} + \cos\theta \mathbf{p}_v + \sin\theta(\mathbf{u} \times \mathbf{p}_v), 0) \, [5]\\
&= ((\mathbf{u} \cdot \mathbf{p}_v)\mathbf{u} + \cos\theta(\mathbf{p}_v - (\mathbf{u} \cdot \mathbf{p}_v)\mathbf{u}) + \sin\theta(\mathbf{u} \times \mathbf{p}_v), 0) \, [6]
\end{aligned}$$
$$(11.8)$$

where [1] is obtained as $p_w = 0$, [2] follows from Equation (11.7), the imaginary part in [3] follows from the theorem of vector triple product that asserts $\mathbf{a} \times (\mathbf{b} \times \mathbf{c}) = (\mathbf{a} \cdot \mathbf{c})\mathbf{b} - (\mathbf{a} \cdot \mathbf{b})\mathbf{c}$, the real part in [3] becomes 0 because $(\mathbf{q}_v \times \mathbf{p}_v) \cdot \mathbf{q}_v = 0$, [4] uses the definition "$\mathbf{q} = (sin\frac{\theta}{2}\mathbf{u}, cos\frac{\theta}{2})$," [5] follows from the theorems of trigonometry, $sin^2\frac{\theta}{2} = \frac{1 - cos\theta}{2}$, $cos^2\frac{\theta}{2} = \frac{1 + cos\theta}{2}$, and $sin2\theta = 2sin\theta cos\theta$, and [6] is obtained simply by rearranging [5].
 In Fig. 11.5-(b), consider the disk along the edge of which p is rotated to p'. The vector connecting the origin $\mathbf{O}$ to the disk center is $(\mathbf{u} \cdot \mathbf{p}_v)\mathbf{u}$. Suppose a pair of orthogonal vectors on the disk. One is $\mathbf{u} \times \mathbf{p}_v$, and the other is $\mathbf{p}_v - (\mathbf{u} \cdot \mathbf{p}_v)\mathbf{u}$ that connects the disk center to p. Fig. 11.5-(c) shows the disk seen from the top. On the disk, p' is the sum of $cos\theta(\mathbf{p}_v - (\mathbf{u} \cdot \mathbf{p}_v)\mathbf{u})$ and $sin\theta(\mathbf{u} \times \mathbf{p}_v)$. When the displacement of the disk, $(\mathbf{u} \cdot \mathbf{p}_v)\mathbf{u}$, is added to the sum, we obtain p'. It is the imaginary part of [6] in Equation (11.8).

A quaternion $\mathbf{q}$ representing a rotation can be converted into a matrix form. If $\mathbf{q} = (q_x, q_y, q_z, q_w)$, the rotation matrix is defined as follows:

$$\begin{pmatrix} 1 - 2(q_y^2 + q_z^2) & 2(q_xq_y - q_wq_z) & 2(q_xq_z + q_wq_y) & 0 \\ 2(q_xq_y + q_wq_z) & 1 - 2(q_x^2 + q_z^2) & 2(q_yq_z - q_wq_x) & 0 \\ 2(q_xq_z - q_wq_y) & 2(q_yq_z + q_wq_x) & 1 - 2(q_x^2 + q_y^2) & 0 \\ 0 & 0 & 0 & 1 \end{pmatrix} \tag{11.9}$$

Proof of Equation (11.9) is given in the following note. Conversely, given a rotation matrix, we can compute the corresponding quaternion.

[Note: Conversion from a quaternion to a rotation matrix]

Notice that each component of $\mathbf{pq}$ presented in Equation (11.1) is a linear combination of p_x, p_y, p_z and p_w. Therefore, $\mathbf{pq}$ can be represented by a matrix-vector multiplication form:

$$\mathbf{pq} = \begin{pmatrix} q_w & q_z & -q_y & q_x \\ -q_z & q_w & q_x & q_y \\ q_y & -q_x & q_w & q_z \\ -q_x & -q_y & -q_z & q_w \end{pmatrix} \begin{pmatrix} p_x \\ p_y \\ p_z \\ p_w \end{pmatrix} = M_{\mathbf{q}}\mathbf{p}$$

Each component of $\mathbf{pq}$ in Equation (11.1) is also a linear combination of q_x, q_y, q_z and q_w, and therefore $\mathbf{pq}$ can be represented by another matrix-vector multiplication form:

$$\mathbf{pq} = \begin{pmatrix} p_w & -p_z & p_y & p_x \\ p_z & p_w & -p_x & p_y \\ -p_y & p_x & p_w & p_z \\ -p_x & -p_y & -p_z & p_w \end{pmatrix} \begin{pmatrix} q_x \\ q_y \\ q_z \\ q_w \end{pmatrix} = N_{\mathbf{p}}\mathbf{q}$$

Rotation represented in terms of quaternions, $\mathbf{qpq}^*$ in Equation (11.6), is then expanded as follows:

$$\begin{aligned} \mathbf{qpq}^* &= (\mathbf{qp})\mathbf{q}^* \\ &= M_{\mathbf{q}^*}(\mathbf{qp}) \\ &= M_{\mathbf{q}^*}(N_{\mathbf{q}}\mathbf{p}) \\ &= (M_{\mathbf{q}^*}N_{\mathbf{q}})\mathbf{p} \\ &= \begin{pmatrix} q_w & -q_z & q_y & -q_x \\ q_z & q_w & -q_x & -q_y \\ -q_y & q_x & q_w & -q_z \\ q_x & q_y & q_z & q_w \end{pmatrix} \begin{pmatrix} q_w & -q_z & q_y & q_x \\ q_z & q_w & -q_x & q_y \\ -q_y & q_x & q_w & q_z \\ -q_x & -q_y & -q_z & q_w \end{pmatrix} \begin{pmatrix} p_x \\ p_y \\ p_z \\ p_w \end{pmatrix} \end{aligned}$$

$M_{\mathbf{q}^*}N_{\mathbf{q}}$ makes a 4×4 matrix. Consider its first element. It is $(q_w^2 - q_z^2 - q_y^2 + q_x^2)$. As $\mathbf{q}$ is a unit quaternion, $q_x^2 + q_y^2 + q_z^2 + q_w^2 = 1$. Then, the first element is rewritten into $(1 - 2(q_y^2 + q_z^2))$. When all of the 4 × 4 elements are processed in a similar manner, $M_{\mathbf{q}^*}N_{\mathbf{q}}$ is converted into Equation (11.9). It is the rotation matrix that transforms p into p'.

11.2.4 Interpolation of Quaternions

Consider two unit quaternions, $\mathbf{p}$ and $\mathbf{q}$, which represent rotations. They can be interpolated using parameter t in the range of $[0,1]$:

$$\frac{sin(\phi(1-t))}{sin\phi}\mathbf{p} + \frac{sin(\phi t)}{sin\phi}\mathbf{q} \qquad (11.10)$$

where ϕ denotes the angle between $\mathbf{p}$ and $\mathbf{q}$. Note that ϕ can be computed using the dot product of $\mathbf{p}$ and $\mathbf{q}$ because $cos\phi = \mathbf{p} \cdot \mathbf{q} = (p_x, p_y, p_z, p_w) \cdot (q_x, q_y, q_z, q_w) = p_x q_x + p_y q_y + p_z q_z + p_w q_w$.

Equation (11.10) represents the so-called *spherical linear interpolation* (slerp). Its proof is given in the following note. Section 11.5.2 presents how quaternions are interpolated for character animation.

[Note: Proof of spherical linear interpolation]

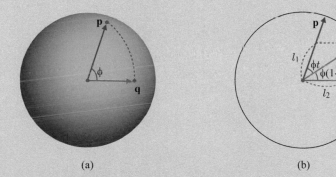

(a)   (b)

Fig. 11.6: Spherical linear interpolation on the 4D unit sphere. (a) Shortest arc between $\mathbf{p}$ and $\mathbf{q}$. (b) Spherical linear interpolation of $\mathbf{p}$ and $\mathbf{q}$ returns $\mathbf{r}$.

The set of all possible quaternions makes up a 4D unit sphere. Fig. 11.6-(a) illustrates $\mathbf{p}$ and $\mathbf{q}$ on the 4D unit sphere. Note that the interpolated quaternion must lie on the shortest arc connecting $\mathbf{p}$ and $\mathbf{q}$. Fig. 11.6-(b) shows the cross section of the unit sphere. It is in fact the great circle defined by $\mathbf{p}$ and $\mathbf{q}$. The interpolated quaternion is denoted by $\mathbf{r}$ and is defined by the parallelogram rule as follows:

$$\mathbf{r} = l_1\mathbf{p} + l_2\mathbf{q} \qquad (11.11)$$

In Fig. 11.6-(b), $sin\phi = \frac{h_1}{l_1}$, and therefore $l_1 = \frac{h_1}{sin\phi}$. As $h_1 = sin(\phi(1-t))$, we can compute l_1 as follows:

$$l_1 = \frac{sin(\phi(1-t))}{sin\phi} \qquad (11.12)$$

Similarly, l_2 is computed as follows:

$$l_2 = \frac{sin(\phi t)}{sin\phi} \tag{11.13}$$

When we insert Equations (11.12) and (11.13) into Equation (11.11), we obtain the slerp function presented in Equation (11.10).

[Note: Quaternions in Direct3D]

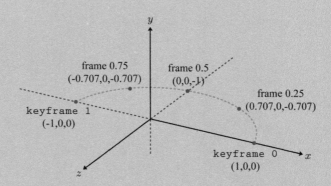

Fig. 11.7: Two keyframes (`keyframe 0` and `keyframe 1`) describe orientations, each represented in a quaternion. The quaternions are interpolated through slerp, and three in-between frames are defined using the interpolated quaternions.

D3DX provides a set of utility functions for handling quaternions. This note shows a sample code using the functions. In the sample code, we have three quaternions:
- `quatP`: 3D vector (1,0,0) to be rotated
- `quatQ0`: NULL (no rotation) defined for `keyframe 0`
- `quatQ1`: Rotation about the y-axis by 180° defined for `keyframe 1`

With a step size 0.25, `quatQ0` and `quatQ1` will be interpolated to generate three quaternions, which are used to rotate `quatP`. See Fig. 11.7. In the sample code, note the following functions:
- `D3DXQuaternionSlerp` for implementing the slerp function presented in Equation (11.10)
- `D3DXQuaternionConjugate` for generating the conjugate needed for Equation (11.6)

```
D3DXQUATERNION quatP(1.0f,0.0f,0.0f,0.0f);
D3DXQUATERNION quatQ0(0,0,0,1);
D3DXQUATERNION quatQ1(0,sinf(D3DX_PI/2.0f),0,cosf(D3DX_PI/2.0f));

D3DXQUATERNION q[5];         // interpolated quaternions
D3DXQUATERNION qc[5];        // quaternions' conjugates
D3DXQUATERNION quatPresult;  // a rotated vector

for(int i=0;i<5;i++) {
  D3DXQuaternionSlerp(&q[i],&quatQ0,&quatQ1,i*0.25f);
  D3DXQuaternionConjugate(&qc[i],&q[i]);
  D3DXQuaternionMultiply(&quatPresult,&q[i],&quatP);
  D3DXQuaternionMultiply(&quatPresult,&quatPresult,&qc[i]);

  fprintf(file,"frame = %f \n",i*0.25f);
  fprintf(file,"Quat Presult: %f %f %f %f \n",
          quatPresult.x,quatPresult.y,
          quatPresult.z,quatPresult.w);
}
```

The above code computes a set of five frames (including the keyframes). Shown below is the output.

```
frame = 0.000000
Quat Presult: 1.000000 0.000000 0.000000 0.000000
frame = 0.250000
Quat Presult: 0.707107 0.000000 -0.707107 0.000000
frame = 0.500000
Quat Presult: 0.000000 0.000000 -1.000000 0.000000
frame = 0.750000
Quat Presult: -0.707107 0.000000 -0.707107 0.000000
frame = 1.000000
Quat Presult: -1.000000 0.000000 -0.000000 0.000000
```

11.3   Hierarchical Modeling and Space Change

An *articulated* body consists of connected rigid components. A good example is a human's skeleton. This section presents the skeleton of a human character and the topic of *space change* for the skeletal model.

11.3.1 Hierarchical Model

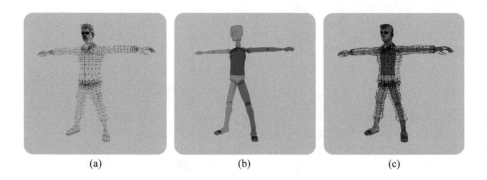

Fig. 11.8: Character mesh and skeleton. (a) Polygon mesh in the default pose. (b) Skeleton. (c) Skeleton embedded into the polygon mesh.

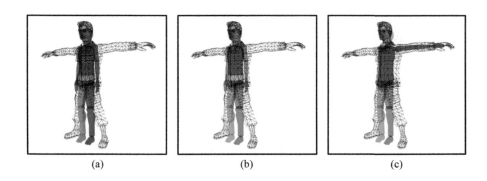

Fig. 11.9: Skeleton editing and embedding. (a) The skeleton template is positioned in the default pose. (b) The splines are deleted except one. Many other bones are also deleted. (c) The left arm is stretched so as to fit into the polygon mesh. This kind of process is repeated for the other bones.

Suppose that, as presented in Chapter 1, an artist uses an interactive 3D modeling package and creates a character represented in a polygon mesh shown in Fig. 11.8-(a). Such an initial pose of the character has many synonyms: default pose, rest pose, dress pose, bind pose, etc. This chapter uses the first term, *default pose*.

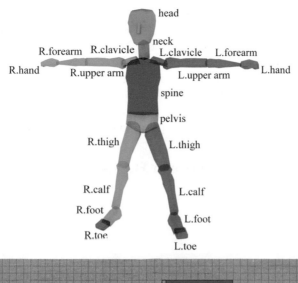

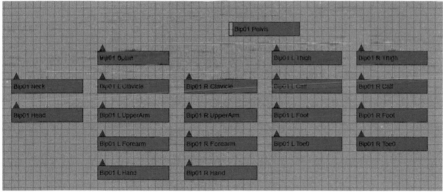

Fig. 11.10: In our example, the soldier character has a simple skeleton composed of 20 bones.

A popular method for animating a character is to use a *skeleton*. As shown in Fig. 11.8-(b), it is composed of *bones*. The skeleton is embedded into the polygon mesh. See Fig. 11.8-(c). When the skeleton is animated, the vertices of the polygon mesh will be accordingly animated.

A template skeleton for a human character is available in 3D modeling packages. Fig. 11.9 shows the process of editing the template 'biped' provided in 3ds Max and embedding it into the character's default pose. (Many bones are deleted from 'biped' to generate a simplified skeleton.) The bones form a *hierarchical structure* of parent-child relationships. Fig. 11.10 shows the bone names of our simplified skeleton and their hierarchy (displayed in 3ds Max). In a character skeleton, the *pelvis* is normally taken as the root node.

So far, the bones are illustrated as if they were surfaces. However, they are not geometric entities. The surface look is provided for user-interface purpose. When the skeleton is embedded into the default pose, a *transform matrix* is automatically computed for a bone. The matrix describes the relative pose of the bone in the skeletal hierarchy. It will be combined with another transform that describes the bone's animation, to determine the positions of the vertices affected by the bone. Sections 11.3.2 and 11.3.3 present the transforms obtained from the default pose, and Section 11.4 presents the rest.

11.3.2   Space Change between Bones

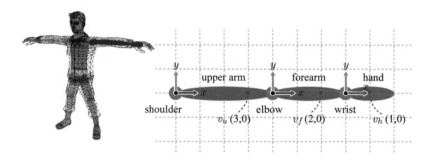

Fig. 11.11:   The soldier's arm is composed of upper arm, forearm, and hand.

The bones are connected at *joints*, which allow the rigid skeleton to animate in an articulated fashion. Fig. 11.11 shows a part of the skeleton in 2D, which consists of three bones (upper arm, forearm, and hand) and three joints (shoulder, elbow, and wrist). Consider the vertices, v_u, v_f, and v_h, which belong to the upper arm, forearm, and hand, respectively. When the forearm moves, for example, v_f has to move accordingly. It is simply achieved if v_f is defined in the forearm's *object space*. (As discussed earlier, an object can be thought of as being stuck to its object space.) Initially, all vertices of the default pose are defined in the world space[1]. Therefore, every world-space vertex of the default pose needs to be transformed into the object space of the bone (which we call *bone space* henceforth) it belongs to. For example, v_f will be transformed into the forearm's bone space so as to have the coordinates (2,0).

---

[1]More precisely, it would be "object space of the character." To avoid confusion with "object space of a bone," we use *world space* instead.

For now, consider the opposite direction, i.e., from the bone space to the world space. If we can compute such a bone-to-world transform, its inverse can be used to convert a world-space vertex into the bone space. This and the next subsections present how to derive the bone-to-world transform and its inverse.

Once the default pose is fixed, each bone's pose relative to its parent is determined. A bone has its own length and conventionally is aligned along the x-axis of its bone space. Suppose that, in Fig. 11.11, the upper arm's length is four. Then, the elbow is located at $(4,0)$ in the upper arm's bone space. If you recall the view transform presented in Chapter 2, it can be easily understood that the *space change* from the forearm's bone space to the upper arm's is simply achieved using the matrix that superimposes the coordinate system of the upper arm onto that of the forearm. In Fig. 11.11, the space-change matrix is just a translation along the x-axis by four units. We call it *to-parent transform* of the forearm in the sense that it transforms a forearm vertex to the space of its *parent*, the upper arm. Let us denote the forearm's to-parent matrix by $M_{f,p}$:

$$M_{f,p} = \begin{pmatrix} 1 & 0 & 4 \\ 0 & 1 & 0 \\ 0 & 0 & 1 \end{pmatrix} \tag{11.14}$$

Consider v_f in Fig. 11.11, whose coordinates are $(2,0)$. Its coordinates in "the bone space of the upper arm" are computed as follows:

$$M_{f,p}v_f = \begin{pmatrix} 1 & 0 & 4 \\ 0 & 1 & 0 \\ 0 & 0 & 1 \end{pmatrix} \begin{pmatrix} 2 \\ 0 \\ 1 \end{pmatrix}$$
$$= \begin{pmatrix} 6 \\ 0 \\ 1 \end{pmatrix}$$

In Fig. 11.11, it can be intuitively understood that, in the upper arm's space, v_f has the coordinates $(6,0)$.

Now consider the to-parent matrix of the hand:

$$M_{h,p} = \begin{pmatrix} 1 & 0 & 3 \\ 0 & 1 & 0 \\ 0 & 0 & 1 \end{pmatrix}$$

It transforms v_h, whose coordinates in the hand's space are $(1,0)$, into the forearm's space as follows:

$$
\begin{aligned}
v'_h &= M_{h,p}v_h \\
&= \begin{pmatrix} 1 & 0 & 3 \\ 0 & 1 & 0 \\ 0 & 0 & 1 \end{pmatrix} \begin{pmatrix} 1 \\ 0 \\ 1 \end{pmatrix} \\
&= \begin{pmatrix} 4 \\ 0 \\ 1 \end{pmatrix}
\end{aligned}
\tag{11.15}
$$

Note that v'_h in Equation (11.15) can be again transformed into the upper arm's space by $M_{f,p}$ of Equation (11.14):

$$
\begin{aligned}
M_{f,p}v'_h &= \begin{pmatrix} 1 & 0 & 4 \\ 0 & 1 & 0 \\ 0 & 0 & 1 \end{pmatrix} \begin{pmatrix} 4 \\ 0 \\ 1 \end{pmatrix} \\
&= \begin{pmatrix} 8 \\ 0 \\ 1 \end{pmatrix}
\end{aligned}
\tag{11.16}
$$

Equation (11.16) can be rephrased as follows:

$$
\begin{aligned}
M_{f,p}v'_h &= M_{f,p}M_{h,p}v_h \\
&= \begin{pmatrix} 1 & 0 & 4 \\ 0 & 1 & 0 \\ 0 & 0 & 1 \end{pmatrix} \begin{pmatrix} 1 & 0 & 3 \\ 0 & 1 & 0 \\ 0 & 0 & 1 \end{pmatrix} \begin{pmatrix} 1 \\ 0 \\ 1 \end{pmatrix} \\
&= \begin{pmatrix} 8 \\ 0 \\ 1 \end{pmatrix}
\end{aligned}
$$

i.e., $M_{f,p}$ and $M_{h,p}$ are concatenated to transform a vertex of the hand to the bone space of its *grandparent*, upper arm.

This observation can be generalized. Given a vertex at a bone, we can concatenate the to-parent matrices so as to transform the vertex into the bone space of any ancestor in the skeleton hierarchy. The ancestor can be of course the *root* node.

11.3.3   World Space to Bone Space

Fig. 11.12-(a) redraws the skeleton of Fig. 11.10, focusing on the parent-child relationships of pelvis, spine, clavicle, upper arm, forearm, and hand. For simple discussion, they are numbered: 1 for pelvis, 2 for spine, etc. From now on, the numbers will be used instead of the bone names. Then, their to-parent matrices are denoted by $M_{2,p}$, $M_{3,p}$, $M_{4,p}$, $M_{5,p}$, and $M_{6,p}$. See the hierarchy in Fig. 11.12-(a). For example, $M_{2,p}$ is the to-parent transform from the bone space of the spine to that of the pelvis.

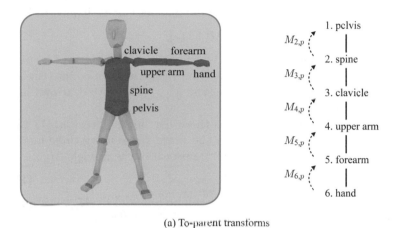

(a) To-parent transforms

(b) From spine to the world

(c) From clavicle to the world

Fig. 11.12: To-parent transforms and inverse world transforms for the default pose.

Consider the root node, pelvis. It has no to-parent matrix but is associated with a transform used to position and orient it in the world space for the default pose. It is the *world transform*. Let us denote the world matrix by $M_{1,d}$, where 1 denotes the pelvis and d stands for default pose.

Now consider the spine's world transform, $M_{2,d}$, which transforms a vertex of the spine into the world space for the default pose. It is defined to be:

$$M_{2,d} = M_{1,d}M_{2,p} \qquad (11.17)$$

i.e., a vertex of the spine is transformed first into the bone space of its parent, the pelvis, by the to-parent matrix $M_{2,p}$, and then transformed into the world space by the world transform of the pelvis, $M_{1,d}$. The dotted arrows in Fig. 11.12-(b) show the path.

The same process can be applied to the other bones. See Fig. 11.12-(c). The clavicle vertex is transformed into the world space using three matrices. They are combined to define the world transform of the clavicle $M_{3,d}$:

$$M_{3,d} = M_{1,d}M_{2,p}M_{3,p} \qquad (11.18)$$

Note that $M_{1,d}M_{2,p}$ in Equation (11.18) can be replaced by $M_{2,d}$ in Equation (11.17). Equation (11.18) can then be simplified as follows:

$$\begin{aligned} M_{3,d} &= M_{1,d}M_{2,p}M_{3,p} \\ &= M_{2,d}M_{3,p} \end{aligned} \qquad (11.19)$$

This reflects the fact that the path followed by the clavicle vertex in Fig. 11.12-(c) includes the path of the spine vertex in Fig. 11.12-(b).

Equations (11.17) and (11.19) can be generalized. The i-th bone's world transform, $M_{i,d}$, is defined as its to-parent transform, $M_{i,p}$, followed by the world transform of its parent, $M_{i-1,d}$:

$$M_{i,d} = M_{i-1,d}M_{i,p} \qquad (11.20)$$

The horizontal arrows in Fig. 11.12-(d) enumerate the world transforms.

So far, we have considered the world transform $M_{i,d}$ from the bone space to the world space. However, what is needed in an articulated-body animation is its *inverse* $M_{i,d}^{-1}$, i.e., a world-space vertex has to be transformed to the space of the bone the vertex belongs to.

When A and B denote matrices, $(AB)^{-1}$ is equivalent to $B^{-1}A^{-1}$. Therefore, $M_{i,d}^{-1}$ is derived directly from Equation (11.20):

$$M_{i,d}^{-1} = M_{i,p}^{-1}M_{i-1,d}^{-1} \qquad (11.21)$$

Fig. 11.12-(e) shows $M_{i,d}^{-1}$s for all bones.

The conclusion in this section is that, once the default pose is fixed, the inverse world transforms $M_{i,d}^{-1}$s can be computed for all bones, colored in red in Fig. 11.12-(e). Computing $M_{i,d}^{-1}$ requires $M_{i-1,d}^{-1}$ to be computed in advance, and therefore we need to do top-down traversal of the skeleton hierarchy, as illustrated in blue arrows in Fig. 11.12-(e). Such $M_{i,d}^{-1}$s will be used in the next section.

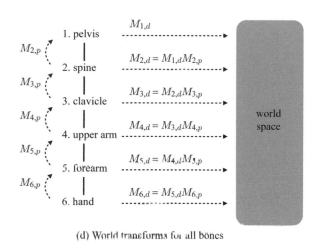

(d) World transforms for all bones

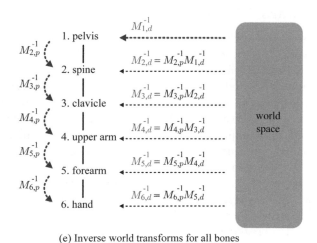

(e) Inverse world transforms for all bones

Fig. 11.12: To-parent transforms and inverse world transforms for the default pose (*continued*).

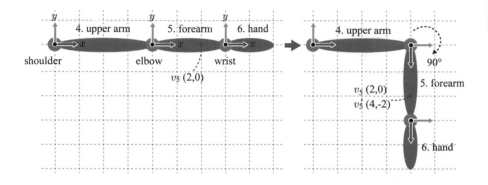

Fig. 11.13: When the forearm is animated, v_5's coordinates remain fixed in its bone space but change with respect to the bone space of its parent (the upper arm) and the world space.

11.4   Forward Kinematics

The inverse of the world transform, $M_{i,d}^{-1}$, presented in the previous section, converts a world-space vertex "in the default pose" to the i-th bone's space. Now the i-th bone is *animated*. Then, the vertices belonging to the bone are accordingly animated. For rendering, the animated vertices should be transformed back to the world space. (Then, they will be transformed to the camera space and so forth, along the pipeline.) Fig. 11.13 shows an example where the forearm is animated. We need a world transform, which we name $M_{5,w}$, for converting "animated v_5" into the world space.

In Fig. 11.13, the forearm is rotated clockwise by 90°. It is −90° counterclockwise. The rotation is about the origin of the forearm's bone space, which is the elbow. Such a transform is named *local transform* in the sense that it is done within the local space (bone space) of a bone. The forearm's local transform is denoted by $M_{5,l}$. Two-dimensional rotation matrix in the homogeneous coordinates is defined as

$$\begin{pmatrix} cos\theta & -sin\theta & 0 \\ sin\theta & cos\theta & 0 \\ 0 & 0 & 1 \end{pmatrix}$$

and therefore $M_{5,l}$ (rotation by −90°) is determined as follows:

$$M_{5,l} = \begin{pmatrix} 0 & 1 & 0 \\ -1 & 0 & 0 \\ 0 & 0 & 1 \end{pmatrix} \qquad (11.22)$$

As the first step for computing the world-space position of "animated v_5," let us find its coordinates in the upper arm's space, which we denote by v_5'. For this purpose, the local transform matrix $M_{5,l}$ in Equation (11.22) is combined with the to-parent matrix $M_{5,p}$ ($M_{f,p}$) defined in Equation (11.14), and is then applied to v_5:

$$v_5' = M_{5,p}M_{5,l}v_5$$

$$= \begin{pmatrix} 1 & 0 & 4 \\ 0 & 1 & 0 \\ 0 & 0 & 1 \end{pmatrix} \begin{pmatrix} 0 & 1 & 0 \\ -1 & 0 & 0 \\ 0 & 0 & 1 \end{pmatrix} \begin{pmatrix} 2 \\ 0 \\ 1 \end{pmatrix}$$

$$= \begin{pmatrix} 4 \\ -2 \\ 1 \end{pmatrix}$$

The dotted grid of Fig. 11.13 may help you understand that v_5' has the coordinates (4,-2) in the upper arm's bone space. This shows that a vertex animated by a bone can be successfully transformed into its parent's space.

The upper arm can also be animated. Let $M_{4,w}$ denote the matrix that transforms the animated vertices of the upper arm into the world space. Then, $M_{5,w}$ for transforming "animated v_5" into the world space is defined as follows:

$$M_{5,w} = M_{4,w}M_{5,p}M_{5,l} \tag{11.23}$$

Considering the hierarchical structure of the skeleton, Equation (11.23) is generalized as follows:

$$M_{i,w} = M_{i-1,w}M_{i,p}M_{i,l} \tag{11.24}$$

When the artist defines the animated pose of the i-th bone, $M_{i,l}$ is obtained, as presented in Equation (11.22). $M_{i,p}$ was obtained from the default pose. (Given the default pose, all of $M_{i,p}$s were immediately computed and fixed, as shown in Fig. 11.12-(a).) Therefore, computing $M_{i,w}$ simply requires $M_{i-1,w}$ (the parent's world transform) to be computed in advance. The skeleton hierarchy implies that we need the world transform of the root node, $M_{1,w}$. It represents the pose of the animated pelvis and is defined by the artist. Then, we can compute the world transforms of all bones "in the animated pose." Fig. 11.14 enumerates the world transforms. For each frame of animation, the skeleton hierarchy is traversed in a top-down fashion. For each bone, $M_{i,l}$ is first computed, and then $M_{i,w}$ is computed using Equation (11.24).

Let v_d denote the world-space vertex "in the default pose." It is transformed into the bone space by $M_{i,d}^{-1}$, which is obtained from the default pose, as shown in Fig. 11.12-(e). The bone-space vertex is then transformed by $M_{i,w}$ to the world-space vertex "in the animated pose." We denote the vertex by v_w. The animated character is rendered using v_ws. The entire process from the default-pose world space to the bone space and back to the animated-pose world space is described as follows:

$$v_w = M_{i,w}M_{i,d}^{-1}v_d \tag{11.25}$$

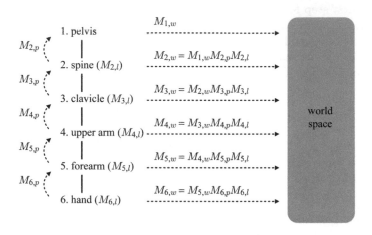

Fig. 11.14: World transforms for all bones in the animated pose.

Kinematics is a field of mechanics that describes the motion of objects without consideration of mass or force[2]. Determining the pose of an articulated body by specifying all bone's transforms is called *forward kinematics*. In Section 11.6, we will see a different method named *inverse kinematics*. It determines the bone transforms of an articulated body in order to achieve a desired pose of the leaf node, such as hand in our hierarchy.

11.5   Skinning and Keyframe Animation

The skeleton is a conceptual structure, and the actual 3D geometry associated with it is the polygon mesh of the character. The polygon mesh deformed by the skeletal motion is often called a *skin*. This section presents how the skin is smoothly deformed.

11.5.1   Skinning

So far, we assumed that a vertex belongs to a single bone. This often leads to unnatural skin deformation. Fig. 11.15-(a) shows the upper arm and forearm connected by the elbow, and three vertices of the mesh (v_1, v_2, and

---

[2]In contrast, dynamics is another field devoted to studying the forces required to cause motions. A simple example was presented in Section 7.2.1 under the name of physics-based simulation.

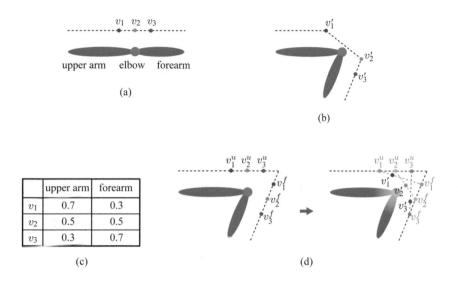

$$
\begin{array}{c|c|c}
 & \text{upper arm} & \text{forearm} \\
\hline
v_1 & 0.7 & 0.3 \\
v_2 & 0.5 & 0.5 \\
v_3 & 0.3 & 0.7 \\
\end{array}
$$

Fig. 11.15: Skinning animation. (a) Vertices on the skin. (b) No blending. (c) Blend weights. (d) Blending.

v_3) near the elbow. Suppose that v_1 belongs to the upper arm whereas v_2 and v_3 belong to the forearm. Fig. 11.15-(b) shows the result when the forearm is rotated. The deformed skin is not smooth.

The problem can be alleviated by making multiple bones affect a vertex and then blending the results, instead of binding a vertex to a single bone. For this purpose, a blending weight is given for each bone affecting a vertex. The weight describes how much a bone contributes to the deformed position of the vertex. Fig. 11.15-(c) shows an example, where the upper arm contributes 70% to v_1's position and the forearm contributes 30%. It looks reasonable because v_1 is closer to the upper arm and therefore is affected more by the upper arm. Similar discussions can be made for the weights given to v_2 and v_3.

Fig. 11.15-(d) illustrates the blending process, where v_1^u, v_2^u, and v_3^u denote the vertex positions transformed by the upper arm's motion, and v_1^f, v_2^f, and v_3^f denote those by the forearm's. Each pair of v_i^u and v_i^f is linearly interpolated using the blend weights given in Fig. 11.15-(c). The result is v_i'. Connecting v_i's generates a smoother skin. This technique is called *vertex blending* or *skinning*.

Skinning is implemented by extending Equation (11.25). See Fig. 11.16-(a) that is copied from Fig. 11.13. Assume that, in addition to the forearm, the hand also affects v_5. As a vertex has different coordinates in different spaces, v_5 is renamed v_6 in the hand's space and has the coordinates (-1,0). Note

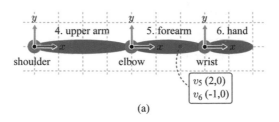

(a)

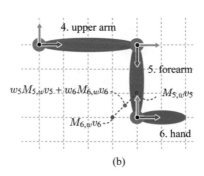

(b)

Fig. 11.16: Vertex blending for skinning. (a) A vertex has different coordinates (v_5 and v_6) in two bone spaces. (b) In the animated pose, v_5 and v_6 have their own world-space positions, and the positions are blended.

that v_5 and v_6 are the results of applying $M_{5,d}^{-1}$ and $M_{6,d}^{-1}$, respectively, to a single world-space vertex of the default pose, which we denote by v_d:

$$
\begin{aligned}
v_5 &= M_{5,d}^{-1} v_d \\
v_6 &= M_{6,d}^{-1} v_d
\end{aligned}
\tag{11.26}
$$

Suppose that the forearm is rotated by $-90°$ and the hand is rotated by $90°$, leading to the animated pose shown in Fig. 11.16-(b). Then, v_5 and v_6 are transformed to the world space by $M_{5,w}$ and $M_{6,w}$, respectively, and are blended using the pre-defined weights w_5 and w_6:

$$
w_5 M_{5,w} v_5 + w_6 M_{6,w} v_6
\tag{11.27}
$$

Equations (11.26) and (11.27) are combined:

$$
w_5 M_{5,w} M_{5,d}^{-1} v_d + w_6 M_{6,w} M_{6,d}^{-1} v_d
\tag{11.28}
$$

Suppose that n bones affect a vertex and their weights sum to 1. Then, the world-space vertex of the animated pose, v_w, is defined by generalizing Equation (11.28):

$$
v_w = \sum_{i=1}^{n} w_i M_{i,w} M_{i,d}^{-1} v_d
\tag{11.29}
$$

11.5.2 Skinning in Keyframe Animation

This subsection presents how the skinning algorithm is implemented in keyframe animation. In a keyframe for skinning, each bone is assigned the key data. Recall that, for each bone i in the animated pose, we need to compute $M_{i,w}$. It is defined as $M_{i-1,w}M_{i,p}M_{i,l}$ in Equation (11.24). The local transform $M_{i,l}$ is (usually) a rotation. The to-parent transform $M_{i,p}$ is a space-change matrix composed of a translation and a rotation. Let us combine $M_{i,l}$ and $M_{i,p}$ into a single matrix and name it Mc. Its upper-left 3×3 sub-matrix represents a combined rotation, and its fourth column represents a combined translation. (If this not clear, read the last paragraph of Section 2.1.2.) For a keyframe, the rotation part of Mc is stored as a quaternion, and the translation is stored as a vector. They form the key data of a bone.

For an in-between frame, both the quaternions and translational vectors of the keyframes are interpolated. The interpolated quaternion is converted into a matrix, as presented in Equation (11.9). The interpolated translation vector fills the fourth column of the matrix, which can then be called the "interpolated Mc." It is combined with the parent bone's world transform $M_{i-1,w}$ so as to complete $M_{i,w}$.

```
for each bone      // default pose
   load Md-

for each frame
   for each bone  // animated pose
      interpolate key data and compute Mc
      compute Mw
      combine Md- and Mw to define Mi
      store Mi into the matrix palette
   invoke vertex shader for skinning
```

Shown above is the pseudo code of skinning for keyframe animation. The first for loop assigns Md- (denoting $M_{i,d}^{-1}$) to each bone. The second for loop is run for each frame of animation. First of all, Mw (denoting $M_{i,w}$) is computed for each bone using "interpolated Mc." Then, Mw is combined with Md- to make a single matrix, Mi. It is stored in a table, called *matrix palette*.

The above code is executed by the CPU. Once the matrix palette is filled with all bones' Mis, the CPU program invokes a vertex shader that implements Equation (11.29). In games, the number of bones affecting a vertex is typically limited to four, for programming efficiency. Then, for each vertex of a polygon mesh, two 1D arrays are assigned, each with four elements. The first array contains indices to the matrix palette, i.e., it points Mis of the affecting bones. The second array contains the blend weights (w_is).

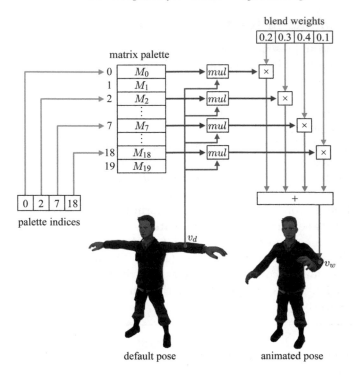

Fig. 11.17: The input to the skinning algorithm is composed of the character's polygon mesh in the default pose, the matrix palette, the indices to the palette, and the blend weights. (The palette indices and blend weights are fixed for a vertex.) The skinning algorithm transforms v_d of the default pose into v_w of the animated pose.

The input to the vertex shader is composed of (1) the polygon mesh in the default pose, (2) the matrix palette storing Mis, (3) a 1D array containing the palette indices, and (4) a 1D array containing the blend weights. Fig. 11.17 illustrates the input set and the flow of skinning animation. Consider v_d. It is a vertex of the polygon mesh in the default pose. Our soldier character has 20 bones, as shown in Fig. 11.10, and therefore the size of the matrix palette is 20. In the current example, the indices of the matrices affecting v_d are (0,2,7,18). Then, v_d is multiplied by each of M_0, M_2, M_7, and M_{18} (through *mul* for matrix-vertex multiplication). The results are combined using the blend weights, (0.2,0.3,0.4,0.1) in the example. The combined is v_w. This algorithm is often called *matrix palette blending*.

The vertex shader processes all vertices in the default pose. Its HLSL code is presented in [Note: Vertex shader for matrix palette blending]. Fig. 11.18-(a) shows two keyframes and three in-between frames of the skin-animated character, and Fig. 11.18-(b) illustrates the superimposed frames.

[Note: Vertex shader for matrix palette blending]

```
void main(float3 Pos : POSITION,              // default pose vertex
          float3 Normal : NORMAL,
          float4 Weight : TEXCOORD0,          // blend weights
          float4 MatrixIndex : TEXCOORD1,     // palette indices
       out float4 oPos : POSITION,
       out float3 oNormal : TEXCOORD0,
  uniform float4 Matrix[60],                  // for 20 bones
  uniform float4x4 WorldViewProj)
{
  float3 weightedPos = 0, weightedNormal = 0;
  for(int i=0; i<4; i++)
  {
    float index = MatrixIndex[i];
    float3x4 boneMatrix = float3x4(Matrix[index+0],
                                   Matrix[index+1],
                                   Matrix[index+2]);
    float3 bonePos = mul(boneMatrix, float4(Pos, 1));
    weightedPos += Weight[i] * bonePos;

    float3x3 Rotation = float3x3(boneMatrix[0].xyz,
                                 boneMatrix[1].xyz,
                                 boneMatrix[2].xyz);
    float3 boneNormal = mul(Rotation, normal);
    weightedNormal += Weight[i] * boneNormal;
  }
  oPos = mul(WorldViewProj, float4(weightedPos, 1));
  oNormal = normalize(weightedNormal);
}
```

(a)   (b)

Fig. 11.18: Skinning for keyframe animation. (a) Keyframes and in-between frames. (b) Superimposed frames.

11.6   Inverse Kinematics

In robotics, an *end effector* refers to the device located at the end of a robotic arm. A good example is a jaw gripper, designed to grasp an object. *Forward kinematics* computes the pose of the end effector as a function of the joint angles of the robotic arm. The reverse process is called *inverse kinematics* (IK). Given the desired pose of the end effector along with the initial pose of the robotic arm, the joint angles of the final pose are calculated.

Even though IK was developed for motion planning in robotics, it is quite relevant to character animation. For example, it is used to compute the leg's joint angles for making the feet land firmly on top of an irregular surface of terrain. By solving IK in real time, the character is able to react spontaneously to an unpredictable environment. IK augments pre-authored animations to avoid the typical computer-generated look.

The IK solutions adopted in the robotics community are largely based on solving a linear system. It involves forming the matrix of partial derivatives called *Jacobian* and computing the (pseudo)inverse of the Jacobian. It is computationally expensive. This section presents two cheaper algorithms which have been popularly adopted for real-time applications.

11.6.1   Analytic Solution

The number of independent variables defining the state of an object is called the *degrees of freedom* (DOF). Consider the shoulder in Fig. 11.19-(a), which is illustrated as a mechanical joint called a *ball joint*. The upper arm may have an arbitrary orientation through up-and-down and left-to-right movements, which are called *pitch* and *yaw*, respectively. We can also rotate the upper arm as if we were using it as a screwdriver. It is called *roll*. Then, the shoulder provides three DOF for the upper arm. In contrast, the elbow is treated like a *hinge joint* as shown in Fig. 11.19-(b). It is a 1-DOF joint.

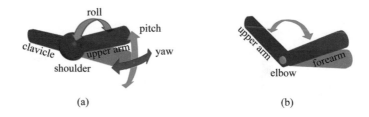

Fig. 11.19: Joints and degrees of freedom. (a) 3-DOF shoulder is often taken as a ball joint. (b) 1-DOF elbow is taken as a hinge joint.

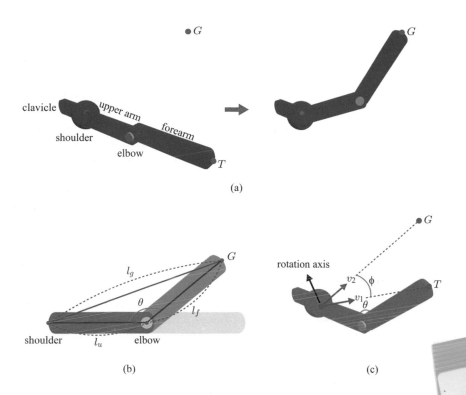

Fig. 11.20: Analytic solution for IK. (a) The final pose of a two-joint a[rm]
is computed given its initial pose and the end effector's goal position G. [(b)]
The joint angle θ of the 1-DOF elbow is computed. (c) The rotation angle[s]
and the rotation axis are computed for the 3-DOF shoulder.

Let us use a two-joint arm to present the *analytic solution* for IK. For simplicity, consider only the position of the end effector. See Fig. 11.20-(a). Given the goal position G and the initial pose of the arm, the *joint angles* of the shoulder and elbow are calculated. Then, the upper arm and forearm will be rotated so as to make the calculated joint angles, and the forearm's tip T will reach G.

The elbow is a 1-DOF joint, and it is straightforward to compute its joint angle. See Fig. 11.20-(b) that illustrates the upper arm and forearm in 2D. The elbow's joint angle is denoted by θ. The lengths of the upper arm and forearm are fixed and are denoted by l_u and l_f, respectively. Given the goal position G, the distance l_g between the shoulder and G becomes also fixed. The *law of cosines* asserts that

$$l_g^2 = l_u^2 + l_f^2 - 2l_u l_f cos\theta \qquad (11.30)$$

Then, θ is computed directly from Equation (11.30):

$$\theta = acos\frac{l_u^2 + l_f^2 - l_g^2}{2l_u l_f} \qquad (11.31)$$

Fig. 11.20-(c) shows the configuration, where the forearm has been rotated to make the elbow's joint angle θ. Now the upper arm should be rotated such that the forearm is accordingly moved and T reaches G. Consider the unit vector v_1 connecting the shoulder and T, and another unit vector v_2 connecting the shoulder and G. If v_1 is rotated by ϕ so as to be aligned with v_2, T will reach G. The rotation angle ϕ is computed using the dot product of v_1 and v_2. (Recall that $v_1 \cdot v_2 = \|v_1\|\|v_2\|cos\phi$.) In addition to the rotation angle, we need the rotation axis. It is perpendicular to the plane spanned by v_1 and v_2 and therefore is determined by their cross product. Then, the upper arm is rotated by ϕ about the rotation axis, and T reaches G.

11.6.2   Cyclic Coordinate Descent

In some applications, analytic solutions are desirable due to their speed and exactness. For a complex chain of bones with many joints, however, an analytic solution may not be feasible. A more general method is needed to solve IK.

Cyclic coordinate descent (CCD) is an optimization-based IK algorithm that is simple but robust. CCD works in an iterative fashion. Each iteration starts from the end effector and works backward along the connected bones. As a result, small adjustments are made to all of the joints, and the distance between the end effector's tip and the goal position is decreased. Then, the next iteration starts.

Fig. 11.21 illustrates how CCD works for the chain of upper arm, forearm, and hand. In Fig. 11.21-(a), the hand is rotated such that it points directly at G. Consider the origin O_h of the hand's space. $\overrightarrow{O_h T}$ is a vector connecting O_h and T (the tip of the hand), and $\overrightarrow{O_h G}$ is similarly defined. $\overrightarrow{O_h T}$ needs to be rotated by θ to get aligned with $\overrightarrow{O_h G}$. The rotation angle θ and the rotation axis are computed using the dot product and cross product of $\overrightarrow{O_h T}$ and $\overrightarrow{O_h G}$, respectively, as presented in the previous subsection.

Now the forearm is rotated. In Fig. 11.21-(b), $\overrightarrow{O_f T}$ is rotated and aligned with $\overrightarrow{O_f G}$. The rotation angle and axis are computed using the dot product and cross product of $\overrightarrow{O_f T}$ and $\overrightarrow{O_f G}$, respectively. Fig. 11.21-(c) shows the rotation result. The same process is performed for the upper arm. The first iteration is completed, and Fig. 11.21-(d) shows the resulting configuration of the chain. The algorithm terminates if the goal is achieved, i.e., if T is equal or close enough to G. Otherwise, the next iteration starts from the end effector, hand. The iterations through the chain are repeated until either the goal is achieved or the pre-defined number of iterations is reached.

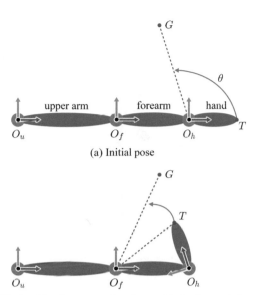

(a) Initial pose

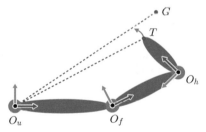

(b) The hand has been rotated, and now it is the forearm's turn.

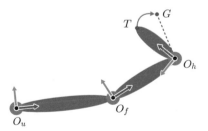

(c) The forearm has been rotated, and now it is the upper arm's turn.

(d) The upper arm has been rotated, and the next iteration starts.

Fig. 11.21: The CCD algorithm processes the chain of bones, one bone at a time, starting from the end effector (the hand in the example). If T does not reach G at the end of an iteration, the next iteration starts.

Fig. 11.22: IK calculation is done for the soldier's arm to make his hand reach the flying ball. Dynamic gazing is also applied to the head bone.

Using IK is a distinguished step many of the contemporary games have taken to accomplish realistic character animations. In a soccer game, for example, IK is solved at real time to make the player's foot reach a flying ball. Fig. 11.22 shows a series of snapshots of the IK-based animation, where the soldier extends his arm to the flying ball. IK has many other uses. For having a character gaze at a randomly moving target, IK is applied to the head bone. There would be no way to make a keyframed animation provide all possible gazing directions. In fact, IK for such dynamic gazing is applied in Fig. 11.22. IK is also widely used in a shooting game to have a soldier aim a gun at the enemies.

Exercises

1. See the figure of the next page. Shown left is the initial pose of the arm. For simplicity, let us take the bone space of the upper arm as the world space. The bone space origins of the forearm and hand are (12,0) and (22,0), respectively, with respect to the world space. From the initial pose, the forearm is rotated by $90°$, and the hand is rotated by $-90°$, to define the pose shown right.

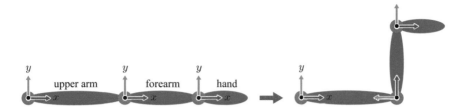

(a) In the initial pose, compute the to-parent matrices of the forearm and hand ($M_{f,p}$ and $M_{h,p}$).

(b) Compute the world matrices of the forearm and hand "in the default pose" ($M_{f,d}$ and $M_{h,d}$).

(c) Compute $M_{f,d}^{-1}$ and $M_{h,d}^{-1}$.

(d) Compute the local transform matrices of the forearm and hand ($M_{f,l}$ and $M_{h,l}$).

(e) Compute the world matrices of the forearm and hand "in the animated pose" ($M_{f,w}$ and $M_{h,w}$).

(f) Consider a vertex v whose coordinates in the forearm's bone space are $(8,0)$. It is affected by two bones, the forearm and hand, which have the same blend weights. Using the vertex blending (skinning) algorithm, compute the world-space position of v "in the animated pose."

2. In Fig. 11.22, dynamic gazing is implemented. Consider the joint connecting the head bone and neck bone. Assume that only the joint is involved in dynamic gazing.

(a) What is the DOF of the joint?

(b) Describe an analytic solution for the dynamic gazing.

Chapter 12

Physics-based Simulation*

Computer games provide a virtual environment, which is usually expected to simulate the real world. Physics-based simulation in games (or simply game physics) serves the purpose by adopting the physics models, which include the physics entities such as mass, velocity, acceleration, force, etc. In games, physics-based simulation is becoming an indispensable component, and many physics engines are available, ranging from high-price commercial engines to open-source engines. Game physics includes a wide spectrum of topics, and we can find many books devoted to it [37, 38].

Section 7.2.1 presented the basics of game physics using a simple example, the particle system. The simple example was even more simplified because the particles were assumed to fly in the free space with no collision. We did not consider, for example, what would happen when the particles ran into each other. Game physics should be able to process such collisions.

In order to process collisions, first of all, we have to perform *collision detection*, which concerns the problems of determining whether, when, and where two or more objects come into contact. Once collision is detected, we have to describe how the objects move after collision. It is called *collision resolution*. This chapter presents two methods for it, *penalty method* and *impulse method*. Section 12.1 presents the penalty method with an example of a particle bouncing on the ground, and Section 12.2 presents the impulse method with an example of billiard game.

The particle and billiard-game examples require quite simple collision detection methods, and they are presented in their respective sections. Collisions between general polygon models are not so simple to detect. Section 12.3 presents a popular method of detecting collisions between polygon models.

12.1 Penalty Method

Consider a particle falling into the ground. Assume that the y-axis of the world space is upward and the zx-plane corresponds to the ground. Then, collision is detected when the y-coordinate of the particle's position becomes zero or negative. This is the simplest example of collision detection!

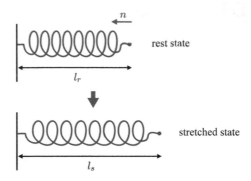

Fig. 12.1: A spring has the rest length l_r and the stiffness constant k_s. It is stretched along the opposite direction of n. If the stretched length is l_s, the spring force is defined to be $k_s(l_s - l_r)n$.

For resolving the detected collision, the penalty method uses a *spring force*, which is one of the most popular and useful forces adopted in game physics. See Fig. 12.1. The spring of the *rest length* l_r is stretched and reaches the length l_s. Then, the spring force f_s is defined by *Hooke's law*:

$$f_s = k_s(l_s - l_r)n \qquad (12.1)$$

where k_s is the spring constant describing the spring's stiffness, and n is the unit vector from the spring end, for which f_s is being computed, to the other end.

Consider the particle falling into the ground, shown in Fig. 12.2-(a). The particle at position s_{i-1} does not yet collide with the ground, but collision is detected at position s_i. In the penalty method, the particle at s_i is *penalized* for penetrating the ground. For this purpose, an imaginary spring is attached between the penetrating point s_i and the ground surface, as shown in Fig. 12.2-(b). The spring is assumed to have zero rest length, i.e., $l_r=0$. Therefore, the stretched spring imparts a force on the particle at s_i. The spring force f_s is computed using Hooke's law in Equation (12.1). Its direction is along the normal n of the ground surface.

Once f_s is computed, the acceleration is determined using Newton's second law, $a = \frac{f_s}{m}$, and is added to the acceleration of gravity g, as shown in Fig. 12.2-(c). The combined acceleration a' is integrated to define the velocity v_{i+1}, i.e., $v_{i+1} = v_i + a't$. See Fig. 12.2-(d). Finally, the average velocity $\frac{v_i + v_{i+1}}{2}$ is integrated to compute the position s_{i+1}, as shown in Fig. 12.2-(e). If you trace s_{i-1}, s_i, and s_{i+1}, you can find that the particle stops its downward motion and is bounced upward. Fig. 12.2-(f) shows the repeated parabolic trajectory of the particle produced by the penalty method.

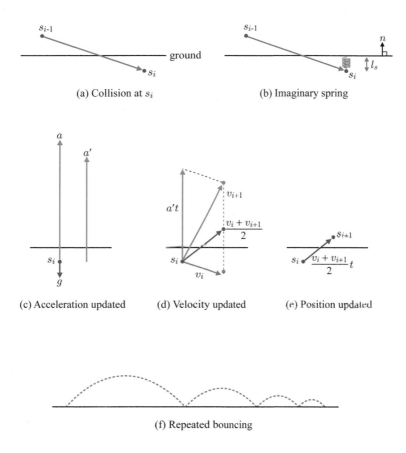

(a) Collision at s_i (b) Imaginary spring

(c) Acceleration updated   (d) Velocity updated   (e) Position updated

(f) Repeated bouncing

Fig. 12.2: A spring imparts a force on the particle at s_i. The spring force and gravity are combined to determine the acceleration a', and then *integration* is performed to update the particle's velocity and position.

The penalty method is easy to implement, and the spring force adopted in the method is neatly integrated with other forces such as gravity. However, the penalty method often reveals a serious problem. Suppose that k_s is underestimated, i.e., is set to a smaller value than desired. Then, the spring force f_s computed by Equation (12.1) becomes small, leading to small vectors for acceleration a' and velocity v_{i+1}. As a result, the new position s_{i+1} might be still under the ground. In contrast, overestimated k_s may lead to an overly large velocity, and the particle might overshoot in an unrealistic manner. We need a trial-and-error process to determine an appropriate value for the spring constant k_s.

12.2   Impulse Method

Even though the penalty method has been widely used in game physics, it is somewhat old-fashioned. An alternative to the penalty method is the impulse method, which is based on the classical principle of *conservation of momentum*. The best example for demonstrating the impulse method is the billiard game. This section presents collision detection and resolution between two billiard balls.

12.2.1   Impulse

Momentum (p) is defined to be mass (m) times velocity (v), i.e., $p = mv$. The principle of conservation of momentum asserts that the total momentum is constant in a closed system. Consider two balls, B_1 and B_2, the masses of which are m_1 and m_2, respectively. If B_1 and B_2 collide, we have the following equation:

$$m_1 v_1 + m_2 v_2 = m_1 v_1' + m_2 v_2' \qquad (12.2)$$

where v_1 and v_2 are the *approaching velocities* before collision, and v_1' and v_2' are the *separating velocities* after collision. Equation (12.2) is rearranged into

$$m_1(v_1' - v_1) = -m_2(v_2' - v_2) \qquad (12.3)$$

Impulse is defined as the "change in momentum." Then, B_1 and B_2 have the following impulses:

$$\begin{aligned} \Delta p_1 &= m_1(v_1' - v_1) \\ \Delta p_2 &= m_2(v_2' - v_2) \end{aligned} \qquad (12.4)$$

Equations (12.3) and (12.4) lead to the following:

$$\Delta p_1 = -\Delta p_2 \qquad (12.5)$$

This asserts that, when two balls collide, the same magnitude of impulse applies in opposite directions.

Let J denote B_1's impulse, Δp_1. Then, Equation (12.4) can be rewritten as follows:

$$\begin{aligned} J &= m_1(v_1' - v_1) \\ -J &= m_2(v_2' - v_2) \end{aligned} \qquad (12.6)$$

Equation (12.6) is rearranged into

$$\begin{aligned} v_1' &= v_1 + \frac{J}{m_1} \\ v_2' &= v_2 - \frac{J}{m_2} \end{aligned} \qquad (12.7)$$

When two balls collide, the *relative separating velocity* ($v_1' - v_2'$) is determined by the *relative approaching velocity* ($v_1 - v_2$) and the *coefficient of restitution* e:

$$v_1' - v_2' = -e(v_1 - v_2) \qquad (12.8)$$

where e is in the range of $[0,1]$. If two clay objects collide and stick to each other, the collision is taken as perfectly inelastic, and e is set to 0. In contrast, collision between two billiard balls is close to perfectly elastic, and e approaches 1.

For computing J, let us insert v_1' and v_2' of Equation (12.7) into Equation (12.8). Then, we obtain the following:

$$
\begin{aligned}
-e(v_1 - v_2) &= v_1' - v_2' \\
&= v_1 + \frac{J}{m_1} - v_2 + \frac{J}{m_2} \\
&= v_1 - v_2 + J(\frac{1}{m_1} + \frac{1}{m_2})
\end{aligned}
\tag{12.9}
$$

The term $(v_1 - v_2)$ representing the relative approaching velocity is abbreviated to v_r, and Equation (12.9) is rewritten as follows:

$$
-ev_r = v_r + J(\frac{1}{m_1} + \frac{1}{m_2})
\tag{12.10}
$$

Equation (12.10) is rearranged into:

$$
-v_r(e+1) = J(\frac{1}{m_1} + \frac{1}{m_2})
\tag{12.11}
$$

Then, impulse J is computed as follows:

$$
\begin{aligned}
J &= -\frac{v_r(e+1)}{\frac{1}{m_1} + \frac{1}{m_2}} \\
&= -v_r(e+1)\frac{m_1 m_2}{m_1 + m_2}
\end{aligned}
\tag{12.12}
$$

This will be used for collision resolution presented in the next subsection.

12.2.2 Impulse-based Collision Resolution

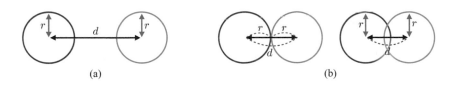

(a)   (b)

Fig. 12.3: Collision detection between balls. (a) No collision. (b) Collision.

Let us first see how collision is detected between two billiard balls. For each frame, the distance d between the centers of the balls is computed. If it is larger than twice the radius r of the ball, there is no collision, as shown in Fig. 12.3-(a). Otherwise, the balls collide, as shown in Fig. 12.3-(b).

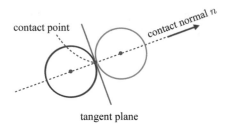

Fig. 12.4:   Collision detection algorithms return the contact point and contact normal. These are used for collision resolution.

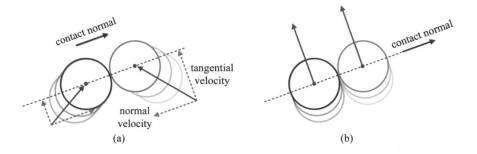

Fig. 12.5:   Normal velocity. (a) The approaching velocity is decomposed into the normal velocity and the tangential velocity. (b) The normal velocity of each ball is zero, and consequently no collision resolution is needed.

In Fig. 12.4, two balls collide at the so-called *contact point*. Consider the tangent plane at the contact point. Its normal is named the *contact normal* and is represented as a unit vector n. For spheres in contact, the contact normal is parallel to the line connecting their centers, which is often called the line of action[1].

Fig. 12.5-(a) shows two balls in contact. The approaching velocity of each ball is illustrated as a solid red arrow. It is decomposed into the *normal velocity* and the *tangential velocity*, which are parallel and perpendicular to the contact normal, respectively. After collision, the normal velocities are changed, but the tangential velocities remain constant. Therefore, only the normal velocities will be considered for collision resolution. Fig. 12.5-(b) shows a special case, where two balls are in contact and moving with the same velocity that is perpendicular to the contact normal. The normal velocity of each ball is zero. Consequently there is no collision to be resolved.

---

[1]In the example of Fig. 12.2-(b), the contact normal is set to the surface normal n of the ground.

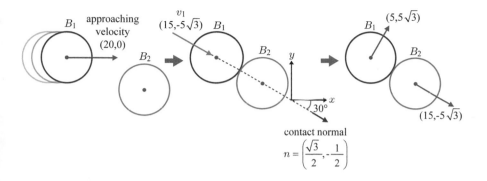

Fig. 12.6: B_1 moves with the approaching velocity (20,0). B_2 is static. The separating velocities of B_1 and B_2 are computed using the impulses.

Now consider the momentum and impulse in Fig. 12.5-(a). When two balls collide, the momentum in the tangential direction is conserved for each ball because the tangential velocity remains constant. In contrast, the normal velocity changes, and so does the momentum in the normal direction. The impulse, defined as the change in momentum, occurs along the normal direction only. Therefore, v_r in Equation (12.12) can be restricted to the normal component of the relative approaching velocity. We will simply call it "relative normal velocity."

Fig. 12.6 shows a top view of the billiard table. With the velocity (20,0), B_1 approaches B_2 that is static. Suppose that, as shown in the middle of the figure, the contact normal is computed as follows:

$$n = (\frac{\sqrt{3}}{2}, -\frac{1}{2}) \tag{12.13}$$

The normal velocity v_1 of B_1 is computed by projecting its approaching velocity to the contact normal:

$$\begin{aligned} v_1 &= ((20,0) \cdot (\tfrac{\sqrt{3}}{2}, -\tfrac{1}{2}))(\tfrac{\sqrt{3}}{2}, -\tfrac{1}{2}) \\ &= (15, -5\sqrt{3}) \end{aligned} \tag{12.14}$$

Assume that, in the example of Fig. 12.6, $m_1 = m_2$ and $e = 1$. As B_2 is static, its normal velocity v_2 is zero. Then, the relative normal velocity v_r that is defined to be $(v_1 - v_2)$ is equal to v_1. Impulse J is computed using Equations (12.12) and (12.14):

$$\begin{aligned} J &= -v_r(e+1)\tfrac{m_1 m_2}{m_1+m_2} \\ &= (-30, 10\sqrt{3})\tfrac{m_1}{2} \\ &= (-15m_1, 5\sqrt{3}m_1) \end{aligned} \tag{12.15}$$

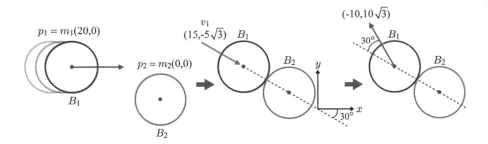

Fig. 12.7: B_1 moves with the approaching velocity $(20,0)$, and collides B_1 that is immovable. B_2's separating velocity is fixed to zero, and the impulse contributes only to the separating velocity of B_1.

The initial momentum p_1 of B_1 is

$$
\begin{aligned}
p_1 &= m_1(20,0)\\
&= (20m_1, 0)
\end{aligned}
\tag{12.16}
$$

Impulse represents the change in momentum, and therefore Equation (12.15) is added to Equation (12.16) to update B_1's momentum:

$$
\begin{aligned}
p_1' &= p_1 + J\\
&= (20m_1, 0) + (-15m_1, 5\sqrt{3}m_1)\\
&= (5m_1, 5\sqrt{3}m_1)
\end{aligned}
\tag{12.17}
$$

Dividing Equation (12.17) by m_1, the *separating velocity* of B_1 is computed. It is $(5, 5\sqrt{3})$. Fig. 12.6 shows how B_1 separates after collision.

The same process is applied to B_2. Recall that, if B_1's impulse is J, the impulse on B_2 is $-J$, as presented in Equations (12.5) and (12.6). Therefore, B_2's impulse is obtained by negating Equation (12.15). It is $(15m_1, -5\sqrt{3}m_1)$ or equivalently $(15m_2, -5\sqrt{3}m_2)$ because $m_1 = m_2$. As B_2 was static, its initial momentum is $(0,0)$. Therefore, the impulse $(15m_2, -5\sqrt{3}m_2)$ is simply set to the momentum after collision. Dividing it by m_2, the separating velocity of B_2 is computed. It is $(15, -5\sqrt{3})$. Fig. 12.6 shows how B_2 separates after collision.

Let us see another example shown in Fig. 12.7. Suppose that B_2 is fixed and immovable. We can then consider m_2 as ∞. In other words, $\frac{1}{m_2} = 0$. Then, impulse J presented in Equation (12.12) is computed as follows:

$$
\begin{aligned}
J &= -\frac{v_r(e+1)}{\frac{1}{m_1}+\frac{1}{m_2}}\\
&= -\frac{v_r(e+1)}{\frac{1}{m_1}}\\
&= (-30m_1, 10\sqrt{3}m_1)
\end{aligned}
\tag{12.18}
$$

When Equation (12.18) is added to Equation (12.16), we have the updated momentum p'_1 of B_1.

$$p'_1 = p_1 + J$$
$$= (20m_1, 0) + (-30m_1, 10\sqrt{3}m_1) \qquad (12.19)$$
$$= (-10m_1, 10\sqrt{3}m_1)$$

Dividing Equation (12.19) by m_1, the separating velocity of B_1 is computed. It is $(-10, 10\sqrt{3})$ and illustrated in Fig. 12.7. Observe that, with respect to the contact normal, the reflection angle is identical to the incident angle, $30°$.

For implementing the billiard game, we have to take another force into account. It is *friction*. The frictional force is opposite in the direction to the velocity of a ball. A simple method for incorporating the frictional force is using a *damping value d*, which is less than 1 and very close to 1. It removes a bit of velocity for each frame, i.e., velocity v_i computed at frame i is multiplied with d. With an appropriate damping value, the billiard balls would stop moving as if the frictional forces were exerted on them.

12.3   Collision Detection

This chapter has the goal of sketching the basics of game physics and uses quite simple objects such as particles and spheres. In reality, however, the game world includes arbitrarily shaped objects represented in polygon meshes. Therefore, game physics has to perform a lot of computation beyond what has been presented so far.

Consider the collision example of two triangle meshes shown in Fig. 12.8. Collision detection requires intersection tests among the triangles. If each object is composed of 1K triangles, for example, we would need 1M triangle-triangle intersection tests (henceforth, triangle tests), which are obviously expensive. When it is required to detect collisions among more than two objects, the computing cost is combinatorially increased.

To save the computing cost, collision detection algorithms are usually implemented in two phases, the *broad phase* and the *narrow phase*. The broad phase excludes all parts of the objects that are out of the bounds of possibility of collision and identifies the remains as the *potentially colliding set* (PCS). Then, the narrow phase performs the pairwise triangle tests within the PCS. The broad phase presented in this section uses the *bounding volumes* and their *hierarchy*. (For a variety of collision detection algorithms, readers are referred to [39].)

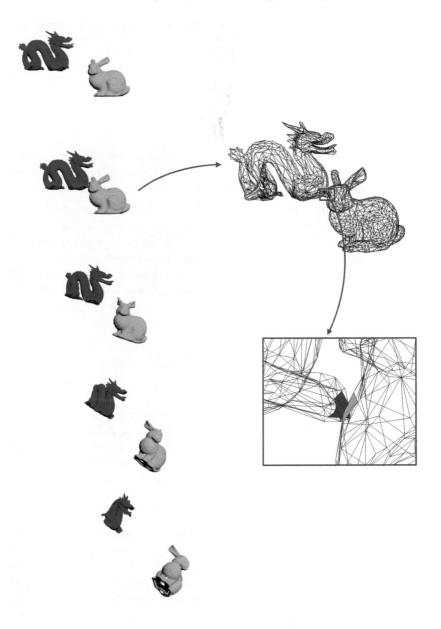

Fig. 12.8: Two models approach each other, collide, and then move apart. In this example, exact collision is detected using the triangle-triangle intersection tests, and the contact points and normals are returned. Using the information, the collision resolution module determines how the models move apart. (The models are provided by the Stanford University Computer Graphics Laboratory.)

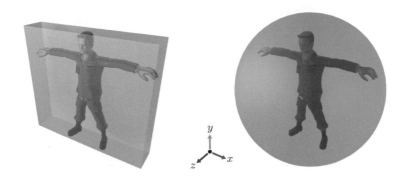

Fig. 12.9: Axis-aligned bounding box (AABB) and bounding sphere.

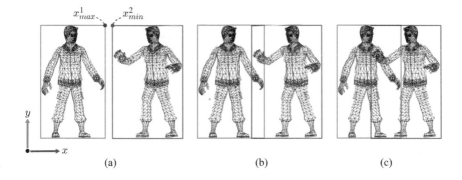

Fig. 12.10: AABBs are tested for overlapping. Only when they overlap, their polygon meshes are tested for collision.

12.3.1 Bounding Volumes and Their Hierarchy

Fig. 12.9 shows two examples of bounding volumes (BVs) for the soldier model: axis-aligned bounding box (AABB) and bounding sphere. This section uses the AABB. BVs are used for preprocessing. Only when the BVs overlap, the polygon meshes within the BVs are tested for collision. In the 2D illustration of Fig. 12.10-(a), an AABB is represented by (x_{min}, x_{max}) and (y_{min}, y_{max}), and the broad phase finds that two AABBs do not overlap because $x^1_{max} < x^2_{min}$. Consequently, the two characters are determined not to collide. No triangle test is invoked.

In contrast, the AABBs overlap in Fig. 12.10-(b). Then, the polygon models within the AABBs make up the PCS, and every pair of triangles (one triangle from the first character, and the other from the second) is tested for intersection. However, no intersection will be found in Fig. 12.10-(b), and

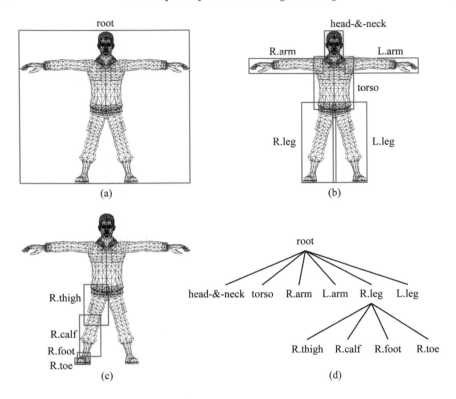

Fig. 12.11:   Bounding volumes are hierarchically organized.

the characters are determined not to collide. In Fig. 12.10-(c), the AABBs overlap, and the triangle test finds intersections between the polygon meshes.

Preprocessing using the BVs increases the overall performance of collision detection. In the example of Fig. 12.10, however, two many polygons are contained in the PCS. If we can reduce the triangle count in the PCS, the time consumed by the triangle test can be reduced, and therefore improved performance can be achieved.

One way to reduce the triangle count is to organize the BVs in a hierarchy. Fig. 12.11-(a) shows the AABB for our soldier character. It contains all polygons of the character and is the *root* of the hierarchy. The polygon mesh is divided into sub-meshes, and an AABB is computed per sub-mesh. Fig. 12.11-(b) shows six smaller AABBs. They are *children* of the root AABB. The division continues. Fig. 12.11-(c) shows four children of the right leg's AABB. Fig. 12.11-(d) shows a part of the bounding volume hierarchy (BVH).

Fig. 12.12 illustrates how the BVHs are traversed at the broad phase. In Fig. 12.12-(a), each BVH is represented as a binary tree. The inputs to the broad phase are the BVH roots, denoted by A and B. Suppose that they are

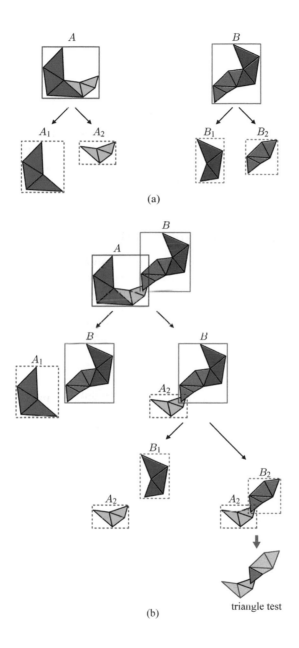

(a)

(b)

triangle test

Fig. 12.12: The broad phase traverses the bounding volume hierarchies to compute the PCS.

found to be overlapped. Without the BVHs, the two polygon meshes would enter the narrow phase for triangle tests. Given the BVHs, however, the broad phase traverses the hierarchies and repeats the BV overlapping tests.

In Fig. 12.12-(b), A is first replaced by its children, A_1 and A_2, and new pairs, (A_1, B) and (A_2, B), are recursively tested for overlapping. (A_1, B) fail the overlapping test and are simply discarded. In contrast, (A_2, B) pass the test. Then, B is replaced by B_1 and B_2, and new pairs, (A_2, B_1) and (A_2, B_2), are recursively tested for overlapping. (A_2, B_1) fail the test and are discarded. (A_2, B_2) pass the test. A_2 and B_2 are the leaf nodes, and therefore the traversal is terminated. (A_2, B_2) form the PCS and enter the narrow phase, where the triangle test is invoked on the PCS. In the example, A_2 and B_2 contain three and four triangles, respectively. Therefore, the triangle test is repeated 12 times.

12.3.2 Triangle-triangle Intersection

Consider two intersecting triangles U and V shown in Fig. 12.13-(a). Their intersection is represented by an edge of two end points p and q. The end points need to be computed to determine the *contact point*. This subsection presents an algorithm for computing p and q.

The surface normal of U is computed using its three vertices and is denoted by (a, b, c). Then, the plane equation of U is defined as follows:

$$f(x, y, z) = ax + by + cz + d = 0 \tag{12.20}$$

By inserting any vertex of U into Equation (12.20), d can be computed, and then the plane equation is determined.

Fig. 12.13-(b) shows a cross-section view of the triangles. If we insert v_1 into $f(x, y, z)$ of Equation (12.20), the perpendicular distance d_1 between v_1 and U is obtained. It is positive because v_1 is located at the *half-space*[2] pointed by U's normal (a, b, c). In contrast, d_2 obtained by inserting v_2 into $f(x, y, z)$ is negative[3].

In Fig. 12.13-(b), the similar triangles lead to the following:

$$\frac{p - v_1}{d_1} = \frac{v_2 - p}{-d_2} \tag{12.21}$$

Rearranging Equation (12.21), we can compute p:

$$p = \frac{d_1}{d_1 - d_2} v_2 - \frac{d_2}{d_1 - d_2} v_1 \tag{12.22}$$

The other end point q in Fig. 12.13-(a) is similarly computed.

---

[2]The equation $ax + by + cz + d = 0$ represents an infinite plane, and it divides the entire 3D space into two half-spaces.

[3]For this reason, d_1 and d_2 are named *signed distances*.

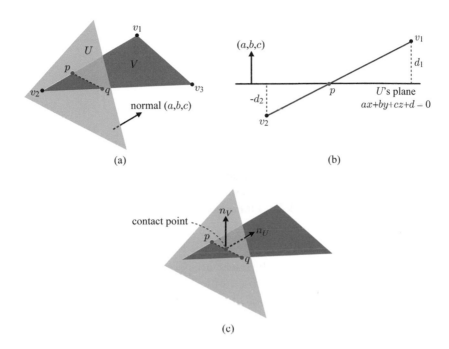

Fig. 12.13: The triangle test returns the contact point and contact normal. (a) The intersection between U and V is an edge bounded by p and q. (b) The end point p is computed using U's plane equation, v_1, and v_2. Similarly, q is computed. (c) The contact point is often set to the midpoint of p and q. The contact normals are often set to the triangle normals of U and V.

When two triangles U and V in the PCS are tested for intersection, they go through some pretests and are also postprocessed. If all vertices of V are found to be located at a half-space of U, for example, the computation presented in Equation (12.22) is not performed, but the triangles are determined not to intersect each other. On the other hand, after p and q are computed, each needs to be tested as to whether it is located inside or outside the triangle U. Because Equation (12.22) does not consider the finite area of U but simply uses the infinite plane where U lies, both p and q may be located outside the triangle. Then, it is probable that the triangles do not intersect, and we need additional postprocessing steps. (Designing these steps is left as an exercise.)

In general, the collision detection module is required to provide the contact points and contact normals for the collision resolution module. In the example of Fig. 12.13-(c), the contact point between U and V is often approximated to the midpoint of p and q in many game physics engines. The contact normals are set to the triangle normals of U and V, denoted by n_U and n_V, respectively.

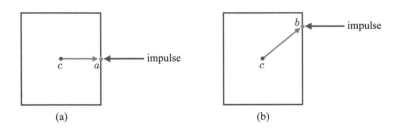

Fig. 12.14:   The center of mass is denoted by c, and a and b represent the contact points. (a) No angular acceleration is generated, and the object does not rotate after collision. (b) Angular acceleration is generated, and the object rotates after collision.

So far, we have considered only linear accelerations for physics-based simulation. When a force is applied to an object, however, the force may induce *angular accelerations* based on the mass distribution of the object, in addition to the linear accelerations. See Fig. 12.14, where c denotes the center of mass of the box, and a and b denote the contact points provided by the collision detection module. As presented earlier, the impulse caused by collision is parallel to the contact normal. The red arrows in the figure represent the impulses. In Fig. 12.14-(a), consider the vector $\vec{ca}$ that connects c and a. The angular acceleration is determined by the cross product of $\vec{ca}$ and the impulse. It is zero in the example, and consequently no angular acceleration is generated. Only the linear acceleration is considered.

In contrast, the cross product of $\vec{cb}$ and the impulse is not zero in Fig. 12.14-(b), and therefore angular acceleration is generated. It is integrated over a time step to produce the change in the *angular velocity*. The angular velocity is integrated to produce the change in object *orientation*. Unlike the case of Fig. 12.14-(a), the box shown in Fig. 12.14-(b) rotates after collision. In the example of Fig. 12.8, the collision resolution module computed the angular accelerations, and consequently the objects were rotated when they moved apart after collision. To bring about realistic simulation, elaborate collision detection and resolution techniques should be adopted. If you are interested, now it is time to pick up a game physics book. Enjoy it!

Exercises

1. Suppose that, in Fig. 12.6, B_2 is not static and its velocity is (8,0). Compute the separating velocities of B_1 and B_2 after collision.

2. Consider a frame composed of m static objects and n moving objects. How many object pairs need to be tested for collision?

3. Section 12.3.2 asserts that, even when p and q are computed in Fig. 12.13, they need to be postprocessed..

   (a) How would you determine whether p (or q) is inside the triangle?

   (b) When p is inside and q is outside the triangle, how would you compute the contact point?

   (c) When both p and q are outside, the line segment connecting them may or may not intersect the triangle. How would you distinguish between the cases?

References

[1] Luna, F.D.: Introduction to 3D Game Programming with Direct3D 10: A Shader Approach. Wordware Publishing Inc., Plano, TX, USA (2008)

[2] Wright, R., Lipchak, B., Haemel, N.: OpenGL®Superbible: Comprehensive Tutorial and Reference, 5th Edition. Addison-Wesley Professional (2010)

[3] Microsoft: The DirectX Software Development Kit (2010) http://msdn.microsoft.com/directx/.

[4] Luebke, D., Watson, B., Cohen, J.D., Reddy, M., Varshney, A.: Level of Detail for 3D Graphics. Elsevier Science Inc., New York, NY, USA (2002)

[5] Hoppe, H.: Optimization of mesh locality for transparent vertex caching. In: Proceedings of the 26th Annual Conference on Computer Graphics and Interactive Techniques. SIGGRAPH '99, New York, NY, USA, ACM Press/Addison-Wesley Publishing Co. (1999) 269–276

[6] Sander, P.V., Nehab, D., Barczak, J.: Fast triangle reordering for vertex locality and reduced overdraw. ACM Transactions on Graphics **26** (2007) 89:1–89:10

[7] Jin, S., Lewis, R.R., West, D.: A comparison of algorithms for vertex normal computation. The Visual Computer **21** (2005) 71–82

[8] Akenine-Möller, T., Haines, E., Hoffman, N.: Real-Time Rendering, 3rd Edition. A. K. Peters, Ltd., Natick, MA, USA (2008)

[9] Clark, J.H.: Hierarchical geometric models for visible surface algorithms. Communications of the ACM **19** (1976) 547–554

[10] Floater, M.S., Hormann, K.: Surface parameterization: a tutorial and survey. In Dodgson, N.A., Floater, M.S., Sabin, M.A., eds.: Advances in Multiresolution for Geometric Modelling. Springer Verlag (2005) 157–186

[11] Everitt, C.: Interactive order-independent transparency (2001) http://developer.nvidia.com/object/Interactive_Order_Transparency.html.

[12] NVIDIA: GPU programming guide - GeForce 8 and 9 series (2008) http://developer.nvidia.com/object/gpu_programming_guide. html.

[13] Persson, E.: Depth in-depth (2007) http://developer.amd.com/ media/gpu_assets/Depth_in-depth.pdf.

[14] Nicodemus, F.E., Richmond, J.C., Hsia, J.J., Ginsberg, I.W., Limperis, T.: Geometrical Considerations and Nomenclature for Reflectance (NBS Monograph 160). National Bureau of Standards (US) (1977)

[15] Phong, B.T.: Illumination for computer generated pictures. Communications of the ACM **18** (1975) 311–317

[16] Oneppo, M.: High level shader language (HLSL) update-introducing version 5.0 (2008) Presentation from GameFest 2008.

[17] Fernando, R., Kilgard, M.J.: The Cg Tutorial: The Definitive Guide to Programmable Real-Time Graphics. Addison-Wesley Longman Publishing Co., Inc., Boston, MA, USA (2003)

[18] Whitted, T.: An improved illumination model for shaded display. Communications of the ACM **23** (1980) 343–349

[19] Goral, C.M., Torrance, K.E., Greenberg, D.P., Battaile, B.: Modeling the interaction of light between diffuse surfaces. SIGGRAPH Computer Graphics **18** (1984) 213–222

[20] Dutré, P., Bala, K., Bekaert, P.: Advanced Global Illumination, 2nd Edition. A. K. Peters Ltd., Wellesley, MA, USA (2006)

[21] Pharr, M., Humphreys, G.: Physically Based Rendering: From Theory To Implementation, 2nd Edition. Morgan Kaufmann Publishers Inc., San Francisco, CA, USA (2010)

[22] Farin, G.E., Hansford, D.: The Essentials of CAGD. A. K. Peters, Ltd., Natick, MA, USA (2000)

[23] Catmull, E., Rom, R.: A class of local interpolating splines. In Barnhill, R., Riesenfeld, R., eds.: Computer Aided Geometric Design. Academic Press (1974) 317–326

[24] Vlachos, A., Peters, J., Boyd, C., Mitchell, J.L.: Curved PN triangles. In: Proceedings of the 2001 Symposium on Interactive 3D Graphics. I3D '01, New York, NY, USA, ACM (2001) 159–166

[25] Blinn, J.F.: Simulation of wrinkled surfaces. SIGGRAPH Computer Graphics **12** (1978) 286–292

[26] Szirmay-Kalos, L., Umenhoffer, T.: Displacement mapping on the GPU - state of the art. Computer Graphics Forum **27** (2008) 1567–1592

[27] Kaneko, T., Takahei, T., Inami, M., Kawakami, N., Yanagida, Y., Maeda, T., Tachi, S.: Detailed shape representation with parallax mapping. In: Proceedings of the ICAT 2001. (2001) 205–208

[28] Hasselgren, J., Munkberg, J., Akenine-Möller, T.: Automatic pre-tessellation culling. ACM Transactions on Graphics **28** (2009) 19:1–19:10

[29] Lindstrom, P., Pascucci, V.: Visualization of large terrains made easy. In: Proceedings of the Conference on Visualization '01. VIS '01, Washington, DC, USA, IEEE Computer Society (2001) 363–371

[30] Green, C.: Efficient self-shadowed radiosity normal mapping. In: ACM SIGGRAPH 2007 courses. SIGGRAPH '07, New York, NY, USA, ACM (2007) 1–8

[31] Crow, F.C.: Shadow algorithms for computer graphics. SIGGRAPH Computer Graphics **11** (1977) 242–248

[32] Williams, L.: Casting curved shadows on curved surfaces. SIGGRAPH Computer Graphics **12** (1978) 270–274

[33] Hasenfratz, J.M., Lapierre, M., Holzschuch, N., Sillion, F.: A survey of real-time soft shadows algorithms. Computer Graphics Forum **22** (2003) 753–774

[34] Dachsbacher, C., Stamminger, M.: Reflective shadow maps. In: Proceedings of the 2005 Symposium on Interactive 3D Graphics and Games. I3D '05, New York, NY, USA, ACM (2005) 203–231

[35] Filion, D., McNaughton, R.: Effects & techniques. In: ACM SIGGRAPH 2008 classes. SIGGRAPH '08, New York, NY, USA, ACM (2008) 133–164

[36] Shoemake, K.: Animating rotation with quaternion curves. SIGGRAPH Computer Graphics **19** (1985) 245–254

[37] Eberly, D.H.: Game Physics. Elsevier Science Inc., New York, NY, USA (2003)

[38] Millington, I.: Game Physics Engine Development (The Morgan Kaufmann Series in Interactive 3D Technology). Morgan Kaufmann Publishers Inc., San Francisco, CA, USA (2007)

[39] Ericson, C.: Real-Time Collision Detection (The Morgan Kaufmann Series in Interactive 3D Technology). Morgan Kaufmann Publishers Inc., San Francisco, CA, USA (2005)

Index

acceleration of gravity, 160, 294
ACMR, 12
affine invariance, 135
affine transform, 25, 31, 45, 74
aliasing, 183
alpha blending, 97
alpha channel, 97
ambient occlusion, 248
ambient reflectance, 111
ambient reflection, 111
angular acceleration, 308
angular velocity, 308
animation, 2
anisotropic filtering, 190
anti-aliasing, 183, 247
approaching velocity, 296
articulated body, 269
aspect ratio, 42, 67
atlas, 92
axis of rotation, 26
axis-aligned bounding box
    (AABB), 82, 303

Bézier curve, 132
Bézier patch, 144, 148
Bézier surface, 141
Bézier triangle, 151, 167
back-face, 56
back-face culling, 56
back-to-front order, 99
ball joint, 286
barycentric coordinates, 151, 213,
    215
basis, 35
basis change, 38, 208
Bernstein polynomial, 134, 143
bilinear interpolation, 73, 141,
    180, 188, 245

bilinear patch, 141
billboard, 164
bone, 271
bone space, 272
bottleneck, 157
bounding sphere, 82, 303
bounding volume, 43, 81, 87, 301
bounding volume hierarchy, 304
broad phase, 301
bump mapping, 197

camera path, 138
camera space, 34, 35, 138
Catmull-Rom spline, 137, 138
center of projection, 45
Cg, 113
chart, 92
clip space, 43, 45
clipping, 43, 53
clockwise rotation, 30
clockwise vertex order, 16, 19, 56
coefficient of restitution, 296
collision detection, 293
collision resolution, 293
color buffer, 23, 95
column vector, 40
conjugate, 262
conservation of momentum, 296
contact normal, 298, 301, 307
contact point, 298, 306
control mesh, 166
control normal, 171
control normal net, 171
control point, 133
control point net, 147, 150, 171
counter-clockwise rotation, 30
counter-clockwise vertex order,
    16, 19, 56